I love
COOKING

Dutch Oven Cookbook

401 Recipes for Campers, Beginners, and Advanced Cooks. Learn How to Cook with a Dutch Oven and Discover New Techniques and Tips for Outdoor Cooking with Family and Friends

Chef Leo Baxter

TABLE OF CONTENTS

I love COOKING

INTRODUCTION

Hello, first I would like to thank you for purchasing this book. In this book, I will show you the advantages and benefits of using a Dutch Oven and how you can benefit from them. The origins of the Dutch Oven date back to the 17th century in the Netherlands (as one might expect from anything with the word "Dutch" in the name). Back then, the most popular cookware was made from expensive materials like copper and brass. And the Dutch were some of the best craftsmen of their time and supplied much of the world's best cookware. But an English craftsman named Abraham Darby thought he could do better. He believed there was a market for cheaper cookware. The key to that was using cheaper materials like cast iron. However, this was a challenge. The Dutch casting process used sand molds to give the finished material a fine finish. The English methods at the time used molds primarily made of clay. Darby and his right-hand man, James Thomas, set about casting iron using sand molds. Their early attempts failed as working with molten iron was different from working with brass which they were accustomed to. But eventually, they succeeded in developing a process for casting iron in sand molds. This made the process cheaper and more efficient. And it allowed them to bring cheaper and more durable cookware to market quickly. I wish you much enjoyment in reading and cooking!

DUTCH OVEN

WHAT IS A DUTCH OVEN?

The classic Dutch Oven is a heavy, black cast-iron pot that is usually heated with charcoal or briquettes and holds heat well. It sits on three legs above the charcoal, which provides the bottom heat. On top, it has a tight-fitting lid that is curved inward and has a high rim so you can place hot coals on top, creating heat.

With practice, you can easily regulate the heat inside the pot. This book will teach you the tricks to understanding how to do it.

Anything that can be cooked in a regular oven can also be cooked in a Dutch Oven. You can cook, stew, fry, and bake in it.

Many Dutch Ovens also have a handle so they can be hung over a campfire. But it's not just for camping, it's also great for making delicious meals at home.

When you stack Dutch Ovens on top of each other, you can use the heat even better.

In different countries, the Dutch Oven has been called different names over time, such as Camp Oven in the USA, Potje in South Africa, Cocotte in France, and Bedourie Oven in Australia.

Modern cast iron pots that are used on the stove or in the oven have a smooth bottom and are often enameled. They do not need to be seasoned and can be cleaned like any other pot.

A Dutch Oven is great for cooking outside all year round, whether it's raining or snowing, while camping, in the backyard, or by a campfire.

ADVANTAGES OF A DUTCH OVEN

Materials

Pure clay is used as the raw material - a naturally occurring material that has been tested for chemical contamination and metals such as lead, cadmium, and arsenic, which are commonly found in conventional cookware. However, this cookware is free from metals and chemicals - a good start, especially as it is marketed as being healthy. No chemicals or glazes are used in the raw material or for finishing the product. This pure clay is inert or non-reactive, even if nothing is added or removed from it.

Multifunctional and versatile

It is probably the most flexible cookware in the kitchen - you can make many dishes such as soups, stews, rice, and other casseroles with it. It is convenient to have a single cookware with so many uses.

Durability

It is a durable and long-lasting cookware that can last for decades with proper care and maintenance.

Even heat distribution

It heats evenly and retains heat well, which eliminates hot spots and ensures that your food cooks evenly.

TIPS FOR BEGINNERS

Use Charcoal

For example, if you want to braise a meat dish in a 12-inch Dutch oven, proceed as follows: 24 briquettes are lit in the starter chimney. The coals are spread on a heat-resistant surface and the Dutch oven is placed on top. Oil is heated in the pot and the meat is browned in 500-gram portions. Then you add the meat with all other ingredients to the Dutch oven and put the lid on. Leave 12 coals under the Dutch oven and place 12 coals evenly on the lid. When the coals have become half ashes, another 24 briquettes are lit in the starter chimney and, when they are glowing, are replaced by the old briquettes. This process can be repeated as often as desired until the meat is cooked. Cooking with the Dutch oven is easier on a grill with a lid or in the oven. This way, neither the briquettes need to be lit nor the ashes disposed of. Cleaning up afterwards is also easier.

Use on a Gas Grill

A Dutch oven works best on a three-burner gas grill. The Dutch oven is placed in the center of the grill and the three burners are turned on at full power. The lid of the gas grill is closed and everything is heated for about 15 minutes. Then oil is heated in the pot and the meat is browned in 500-gram portions. Then add the meat with all the ingredients to the Dutch oven and put the lid on. Turn off the middle burner and only leave the left and right burners on full power. After 10 minutes, stir the contents in the Dutch oven. Once the contents are boiling, reduce the heat of the two remaining burners to half power and after another 10 minutes, further reduce to 40% power. Now the stew can simmer until it's ready.

MASHED POTATOES

Serving:4 - Preparation time: 50 min

Ingredients:

- 12 medium potatoes
- 10 grams of butter
- 6 tablespoons milk nutmeg
- Salt and pepper

Preparation:

1. Peel the potatoes, wash, quarter and cook in the Dutch Oven in lightly salted, boiling water until very soft.
2. Mash the potatoes through a potato ricer (alternatively, you can mash the potatoes, but the mashed potatoes will not be as fluffy.)
3. Fold the milk and butter into the potato mixture and mix well.
4. Season with salt, pepper and nutmeg.
5. Serve and enjoy.

FRIED POTATOES

Serving:4 - Prep time: 45 minutes

Ingredients:

- 10 medium potatoes
- 2 onions
- 1 clove of garlic
- 1 tsp paprika powder
- Salt and pepper
- 6 tablespoons olive oil

Preparation:

1. Wash potatoes, peel and cut into very thin slices.
2. Peel and finely chop the onions and garlic.
3. Heat the oil in the Dutch Oven. Fry the onions and garlic until golden brown. Then add the potatoes and sauté for 20 to 30 minutes with the lid closed. Stir occasionally.
4. Season with pepper, paprika powder and salt.
5. Serve and enjoy.

POTATO PANCAKES

Serving:4 - Preparation time: 25 min

Ingredients:

- 10 medium potatoes
- 3 onions
- Olive oil
- Salt and pepper

Preparation:

1. Peel the potatoes and onions and puree them in a blender.
2. Pour the mixture into a strainer to allow the liquid to drain.
3. Then put in a bowl and add salt to taste and mix well.
4. Heat the oil in the Dutch oven and pour the mixture into the oil in tablespoon-sized portions and flatten slightly. Small round flatbreads are made in the Dutch oven.
5. Fry the donuts on both sides until golden brown.
6. Serve with applesauce or crème fraîche and salmon and enjoy.

DUTCH FRIED POTATOES

Serving:6 - Prep time: 45 minutes

Ingredients:

- 8 medium red, Yukon Gold, or chestnut potatoes, thinly sliced
- 1 medium onion diced
- 225 g diced bacon
- 1 jalapeño seed, diced
- 300 g cheddar cheese
- 1 teaspoon of salt

Preparation:

1. On about half the coals, cook the bacon until tender. It will crisp up as it cooks with the potatoes. Remove the bacon from the dutch oven coals, leaving about 2 tablespoons of bacon grease on the bottom of the dutch oven. Layer half the sliced potatoes in the bottom of the Dutch Oven and sprinkle with half a teaspoon of salt.
2. Top the potatoes with half the onion, half the jalapeños (if desired), half the bacon, and then half the cheese.
3. Repeat the layers with the remaining ingredients and place the lid on the Dutch Oven. Place 9 coals in the bottom and 18 coals in the bottom of a Dutch Oven on a stand or secure surface. This should be heated to around 180°C.
4. Check these regularly and adjust the coals if necessary. Add more as the original coals wear off.
5. If the bottom of the potatoes is cooking too quickly despite turning off the charcoal, add 1/3 cup of water to the bottom.

PUMPKIN FRIES

Serving:4 - Preparation time: 25 min

Ingredients:

- 1 kg Hokkaido pumpkin
- 6 tablespoons olive oil
- 2 tsp paprika powder
- 2 teaspoons curry
- Salt and pepper

Preparation:

1. Halve the pumpkin, remove the seeds and cut the flesh into small chips.
2. Prepare a large bowl, put the fries in it and add the olive oil and spices and mix well.
3. Place the pumpkin strips in the Dutch Oven and bake for approx. 15 minutes at medium heat from below and high heat from above.
4. Serve and enjoy the finished pumpkin fries.

POTATO AND CHICKPEA BALLS

Serve:4 Preparation time: 25 minutes

Ingredients:

- 8 medium potatoes
- 800 g of chickpeas
- 2 onions
- 1 bunch of parsley
- 4 tablespoons olive oil
- Salt pepper

Preparation:

1. Peel, wash and quarter the potatoes and cook in a Dutch oven with salted water until soft. Take out and set aside.
2. Then cook the chickpeas with water in the Dutch oven until soft. Remove and add to the potatoes.
3. Peel and chop the onion.
4. Mix all three ingredients well in a bowl.
5. Chop and add the parsley and season the mixture with salt and pepper.
6. Form small balls from the dough and fry in the Dutch oven with oil until golden brown on all sides.
7. Serve and enjoy.

POTATO WEDGES

Serving:4 - Preparation time: 50 min

Ingredients:

- 12 medium potatoes
- 3 tablespoons olive oil
- 1 tablespoon rosemary
- 200 g of grated parmesan
- 1 tablespoon curry powder
- Salt and pepper

Preparation:

1. Wash the potatoes thoroughly, cut into quarters and place in a bowl. Add oil, pepper, salt and curry powder and mix well.
2. Place the potatoes, skin side down, in the lightly oiled Dutch Oven.
3. Bake at low heat from below and high heat from above for about 20 minutes. Then sprinkle the parmesan on top and bake for another 20 minutes until the cheese has melted. When the potato wedges are soft on the inside and golden brown at the corners, they're done.
4. Serve and enjoy.

ROSEMARY POTATOES

Serving:4 - Preparation time: 30 min

Ingredients:

- 10 medium potatoes
- 1 tablespoon of butter
- 1 clove of garlic
- 1 tablespoon of olive oil
- 1 tsp fresh thyme
- 1 tablespoon fresh rosemary
- Salt and pepper

Preparation:

1. Wash, quarter and cook potatoes until firm and slightly chewy.
2. Peel and chop the garlic. Wash and chop the thyme and rosemary.
3. Heat the oil and butter in the Dutch Oven. Fry garlic. Then add the potatoes and fry for 5 to 10 minutes until golden brown.
4. Add rosemary and thyme and mix well. Fry again for a minute.
5. Season with salt and pepper.
6. Serve and enjoy.

BAKED POTATOES WITH HERB QUARK

Serving:4 - Preparation time: 60 min

Ingredients:

- 4 large potatoes
- 2 tablespoons of thyme
- 2 tablespoons olive oil
- 150 grams of cottage cheese
- 4 tablespoons of milk
- 5 tablespoons mixed herbs
- Salt and pepper
- Parsley to decorate

Preparation:

1. Wash potatoes and prick lightly on several sides.

2. Tear four squares of aluminum foil to wrap the potatoes.
3. Brush aluminum foil with oil. Place the potatoes on the aluminum foil and season with salt and pepper. Then wrap well.
4. Place in the Dutch Oven and bake for approx. 45 to 55 minutes over medium heat from below and high heat from above. To check, poke a fork in the potato and see if it's soft.
5. For the herb quark: Mix the milk, quark, mixed herbs, pepper and salt well.
6. Cut the potatoes open slightly and add the herb quark to the potatoes. Decorate with parsley.
7. Serve and enjoy.

SWEET YAMS

Serving:4 - Preparation time: 60 minutes

Ingredients:

- 4 sweet potatoes
- 20 grams of butter
- 20 grams of brown sugar
- 50 ml orange juice ½ tsp cinnamon
- 1 tsp lemon juice
- 1 tsp lemon zest

Preparation:

1. Peel, wash and slice the sweet potatoes.
2. Melt the butter in the Dutch oven.
3. Mix the orange juice, sugar, lemon juice and cinnamon well.
4. Put the sweet potatoes in the Dutch Oven and pour the sauce over them.
5. Cover and cook in the Dutch Oven for approx. 30 minutes over low heat from below and medium heat from above. Then sprinkle lemon zest on top, bake on high heat for another 20 until sweet potatoes are slightly crispy.
6. Serve and enjoy.

BREAKFAST

Spicy pancakes

Serving:4 - Preparation time: 10 min

Ingredients:

- 800 ml natural yoghurt
- 8 eggs
- 8 tablespoons of porridge
- 4 tablespoons herbs
- Oil for frying
- 4 tomatoes
- 4 lettuce leaves
- 1 cucumber
- Salt and pepper

Preparation:

1. Whisk the eggs with the rolled oats in a bowl and season with salt and pepper.
2. Pour the mixture into the Dutch Oven and lightly brown both sides with a little oil.
3. Wash vegetables and cut into small pieces. Mix the yoghurt with the herbs and season with salt and pepper.
4. Serve everything together and enjoy.

HEFEZOPF

Serving:4 - Preparation time: about 1-2 hours

Ingredients:

- 1 kg of wheat flour
- 1 yeast loaf
- 3 eggs
- 1 yeast cube
- 150 grams of butter
- 100 grams of sugar
- ½ liter of milk
- 1 tbsp lemon zest

Preparation:

1. Dissolve the yeast in a bowl of lukewarm milk. Add sugar and mix everything well. Add the flour, eggs and lemon zest to the bowl and mix to form a dough. Then add the butter and salt and knead again.
2. Cover the dough with a damp cloth and let it rise for about 2 hours.
3. Dust the dough with flour, knead again and divide into 3 equal parts.
4. Roll the pieces of dough into long strands and braid them into a braid. Sprinkle with granulated sugar.
5. Put the braid in the Dutch Oven and let it rise for 30 minutes. Close the Dutch Oven, place 9 briquettes under and 6 briquettes over the oven and heat up.
6. Bake the yeast braid for about 50 minutes. Spread with butter and enjoy

BREAKFAST CUTS

Serving:1 - Preparation time: 10 minutes

Ingredients:

- 1 slice of wholemeal bread
- 1 tsp cream cheese
- 1 teaspoon of chives
- 2 slices of semi-hard cheese
- Salt and pepper

Preparation:

1. Preheat the Dutch Oven to 175° Celsius.
2. Meanwhile spread cream cheese on the bread slice, sprinkle with chives, season with salt and pepper and place the sliced cheese on top.

3. Add the bread to the pan and toast for 5 minutes with the lid closed.

SCRAMBLED EGGS WITH SALMON

Serving:1 - Preparation time: 20 minutes

Ingredients:

- 2 eggs
- 50 g smoked salmon
- 2 tablespoons yogurt
- 1 shallot
- ½ clove of garlic
- ½ tsp dill, chopped
- ½ tsp horseradish, grated
- Nutritional information per serving
- Calories: 278.3 kcal
- Carbohydrates: 3.4 g
- Fat: 18.4 g
- Egg white: 22.8 g

Preparation:

1. First, the shallot is peeled, halved and cut into small cubes. The garlic clove is finely chopped.
2. Then the lid of the Dutch Oven is turned over and put on. The scrambled eggs are prepared in the lid.
3. Put the butter in the lid and pour in the diced shallots and garlic.
4. Sweating at 175° Celsius.
5. Now put the eggs together with the yoghurt and the dill in a mixing bowl and whisk.
6. Add the egg mixture to the onions and garlic and allow to set.
7. As long as the egg mixture is not completely set, place the smoked salmon on top and let it set
8. Finally refine with horseradish and enjoy.

POWER BOWL

Serving:2 - Preparation time: 15 min

Ingredients:

- 12 tablespoons millet-buckwheat porridge
- 600 ml oat drink
- 4 apples
- 4 bananas
- 4 teaspoons of flaxseed
- 4 tablespoons of cranberries
- 4 tablespoons of walnuts
- 6 mint leaves

Preparation:

1. Bring the oat drink to a boil in the Dutch oven and add the porridge.
2. Peel and cut two apples and two bananas into small pieces and add them as well.
3. Puree the mixture with a blender.

4. Peel the other apples and bananas and cut into small pieces.
5. Arrange the finished dish and decorate with banana and apple pieces.

PORRIDGE WITH COCONUT FLAKES

Serving:4 - Preparation time: 15 min

Ingredients:

- 1l almond milk
- 10 tablespoons of flaked almonds
- 2 tablespoons chopped almonds
- 4 tablespoons coconut flakes
- 4 bananas
- 2 apples
- 2 pears
- Cinammon

Preparation:

1. Peel and slice two bananas and peel and mash two bananas with a fork.
2. Wash, core and cut the apples and pears into small pieces.
3. Add the flaked almonds and almond milk to the Dutch Oven and bring to the boil, stirring constantly. Then remove from the embers.
4. Mix all ingredients in a bowl and season with cinnamon if necessary.
5. Arrange on deep plates and enjoy the finished porridge.

DANISH BABE

Serving:2 - Preparation time: 20 minutes

Ingredients:

- 3 eggs
- 1 apple
- 125 grams of flour
- 175 ml milk
- 2 tablespoons butter
- 2 tablespoons of sugar

Preparation:

1. Preheat the oven to 200 °C.
2. Put the butter in the Dutch Oven and melt. Peel, core and cut the apple.
3. Then place in the oven and refine with sugar.
4. Put the flour, 1 tablespoon sugar, 1 tablespoon salt and some cinnamon in a bowl and mix. Then add eggs and milk and mix again.
5. Add the batter to the apples and bake for about 20 minutes. Refine with powdered sugar and serve.

PEPPER SALMON QUICHE

Serving:4 - Prep time: 45 minutes

Ingredients:

- 100 g low-fat quark
- 3 tablespoons sesame oil
- 1 egg yolk
- 3 eggs
- 2 teaspoons of baking soda
- 200 g wholemeal spelled flour
- 2 peppers 4 tablespoons of water
- 1 small zucchini
- 1 clove of garlic
- 2 tablespoons fresh thyme
- 250 g salmon fillet
- 100 ml milk
- Salt and pepper

Preparation:

1. Chop the garlic, slice the zucchini and cut the peppers into strips. Cut the salmon into bite-sized pieces.
2. Mix together the quark, oil, egg yolk, water and ½ tsp salt. Then add flour and baking powder and mix well.
3. Spread the batter on the bottom of the Dutch Oven. Grease a little beforehand. Prick the base several times with a fork.
4. Whisk together the eggs, milk, garlic, half the thyme and season with salt and pepper.
5. Spread the salmon and vegetables on the dough and pour the egg milk over it.
6. Bake in the Dutch oven with the lid closed (medium heat from below and above for approx. 35 minutes).
7. Serve sprinkled with thyme and enjoy.

FLYING DUTCHMAN

Serving:2 - Preparation time: 30 minutes

Ingredients:

- 1 stalk of rhubarb
- 7 grams of baking powder
- 25 g sugar (white)
- 10 grams of vanilla sugar
- 50 ml apple cider vinegar
- 200 ml milk
- 1 tablespoon butter
- 2 tablespoons sugar (white)
- 5 tablespoons of water
- 1 tsp starch
- 2 tablespoons powdered sugar
- 1 pinch of salt and cardamom

Preparation:

1. Preheat the oven to 180 °C and place the Dutch Oven in the oven.

2. Put the flour, baking powder, vanilla sugar, sugar, apple cider vinegar, milk, butter and a pinch of salt in a bowl and knead into a dough.
3. Melt butter in Dutch oven. Put the batter in the Dutch Oven and bake for about 30 minutes. Wash and chop the rhubarb.
4. Put the rhubarb, sugar and cardamom in a bowl of water and heat. In another saucepan, add the cornstarch and water and stir. Add to the pot with the rhubarb.
5. Remove the Dutch Oven from the oven and turn the baby over. Dust with icing sugar and serve with rhubarb compote.

CASSEROLE

Serving:8 - Preparation time: 20-30 minutes

Ingredients:

- 3 cups hash browns
- 400 g fresh sausage, crumbled
- 6 eggs beaten
- 1 cup cheddar cheese, grated
- Cookie dough, enough for 6 cookies
- 4 tablespoons of butter or oil

Preparation:

1. Preheat the Dutch Oven over a campfire or on a wire rack.
2. Place the sausage in the Dutch Oven with half the butter or oil and fry until brown, stirring occasionally. Remove from the oven and set aside.
3. Add the hash browns with the remaining butter or oil. Fry and turn on one side.
4. Place the bratwurst on the rösti. Add the beaten eggs to the sausage running down all the bottom layers.
5. Sprinkle the egg with cheese. Pour large amounts of cookie dough onto the tops of the eggs until everything is covered. Put the Dutch Oven lid on and make sure it is secure. Place the Dutch Oven in the fire directly over some glowing coals but away from the flames. Add 4-8 large glowing coals on top of the lid.
6. Check and rotate the oven occasionally to ensure that ash does not get into the food when you open the lid.
7. Breakfast is ready when the biscuits are brown on the inside. Cut out large pieces as a portion.

MUSHROOM OMELET

Serving:4 - Preparation time: 15 min

Ingredients:

- 1 pepper
- 250 grams of mushrooms
- 10 eggs 100 g grated Gouda
- Olive oil for frying
- Salt and pepper

Preparation:

1. Wash the peppers, deseed, remove the stalk and cut into small pieces. Wash the mushrooms and cut into thin strips.
2. Put the eggs in a bowl, season with pepper and salt and whisk well with the grated Gouda.
3. Put olive oil in the Dutch Oven and fry the vegetables well. Close the lid and let the vegetables cook.
4. Add the egg and cheese mixture and fry over low heat, top and bottom, until the egg and cheese mixture is good, 10 minutes.
5. The omelette is ready. Enjoy your meal!

STUFFED PORK CHOPS

Serving:8 - Prep time: 45 minutes

Ingredients:

- 1 packet of pork stuffing
- 3/4 tsp seasoned salt
- Garlic powder
- 1/2 teaspoon coarsely ground pepper
- 1 can (110 g) cream of mushroom soup, undiluted
- 1/4 cup 2% milk
- 1 cup of smoked Gouda
- 1 small apple, finely chopped
- 1/2 cup chopped pecans, toasted
- 8 boneless pork chops (170 g each)
- 2 tablespoons olive oil
- Chopped fresh chives or
- Parsley, optional

Preparation:

1. Prepare the filling according to the instructions on the package. Cool down a bit. In a small bowl mix the spices. In another bowl, whisk the soup and milk together until well combined. Stir cheese, apple, and pecans into cooled filling. Cut a pocket horizontally in the thickest part of each loin. Fill with stuffing. Brush outside of chops with 1 tablespoon oil; Sprinkle with spice mix.
2. In a Dutch oven, heat the remaining oil over medium-high heat. Place the pork chops in a skillet, filling cut-side up and spreading evenly. Pour soup mixture around the chops; bring to a boil. Reduce heat; Cover and simmer for 35-40 minutes or until the pork is no longer pink and wait until a thermometer inserted into the stuffing reads 165°C.
3. Remove from heat; Leave on for 5 minutes. Place chops in a bowl. spoonful of sauce on top. Sprinkle with chives if you like. Cast iron pot (or smaller) and lid for heating. Heat for 20 to 30 minutes.

PANCAKES

Serving:4 - Preparation time: 30 minutes

Ingredients:

- 6 eggs

- 150 grams of flour
- 120 grams of cane sugar
- 100 grams of blueberries
- 350 ml milk
- 5 tablespoons butter
- 1 vanilla bean
- 1 pinch of salt and powdered sugar
- 1 tablespoon lemon juice

Preparation:

1. Preheat the grill and Dutch oven to 220°C.
2. Beat the eggs until fluffy. Scrape the pulp of the vanilla bean. Wash blueberries under cold water.
3. Mix the vanilla bean and sugar in a bowl.
4. Add the flour, milk, lemon juice, salt and vanilla sugar to the eggs and mix well.
5. Place 3 tablespoons of butter in a Dutch oven and heat. Then put the batter in the Dutch Oven and add the blueberries.
6. Bake everything for about 25 minutes at 200 °C. Put 2 tablespoons of butter on the oven pancake and let it melt. Dust with powdered sugar and serve

BAKED BEANS

Serving:4 - Preparation time: 10 minutes

Ingredients:

- 4 cans of baked beans
- 250 grams of bacon
- 150 ml maple syrup
- 3 tablespoons brown sugar
- 2 tablespoons hot sauce
- Some oil
- 1 pinch of salt

Preparation:

1. Cut the bacon into bite-sized pieces and sauté in a little oil.
2. Place the beans in the Dutch Oven and let simmer.
3. Refine with maple syrup, sugar, hot sauce and salt.
4. Simmer for a few minutes.
5. Divide the baked beans among plates and serve with some bacon or scrambled eggs, if desired.

MINERS breakfast

Serving:6 - Preparation time: 25 minutes

Ingredients:

- 1 kg sausage (raw)
- 1 kg potatoes (grated)
- 8 eggs
- 250 g cheese (grated)

Preparation:

1. Place the Dutch Oven on hot embers.

2. Fry the sausage meat. Remove the sausage from the oven and let drain.
3. Pour the sauce into the Dutch Oven, roast the potatoes in the sauce and distribute.
4. Put the sausage mixture on the potatoes.
5. Beat eggs, season and add to Dutch oven and sprinkle with cheese.
6. Cover the closed pot with embers and cook for about 25 minutes.

BERRY MUFFINS

Serving:1-2 - Prep time: 20 minutes

Ingredients:

- 2 1/2 cups berries
- 1 tablespoon of sugar
- Muffin or vanilla cake mix

Preparation:

1. Mix your favorite berries with a few tablespoons of sugar. Be sure to save some of the mixture, but transfer the rest to a cast-iron skillet.
2. Top the berries with your favorite muffin or vanilla cake mix, prepared according to package directions.
3. Place the lid on the fire pot and slide it onto hot coals. Bake for about an hour. Scatter over the extra macerated berries just before serving

SUPER BOWL

Serving:2 - Preparation time: 15 min

Ingredients:

- 12 tablespoons millet-buckwheat porridge
- 600 ml oat drink
- 4 apples
- 4 bananas
- 4 teaspoons of flaxseed
- 4 tablespoons of cranberries
- 4 tablespoons of walnuts
- 6 mint leaves

Preparation:

1. Bring the oat drink to a boil in the Dutch oven and add the porridge.
2. Peel and cut two apples and two bananas into small pieces and add them as well.
3. Puree the mixture with a blender.
4. Peel the other apples and bananas and cut into small pieces.
5. Arrange the finished dish and decorate with banana and apple pieces

BAGEL WITH CHEESE AND EGG

Serving:2 - Preparation time: 15 minutes

Ingredients:

- 4 eggs
- 2 rolls
- 2 spring onions
- 1 jalapeno
- 1 avocado
- 4 tablespoons parmesan cheese
- 2 tablespoons butter
- Some garlic and sriracha
- 1 pinch of salt and pepper

Preparation:

1. Slice the bagels and add 2 tablespoons butter to the Dutch oven. Sear briefly on the grill.
2. Rub bagels with garlic.
3. Briefly dig the Dutch Oven into glowing coals.
4. Butter the bagels and place in the Dutch Oven.
5. Crack the eggs and spread them on the bagels. Sprinkle with cheese and bake for about 10 minutes.
6. Chop green onions and jalapeño. Also, halve the avocado and cut into small pieces. Then the bagels with green onions and jalapeño
7. sprinkle.
8. Refine with avocado and season with some Sriracha sauce and serve.

BACON WITH CHEESE AND EGGS

Serving:8 - Preparation time: 25 minutes

Ingredients:

- 450 g bacon strips, chopped
- 1 package (550 g) chilled fried potatoes
- 8 large eggs
- 1/2 cup of coffee creamer
- 1/2 to 1 teaspoon pepper sauce, optional
- 2 cups grated cheddar cheese

Preparation:

1. Prepare a medium to high temperature grill with 32-36 charcoal briquettes.
2. Fry the bacon in a Dutch oven over the campfire until crispy, stirring occasionally. Remove with a slotted spoon.
3. Gently press the potatoes onto the bottom and Dutch Oven. In a small bowl, whisk together the eggs, heavy cream, and pepper sauce, if desired, until well combined. Pour this over the potatoes; Sprinkle with cooked bacon and cheese.
4. Cover the Dutch Oven. When the briquettes are covered with white ash, set the Dutch Oven directly to 16-18 briquettes. Using long-handled tongs, place 16-18 briquettes on the pan lid.
5. Cook for 20-25 minutes, or until eggs are completely set and cheese is melted. To inspect the unit, use pliers to gently lift the lid. Fry for 5 minutes longer if necessary.

OMELETTE

Serving:2 - Preparation time: 10 minutes

Ingredients:

- 4 eggs
- 50 ml milk
- ½ zucchini
- ½ stick of celery
- 1 shallot
- 30 grams of broccoli
- 2 tablespoons butter
- Salt and pepper

Preparation:

1. First, peel, halve and dice the shallot. Cut zucchini and celery into small pieces.
2. Put the butter in the Dutch Oven and fry the vegetables in it.
3. Crack the eggs into a bowl and mix in the milk, salt and pepper.
4. Pour the egg mixture over the vegetables and let it set at 175° Celsius.

ASIA SCRAMBLED EGGS

Serving:4 - Preparation time: 15 min

Ingredients:

- 2 cm ginger
- 1 bunch of spring onions
- 6 eggs 6 tablespoons coconut milk
- 200 g of bean sprouts
- Salt and pepper

Preparation:

1. Peel ginger and cut into small pieces. Wash the spring onions and cut into small pieces.
2. Place eggs and coconut milk in a small bowl and mix with salt, pepper and ginger.
3. Heat the olive oil in the Dutch Oven and pour the egg mixture into the Dutch Oven and stir well. Fry for about 10 minutes on low heat.
4. Wash sprouts, sweat in a little water and drain.
5. Decorate the finished dish with sprouts and serve.

GOOD MORNING PAN

Serving:4 - Prep time: 40 minutes

Ingredients:

- 6 tomatoes
- 1 onion
- 100 grams of feta
- 3 peppers
- 1 jalapeno
- 8 eggs
- Paprika powder
- Salt and pepper
- Oil for frying
- Freshness

Preparation:

1. Peel and chop onions. Wash the peppers and jalapeños, remove the stalk, deseed and cut into small pieces. Wash and finely chop the parsley. Wash the tomatoes, remove the stalk and dice.
2. Heat the oil in the Dutch Oven and sauté the onions, tomatoes, jalapeños and peppers until tender, about 5 minutes. Season with salt, pepper and paprika. Add the feta and cook another 5 minutes until the feta is melted.
3. Make 8 holes in the mixture and crack the eggs and place them in the holes.
4. Cook the eggs with the lid on over low heat from below and medium heat from above until the whites are set and the yolks are still soft.
5. Serve with parsley and enjoy.

CHEESE OMELET

Serving:4 - Preparation time: 15 min

Ingredients:

- 8 tablespoons chia seeds 6 eggs
- 20 g Parmesan cheese
- 120g Gouda
- Pepper and Nutmeg

Preparation:

1. Finely grate the parmesan and fry in the Dutch oven with oil.
2. Put eggs in a bowl and whisk well. Season to taste with pepper and nutmeg.
3. Place the eggs in the saucepan on top of the fried parmesan.
4. Add the Gouda and fry everything together until golden brown.
5. Serve and enjoy.

PORRIDGE WITH OATS

Serving:1 - Preparation time: 30 minutes

Ingredients:

- 40 grams of rolled oats
- 200 ml almond milk
- 1 kiwi
- 20 grams of blueberries
- • ½ pear
- • ½ packet vanilla sugar
- • 1 tablespoon of honey
- • 1 tbsp lemon balm, chopped

Preparation:

1. First put the almond milk in the Dutch Oven.
2. Add the rolled oats, vanilla sugar and honey and simmer at 175° Celsius for 5 minutes with the lid open.
3. Meanwhile, cut the fruit into small cubes.
4. Take the pot off the fire and add the fruit cubes with the lemon balm. Mix well and let the porridge steep for 15 minutes.

PANCAKES WITH CHIA SEEDS

Serving:4 _ Preparation time: 15 min

Ingredients:

- 8 tablespoons of chia seeds
- 8 bananas
- Butter for frying 8 eggs
- Some cinnamon
- Fruit of your choice

Preparation:

1. Mash bananas with a fork and place in a bowl.
2. Add chia seeds and eggs and mix well. Let stand 5 minutes for the chia seeds to swell up a bit.
3. Place the Dutch Oven lid upside down on the embers. Melt the butter on the lid and put the dough on the lid. Fry until golden brown on both sides.
4. Serve sprinkled with cinnamon and fruit and enjoy.

SCRAMBLED EGGS

Serving:1 - Preparation time: 10 minutes

Ingredients:

- 2 eggs
- 1 tbsp bacon
- 2 tablespoons yogurt
- 1 tablespoon mountain cheese, grated
- 2 sage leaves

Preparation:

1. First, finely chop the sage leaves. And cut the bacon into cubes.
2. Put the bacon in the lid of the Dutch oven and roast at 175° Celsius.
3. Meanwhile, put the eggs in a bowl. Add yoghurt, cheese and sage and mix well.
4. Add the egg mixture to the bacon and stir.

SMOKED SALMON

Serving:4 - Preparation time: 60 min

Ingredients:

- 600 g salmon fillet
- 400g smoking chips (beech)
- 2 tablespoons oregano
- 20 g coarsely ground pepper
- coarse sea salt

Preparation:

1. Season the salmon with oregano, salt and pepper and place in an aluminum bowl. The aluminum pan is important because the liquid that comes out of the salmon as it smokes could snuff out the smoke chips.
2. Distribute smoking chips evenly on the bottom of the Dutch Oven and place a stacking grate on top.
3. Place the aluminum tray on the grid.
4. Heat the Dutch Oven from below with as much heat as possible. Keep lid closed and do not place coals on lid. Be careful, the bottom of the pan gets very hot.
5. Do not open the lid while the smoking chips are smoldering as the smoking chips may burst into flames with exposure to more oxygen. The heat ensures that the fish is cooked.
6. The fish should be golden between half an hour and an hour. When this is achieved, the fish is ready to serve.
7. Serve warm or cold and enjoy.

PANCAKES WITH YOGURT

Serving:4 - Preparation time: 10 min

Ingredients:

- 800 ml natural yoghurt
- 8 eggs
- 8 tablespoons of porridge
- 4 tablespoons herbs
- Oil for frying
- 4 tomatoes
- 4 lettuce leaves
- 1 cucumber
- Salt and pepper

Preparation:

1. Whisk the eggs with the rolled oats in a bowl and season with salt and pepper.
2. Pour the mixture into the Dutch Oven and lightly brown both sides with a little oil.
3. Wash vegetables and cut into small pieces. Mix the yoghurt with the herbs and season with salt and pepper.
4. Serve everything together and enjoy.

CAZUELA AL DENTE

Serving:6 - Preparation time: 30 minutes

Ingredients:

- 8 tablespoons chia seeds 6 chicken drumsticks
- 3 cups diced peeled butternut squash (diced)
- 6 small potatoes, peeled
- 6 pieces of fresh or frozen corn on the cob
- 3 carrots, cut into pieces
- 3 cans of chicken broth
- Warm cooked rice

- Pepperoni sauce to taste
- Season with salt and pepper
- Chopped fresh coriander or parsley

Preparation:

1. Place the chicken, squash, potatoes, corn, carrots and broth in a large soup kettle or Dutch oven. Bring to a boil and reduce the temperature; cover and simmer 25 minutes, or until chicken is tender and vegetables are tender.
2. Serve with rice in a shallow soup bowl. Serve with hot pepper sauce, salt, pepper and coriander or parsley.

SALMON OMELETTE WITH CUCUMBER

Serving:4 - Preparation time: 15 min

Ingredients:

- 160 g smoked salmon
- 1 cucumber
- 8 eggs
- 50 ml milk
- 2 tsp chopped parsley
- Salt and pepper
- Olive oil

Preparation:

1. Cut salmon and cucumber into small pieces.
2. Mix eggs with milk and parsley and season with salt and pepper.
3. Heat the olive oil in the Dutch oven and fry the salmon briefly. Spread evenly. Then pour the egg mixture into the saucepan. Simmer on low for about 10 minutes.
4. Serve the finished omelette with the cucumber slices and enjoy.

APPLE CAKE

Serving:4 - Prep time: 55 min

Ingredients:

- 300 grams of wheat flour
- 400 ml milk
- 6 eggs
- 1 pinch of salt
- Butter
- 6 apples
- 6 teaspoons of cane sugar
- 2 teaspoons of cinnamon
- 100 g powdered sugar

Preparation:

1. Put the flour, milk and salt in a bowl and mix well with a whisk.
2. Put the eggs in a small bowl and beat them. Carefully pour the eggs into the flour mixture, whisking constantly.

3. Let the dough stand for about 30 minutes. Meanwhile, mix together the cinnamon, sugar, and powdered sugar in a small bowl.
4. Peel and cut the apples into small pieces and mix with the cane sugar.
5. Place the Dutch Oven lid upside down on the embers. Fry the apples in the Dutch Oven lid with a little butter on both sides.
6. Then use a ladle to put small amounts of batter in the Dutch Oven lid and fry on both sides.
7. Serve the finished apple pancakes sprinkled with cinnamon sugar and enjoy.

CHILAQUILENE

Serving:1-2 - Prep time: 15 minutes

Ingredients:

- Tortilla chips
- 2 tomatoes
- cooking oil
- 1 onion
- 1/2 jalapeño, diced
- 2 eggs

Preparation:

1. Prepare the finished tortilla.
2. Start by roasting two tomatoes in an oiled cast iron skillet over hot coals. Fry until light bubbles form and set aside.
3. Add a little more oil to your pan and sauté a diced onion. Add a few large handfuls of tortilla chips, along with the tomatoes and half a diced jalapeño. Fry just until hot.
4. Refine with boiled eggs, how you like them best. Throw in some cilantro, quest fresco, and sliced avocado, and you have delicious campfire-cooked chilaquiles.

GREEN GARLIC BEANS

Serving:12 - Preparation time: 10 minutes

Ingredients:

- 1.3 kg fresh green beans, trimmed
- 1 tablespoon sesame oil
- 1 tablespoon canola oil
- 1 shallot, finely chopped
- 6 garlic cloves, chopped
- 2 teaspoons of salt
- Pepper
- Tablespoon of sesame seeds, toasted

Preparation:

1. In a Dutch Oven, bring 10 cups of water to a boil. Add green beans; Cook uncovered for 6-8 minutes or until tender.

2. Meanwhile, heat oils in a small skillet over medium-high. Add shallots, garlic, salt and pepper; cook and stir 2-3 minutes or until tender.
3. Drain green beans and return to Dutch Oven. add shallot mixture; mix to coat. Sprinkle with sesame.

COCONUT MASH

Serving:4 - Preparation time: 15 min

Ingredients:

- 1l almond milk
- 10 tablespoons of flaked almonds
- 2 tablespoons chopped almonds
- 4 tablespoons coconut flakes
- 4 bananas
- 2 apples
- 2 pears
- Room

Preparation:

1. Peel and slice two bananas and peel and mash two bananas with a fork.
2. Wash, core and cut the apples and pears into small pieces.
3. Add the flaked almonds and almond milk to the Dutch Oven and bring to the boil, stirring constantly. Then remove from the embers.
4. Mix all ingredients in a bowl and season with cinnamon if necessary.
5. Arrange on deep plates and enjoy the finished porridge.

APPLE PANCAKES

Serving:4 - Prep time: 55 min

Ingredients:

- 300 grams of wheat flour
- 400 ml milk
- 6 eggs
- 1 pinch of salt
- Butter 6 apples
- 6 teaspoons of cane sugar
- 2 teaspoons of cinnamon
- 100 g powdered sugar

Preparation:

1. Put the flour, milk and salt in a bowl and mix well with a whisk.
2. Put the eggs in a small bowl and beat them. Carefully pour the eggs into the flour mixture, whisking constantly.
3. Let the dough stand for about 30 minutes. Meanwhile, mix together the cinnamon, sugar, and powdered sugar in a small bowl.
4. Peel and cut the apples into small pieces and mix with the cane sugar.

5. Place the Dutch Oven lid upside down on the embers. Fry the apples in the Dutch Oven lid with a little butter on both sides.
6. Then use a ladle to put small amounts of batter in the Dutch Oven lid and fry on both sides.
7. Serve the finished apple pancakes sprinkled with cinnamon sugar and enjoy.

ENGLISH BREAKFAST

Serving:1 - Preparation time: 10 minutes

Ingredients:

- 2 small sausages
- 2 slices of bacon
- 60 g of baked beans
- 1 tomato
- 1 egg
- 1 tsp oil
- Salt and pepper
- Nutritional information per serving
- Calories: 424.4 kcal
- Carbohydrates: 13.8 g
- Fat: 28.7 g
- Egg white: 24.7 g

Preparation:

1. First, the oil is poured into the Dutch Oven.
2. Then halve the tomato and add to the Dutch Oven along with the other ingredients. Lay the tomatoes cut side down.
3. With the lid closed, the English Breakfast is fried at 175° Celsius.
4. Finally, season with salt and pepper.

DELICIOUS DUTCH OVEN BRUNCH

Serve:12 - Prep time: 20-30 minutes

Ingredients:

- 2 (340 g) sausage (of your choice)
- 6 slices of sourdough bread, cut into bite-sized pieces
- 4 cups mild cheddar cheese, sliced
- 8 eggs
- 2 1/4 cups milk
- 1 teaspoon dry mustard
- 5 spring onions, sliced
- 2 cups fresh mushrooms, roughly chopped
- Spring onions (from above) and fresh tomatoes for serving

Preparation:

1. Set the Dutch Oven to medium temperature and roast the bratwurst. When they're done, cut them into bite-sized pieces.
2. When they're done, take them out of the pot and add some hot water. Spray with non-stick cooking spray.

3. Put the bread cubes on the bottom of the pan.
4. Garnish with 3 cups of cheese, then top the sausage pieces with mushrooms.
5. Whisk together the eggs, milk, mustard and the bottom of the spring onions.
6. Pour over. Cover and refrigerate for 8 hours or overnight.
7. Remove from the fridge about 30 minutes before baking. Preheat the oven to 180°C.
8. Bake 55 minutes. Remove lid, cover with remaining cup of cheese, bake an additional 5 minutes or until cheese is melted.
9. Leave to rest for 5-10 minutes before serving. Refine with fresh tomatoes and spring onions.

FARMER'S BREAKFAST WITH A DIFFERENCE

Serving:1 - Preparation time: 20 minutes

Ingredients:

- 1 small boiled potato
- 2 slices of bacon
- 1 Debrecen sausage
- 1 tbsp corn
- 1 chilli, red
- 2 eggs
- 1 tablespoon cheddar, grated
- 1 tsp oil
- Salt and pepper
- Nutritional information per serving
- Calories: 464 kcal
- Carbohydrates: 13.7 g
- Fat: 33.2 g
- Egg white: 24.2 g

Preparation:

1. First cut the potatoes, bacon and sausages into small cubes. Finely chop the chili and whisk in the eggs.
2. Place the diced potatoes, bacon and sausages with the corn in the Dutch oven and fry briefly at 190° Celsius.
3. Then push everything to the side
4. Now add the beaten egg and fry until scrambled. Then sprinkle the grated cheese on top and let it melt.
5. Season with salt and pepper and serve with potatoes, bacon, sausage and corn.

PANCAKES

Serving:4 - Preparation time: 15 min

Ingredients:

- 8 eggs
- 200 grams of cream cheese
- Olive oil for frying
- (370 kcal/serving

Preparation:

1. In a bowl, beat the eggs and cream cheese until fluffy.
2. Place the Dutch Oven lid upside down on the embers and heat the oil in the Dutch Oven lid.
3. Place the batter in the lid and sear on both sides.
4. Serve and enjoy.

QUICHE LORRAINE

Serving:4 - Preparation time: 30 min

Ingredients:

- 1 onion
- 150 grams of bacon
- 250 g grated Emmental cheese
- 6 eggs
- 125 ml cream
- Paprika powder
- Salt and pepper
- Olive oil for frying

Preparation:

1. Peel and chop the onion. Prepare the Dutch Oven by placing the pot on top of the charcoal briquettes.
2. Heat the oil in the Dutch oven and sauté the onions in it until translucent.
3. Add the bacon and Emmental and stir in.
4. Mix eggs and cream in a bowl and pour over the remaining ingredients.
5. Put the lid on and place the remaining charcoal briquettes on top.
6. Let the quiche cook for about 20 minutes until the eggs are completely set.
7. Serve and enjoy.

FRENCH TOAST

Serving:6 - Preparation time: 10 minutes

Ingredients:

- 6 slices of toast
- 2 eggs
- 150 ml milk
- 1 tablespoon of sugar
- 1 tablespoon vanilla sugar
- 2 teaspoons of cinnamon
- Some fruits
- Maple syrup
- Powdered sugar
- Butter
- 1 pinch of salt

Preparation:

1. Put the milk, eggs, sugar, salt and some cinnamon in a bowl and mix well. Pour the mixture into a flat mold. Let toast soak.
2. Place the Dutch Oven on the grill and preheat the grill to 180 degrees.

3. Put the butter in the Dutch Oven and melt. Add the toast and toast.
4. Serve French toast with fruit and enjoy.

DELICACIES FOR EARLY RISERS

Serving:6 - Preparation time: 25 minutes

Ingredients:

- 1/2 cup - 1 cube of butter
- 9 eggs
- 1 1/2 cups milk
- 1 tablespoon of vanilla
- Zest of a lemon
- 1 1/2 cups flour
- Salt
- 4 cups of berries
- Powdered sugar
- Lemon, if desired

Preparation:

1. Using a stove, prepare 24 charcoals.
2. 2. In a large bowl, whisk together the eggs, milk, vanilla, and lemon zest (this can be done ahead of time). When ready to cook, add the flour and salt and beat until well combined.
3. 3. When the coals are nice and hot, place 8 coals directly under the Dutch Oven. Add butter cubes and let melt. Pour the melted batter into the saucepan, cover and place the remaining 16 coals in the lid.
4. 4. Turn the lid a quarter turn every 5 minutes and let the treat cook until set, about 25 minutes. It should puff up to the lid and when the lid is removed it will fall off. Remove from stove.
5. 5. Top with berries, powdered sugar and a squeeze of lemon. Replace the lid and allow the berries to warm before serving. Cut into 6 slices.

GOOD MORNING POT

Serving:4 - Prep time: 40 minutes

Ingredients:

- 6 tomatoes
- 1 onion
- 100 grams of feta
- 3 peppers
- 1 jalapeno
- 8 eggs
- Paprika powder
- Salt and pepper
- Oil for frying
- Fresh parsley

Preparation:

1. Peel and chop onions. Wash the peppers and jalapeños, remove the stalk, deseed and cut into small pieces.

Wash and finely chop the parsley. Wash the tomatoes, remove the stalk and dice.
2. Heat the oil in the Dutch Oven and sauté the onions, tomatoes, jalapeños and peppers until tender, about 5 minutes. Season with salt, pepper and paprika. Add the feta and cook another 5 minutes until the feta is melted.
3. Make 8 holes in the mixture and crack the eggs and place them in the holes.
4. Cook the eggs with the lid closed over low heat from below and medium heat from above until the whites are set and the yolks are still soft.
5. Serve with parsley and enjoy.

CAPPUCCINO

Serving:1-2 - Prep time: 20 minutes

Ingredients:

- Ground coffee
- milk, optional)

Preparation:

1. Heat 150 ml milk over the stove. Pour the warm milk into a jar with a lid and shake vigorously.
2. Pour the espresso into a cup and top up with the frothed milk. For a touch of sweetness, we recommend a dash of maple syrup.

MUSHROOM OMELETTE

Serving:4 - Preparation time: 15 min

Ingredients:

- 1 pepper
- 250 grams of mushrooms
- 10 eggs
- 100 g grated Gouda cheese
- Olive oil for frying
- Salt and pepper

Preparation:

1. Wash the peppers, deseed, remove the stalk and cut into small pieces. Wash the mushrooms and cut into thin strips.
2. 2. Put the eggs in a bowl, season with pepper and salt and whisk well with the grated Gouda.
3. 3. Put olive oil in the Dutch Oven and fry the vegetables well. Close the lid and let the vegetables cook.
4. 4. Add the egg and cheese mixture and fry over low heat, top and bottom, until the egg and cheese mixture is good, 10 minutes.
5. 5. The omelette is ready. Enjoy your meal!

SEASONAL BREAKFAST FRITTATA

Serving: 2-3 - Prep time: 35 minutes

Ingredients:

- 300 grams of Italian sausage
- 6 large eggs
- 1 cup half and half
- Salt and pepper
- Red pepper flakes
- 2 large handfuls of spinach or Swiss chard
- 225 g feta, crumbled
- 1 large, ripe tomato, roughly chopped

Preparation:

1. Preheat the Dutch Oven to 180°C
2. 2. Cook sausage in a pan over medium heat. Remove grease and drain, but do not wipe clean.
3. 3. Whisk together the eggs, cream, salt, pepper and paprika flakes in a bowl and stir until fluffy.
4. 4. Add sausage, greens, feta and tomato.
5. 5. Pour into a skillet and fry over medium-high heat until edges are set and holding together.
6. 6. Place the pan in the oven and bake for 25-30 minutes until the top of the frittata.

HEARTY PORRIDGE

Serving:1 - Preparation time: 30 minutes

Ingredients:

- 40 grams of rolled oats
- 200 ml vegetable broth
- 1 tbsp peas
- 40 grams of carrots
- ½ apple
- 1 clove of garlic
- 1 tablespoon butter
- 1 pinch curry powder
- 2 spring onions, chopped
- Salt and pepper

Preparation:

1. First, peel and dice the carrots and apple, finely chop the garlic.
2. 2. Put the butter in the Dutch Oven and sauté the carrots, apple and garlic in it.
3. 3. Then add curry powder and rolled oats and roast while stirring constantly.
4. 4. Now pour in the vegetable stock and add the peas. Season with salt and pepper.
5. 5. Cook with the lid closed and 175° Celsius for 5 minutes.
6. 6. Then remove from the fire, stir and leave to swell for 15 minutes.
7. 7. Finally add the spring onions, stir and enjoy.

SCRAMBLED EGGS WITH FETA AND OLIVES

Serving:4 - Preparation time: 20 min

Ingredients:

- 250 grams of feta
- 30 olives
- 6 tablespoons milk 8 eggs
- Salt and pepper
- Olive oil for frying

Preparation:

1. Put the eggs and milk in a bowl and stir. Pit and chop the olives.
2. 2. Heat the oil in the Dutch oven and add the olives with the egg.
3. 3. As soon as the egg is golden brown, spread the feta cheese over it and let it melt briefly
4. 4. Serve and enjoy.

PANCAKE

Serving:4 - Preparation time: 30 minutes

Ingredients:

- 8 eggs
- 200 ml milk
- 400 ml broth
- 1 bunch of parsley, chopped
- Nutmeg, ground
- Salt and pepper

Preparation:

1. First put all the ingredients in a bowl and mix well.
2. 2. Then pour into 4 fireproof bowls and fill the bottom of the Dutch Oven with approx. 3cm of water.
3. 3. Place the shells in the pot and leave to set for 25 minutes at 160° Celsius with the lid closed.

CRISPY HAM

Serving:1 - Preparation time: 10 minutes

Ingredients:

- 4 slices of bacon
- 1 tablespoon of honey
- 1 pinch of cayenne pepper
- some oregano, dried

Preparation:

1. First put the honey, cayenne pepper and oregano in a bowl and stir.
2. 2. Brush the bacon with the marinade.
3. 3. Preheat the Dutch Oven to 190° Celsius.
4. 4. Turn the lid over and place the bacon on the lid.
5. 5. Fry until crispy and enjoy.

BRAISED CHICKEN ON POTATOES

Serving:6 - Preparation time: 13 h 30 min

Ingredients:

- 4 chicken thighs
- 3 leeks
- 700 grams of potatoes
- 2 onions
- 2 tablespoons olive oil
- 3 cloves of garlic
- 2 pieces of bacon rind
- 250 ml cream
- 100 ml milk
- 300 g Parmesan cheese
- Salt and pepper

Preparation:

1. Peel and chop the garlic. Rub chicken thighs with garlic. Leave in the fridge for 1 night.
2. 2. Peel potatoes and onions. Cut into small pieces along with the leek.
3. 3. Add oil to the Dutch Oven. Then fill with potatoes, leeks and onions. Season with salt and pepper. Pour over the parmesan and finish with cream and milk.
4. 4. Place the legs on the mixture and cook for about 1 ½ hours over a low heat from below and high heat from above. The dish is ready when the skin is nice and crispy.
5. 5. Serve and enjoy.

CHICKEN WITH 40 CLOVES OF GARLIC

Serving:8 - Prep time:

Ingredients:

- 2 kg fat young chicken
- 1 cup olive oil
- 40 cloves of garlic
- 1 bay leaf
- 2 sticks of celery
- 1 bunch of yarn
- 1 bouquet of fresh spices
- (parsley, sage, thyme, rosemary)
- Salt and pepper

Preparation:

1. Wash and cut the celery into pieces.
2. Salt and pepper the inside of the chicken and add a bouquet garnier.
3. 3. Pour the olive oil into the Dutch Oven and add all the unpeeled garlic cloves, fresh herbs, bay leaf and celery.
4. 4. Roll the chicken in it several times so that it is well coated with oil.

5. 5. Fry with the lid closed over low heat from below and medium heat from above for approx. 1 ½ hours.
6. 6. Serve and enjoy.

CHICKEN ON POTATOES

Serving:4 - Preparation time: 100 min

Ingredients:

- 4 chicken thighs
- 8 potatoes
- 600 ml chicken broth
- 4 cloves of garlic
- 2 onions
- Thyme sprigs
- Rosemary sprigs
- Pepper and salt
- Olive oil
- Some paprika powder

Preparation:

1. Salt and pepper the chicken thighs and rub with paprika powder. Peel and quarter the potatoes. Peel and thinly slice the onions and garlic.
2. Put some oil in the Dutch Oven. Then spread the potato pieces evenly over the base. Cover with chicken broth.
3. Then add garlic and onions. Finally, spread the chicken thighs over the potatoes and garnish with rosemary and thyme.
4. Cook over low heat from below and high heat from above for about 80 to 90 minutes. Finished!
5. Serve and enjoy.

CHICKEN IN GINGER AND PINEAPPLE MARINADE

Serving:4 - Prep time: 1 day 30 minutes

Ingredients:

- 4 chicken breasts
- 2 tablespoons of soy sauce
- 2 tablespoons of raspberry vinegar
- 1 small can of pineapple
- 2 tablespoons of sherry
- 1 pinch of Sambal Oelek
- 1 teaspoon mustard powder
- 2 cloves of garlic
- 2 cm ginger
- 2 sprigs of tarragon
- 2 tablespoons cashew nuts
- Olive oil for frying

Preparation:

1. For the marinade, mix together the soy sauce, vinegar, pineapple juice, sherry, sambal oelek, mustard powder, crushed garlic cloves, minced ginger and tarragon leaves.
2. Place the chicken breast fillets in the marinade and leave to soak overnight. Turn the chicken occasionally.
3. Then drain and fry on all sides in the Dutch oven with a little olive oil.
4. Put the nuts and pineapple in the Dutch Oven and roast for 3 minutes. Then add the marinade and simmer for another 10 minutes.
5. Serve and enjoy immediately.

CHICKEN WITH FENNEL

Serving:4 - Prep time: 40 minutes

Ingredients:

- 4 chicken breasts
- 2 bulbs of fennel
- 2 onions
- 2 carrots
- 2 lemons
- 4 tablespoons olive oil
- 2 tablespoons of fennel seeds
- 200 ml vegetable broth
- 1 sprig of dill
- Salt and pepper

Preparation:

1. Peel the onion, carrot and fennel and cut into small pieces. Cut the lemon into small slices. Season chicken breast with salt and pepper.
2. Heat the olive oil in the Dutch Oven. Fry the onion, fennel, fennel seeds, carrots and lemon. Add the chicken breast and sauté for 2 minutes.
3. Then bake with the lid closed over low heat from above and below (approx. 6 briquettes each) for approx. 15 to 20 minutes.
4. Serve the finished dish decorated with dill and enjoy.

CHICKEN AND TARRAGON

Serving:4 - Preparation time: 30 min

Ingredients:

- 400 grams of spaghetti
- 4 chicken drumsticks
- 2 glasses of dry white wine
- 150 ml cream
- Fresh tarragon
- Spiced pepper
- Salt and pepper
- Oil for frying

Preparation:

1. Cook spaghetti until firm and slightly tough.

2. Finely chop the tarragon and gently sweat from below with the seasoned pepper and white wine in the Dutch oven over a medium heat for 7 to 8 minutes. Take out and set aside.
3. Season chicken with salt and pepper. Put some oil in the Dutch Oven and fry the chicken until golden brown.
4. Gradually pour the tarragon wine over the chicken. Make sure the tarragon wine has completely evaporated before pouring more tarragon wine over the chicken. It's easy to burn if you wait too long, so be careful!
5. When the meat is done, fold the cream into the sauce. Season with salt and pepper.
6. Serve with the spaghetti and enjoy.

CHICKEN IN PEANUT SAUCE FROM AFRICA

Serving:4 - Preparation time: 60 min

Ingredients:

- 1 chicken
- 3 tablespoons peanut sauce
- 1 bouillon cube
- 750ml of water
- 1 tsp tomato paste
- 1 can of tomatoes
- 1 onion
- 1 hot pepper
- 500 grams of mushrooms
- 500 grams of carrots
- 2 cloves of garlic
- Some lemon juice
- Oregano, laurel
- Thyme
- Salt and pepper

Preparation:

1. Cut the chicken into small pieces. Peel and finely chop the onions and garlic. Cut the peppers into fine rings.
2. Clean mushrooms and carrots and cut into thin slices.
3. Then add the water, chicken, peanut sauce, bouillon cube, tomato paste, chopped tomatoes, onion, pepperoni and spices to the Dutch Oven and simmer for 20 minutes.
4. Add the vegetables and cook for another 30 minutes over high heat from below and low heat from above.
5. Then add the garlic and some lemon juice and season again with salt and pepper. Finished!
6. Serve and enjoy.

CHICKEN BREAST WITH CARROT SAUCE

Serving:4 - Preparation time: 100 min

Ingredients:

- 3 carrots
- 1/8 l chicken broth
- 100 ml whipping cream
- 4 chicken breasts

- 1 tablespoon of clarified butter
- ½ tsp cornstarch
- 2 tablespoons of dry white wine
- Salt and pepper
- Some nutmeg
- Parsley leaves

Preparation:

1. Peel and finely grate the carrots. Place in the Dutch Oven with the broth and cook. Reduce the liquid by half. Then take it out. Place in a sieve, squeeze out the liquid well and collect in a container.
2. Salt and pepper the chicken breasts and sauté in the Dutch oven for about 2 minutes on each side.
3. Pour the cream over the carrot juice, put it in the Dutch Oven and let it boil down a bit. Mix the cornstarch with the white wine, add to the sauce and bind with it. Season with salt and pepper.
4. Arrange everything together on plates and decorate with nutmeg and parsley leaves. Serve and enjoy.

DUCK IN RED WINE SAUCE

Serving:2 - Prep Time: 30 mi

Ingredients:

- 180 g duck breast fillet
- 100 grams of kale
- 1 red onion
- 1 tablespoon of parsley
- 1 tsp tomato paste
- 80 ml of red wine
- 300 ml beef broth
- Sea salt and pepper
- Olive oil for frying

Preparation:

1. Cut the kale into small slices. Peel the red onion and cut into small pieces.
2. Place the kale and onions in the Dutch Oven with a little oil and sauté. Season with salt and pepper. Add beef broth, red wine and tomato paste and mix well. Simmer for 5 minutes. Season with parsley, salt and pepper.
3. Place the duck in the Dutch Oven and simmer together for about 30 minutes.
4. Serve immediately and decorate with some parsley. Finished! Enjoy your meal!

CHICKEN BREAST IN CREAMY MUSHROOM SAUCE

Serving:4 - Preparation time: 35 min

Ingredients:

- 2 onions
- 2 sprigs of marjoram

- 500 g mixed mushrooms
- 40 grams of margarine
- 4 chicken breasts
- Salt and pepper
- ¼ tsp cinnamon
- ¼ tsp allspice
- 125 ml cream
- ¼ l instant sauce
- 2 tablespoons brandy

Preparation:

1. Peel and dice the onion. Clean the mushrooms and cut into pieces.
2. Sauté the diced onions, marjoram leaves and pieces of mushroom in the Dutch Oven with a little margarine. Take out and keep warm.
3. Season the chicken breasts and fry in the Dutch oven.
4. Add the mushrooms, cream and gravy and simmer for about 20 minutes with the lid closed and over medium heat from above and below. Season to taste with salt, pepper and brandy. Finished!
5. Serve and enjoy.

AROMATIC CHICKEN BREAST WITH CHILI

Serving:2 - Prep time: 40 minutes

Ingredients:

- 250g chicken breast
- ½ lemon
- 100 grams of kale
- 1 red onion
- 2 tomatoes
- 1 cm ginger
- 1 chili pepper
- 2 tablespoons of capers
- 2 tablespoons of parsley
- ½ lemon
- 100 grams of buckwheat
- 1 tablespoon of olive oil

Preparation:

1. Cut the tomatoes into small pieces and puree in a blender with the chilli, capers, parsley and lemon juice.
2. Oil the chicken breasts with a teaspoon of turmeric, lemon juice and olive oil and leave to stand for about 10 minutes.
3. Place the chicken breasts in the Dutch Oven and fry briefly and hot.
4. Peel and finely chop the onion and ginger. Add to the Dutch Oven along with the kale and roast for a further 7 minutes.
5. Prepare the buckwheat according to package directions and serve with the chicken, vegetables and tomato salsa and enjoy.

TURKEY WITH TOMATO MARINADE

Serving:2 - Preparation time: 20 min

Ingredients:

- 2 turkey breasts
- 1 chili pepper
- 2 cloves of garlic
- 2 tsp paprika powder
- ½ lemon
- 2 tablespoons tomato paste
- 4 tablespoons olive oil
- Sea salt and pepper

Preparation:

1. Lightly score the turkey breast on all sides to add the marinade.
2. Peel the garlic cloves and cut into small pieces with the chili pepper.
3. Place spices, juice of half a lemon, tomato paste and olive oil in a small bowl and mix together. Season with salt and pepper.
4. Brush the turkey breast with all of the marinade and place in the Dutch Oven. Fry on all sides until the turkey breast is done.
5. Season with sea salt and pepper. Finished! Good Appetite.

CILANTRO CHICKEN

Serving:4 - Prep time: 40 minutes

Ingredients:

- 1 bunch coriander
- 4 chicken breasts
- 1 tsp cornstarch
- 1 tablespoon of water
- 2 tablespoons cream
- 85 grams of yoghurt
- 175 ml chicken broth
- 2 tablespoons lemon juice
- 2 cloves of garlic
- 1 shallot
- 1 tomato
- Salt and pepper
- Olive oil for frying

Preparation:

1. Clean and chop the coriander. Peel and finely chop the garlic and shallot. Skin, deseed and dice the tomato.
2. Season the chicken with salt and pepper and sear on all sides with a little oil. Wrap in aluminum foil and keep warm.
3. Mix the starch and water and stir in the yoghurt and cream.
4. Add the chicken broth to the Dutch Oven with the lemon juice, garlic and shallot and let simmer. Then add the tomato to the yoghurt mixture, salt and pepper and

place in the Dutch Oven. Simmer for another 10 minutes.
5. Add cilantro and chicken and simmer for 5 minutes. Season if necessary. Finished!
6. Serve and enjoy.

CHICKEN WITH FRUIT FILLING

Serving:4 - Preparation time: 60 min

Ingredients:

- 1 chicken
- 1 banana
- 1 apple
- 1 tablespoon of raisins
- 2 tablespoons brandy
- 1 tsp Tabasco
- 1 teaspoon grated lemon zest
- 1 tablespoon of lemon juice
- 1 tablespoon of butter
- Salt and pepper

Preparation:

1. Peel the banana and cut into pieces. Wash, core and cut the apple into pieces. Lightly salt and pepper the chicken inside and out.
2. Mix together the banana, apple, raisins, tabasco and lemon zest and stuff into the chicken.
3. Sew the chicken shut, brush with brandy and lemon juice and drizzle with melted butter.
4. Place the chicken in the Dutch Oven and roast with the lid closed over medium heat from above and low heat from below for approx. 45 minutes. Meanwhile, drizzle with butter.
5. Serve and enjoy.

AFRICAN CHICKEN

Serving:4 - Preparation time: 50 min

Ingredients:

- 4 chicken breast fillets
- 4 cloves of garlic
- ½ chili pepper
- 1 cm ginger
- 150 ml of tomato paste
- 50 ml balsamic vinegar
- 3 tablespoons of honey
- 1 tablespoon of sugar
- 150 ml Dijon mustard
- 300 ml cream
- 200 ml milk
- 4 onions
- Pepper and salt
- ½ tsp nutmeg
- ½ tsp cardamom
- ½ tsp turmeric
- 1 pinch of cinnamon

- 2 tablespoons olive oil

Preparation:

1. Peel the onions, ginger and garlic. Chop the garlic and ginger and cut the onion into fine rings. Cut the chili into fine rings. Put all the spices in a bowl and mix well.
2. Take the chicken breast fillets, rub with the spice mixture and leave for half an hour. Heat the oil in the Dutch oven. Sweat onions, ginger and garlic. Add the chicken breast fillets and sauté. Then add sugar and honey.
3. Then put the remaining ingredients in the Dutch Oven and mix well. Put the lid on and simmer for about 1 hour.
4. Serve with rice and enjoy.

MEDITERRANEAN SALMON FILLET

Serving:4 - Prep time: 40 minutes

Ingredients:

- 1 kg of salmon
- 3 cloves of garlic
- 6 dried tomatoes
- 4 tablespoons olive oil
- 10 black olives
- 1 lemon
- 4 large tomatoes
- 100 ml of white wine
- Salt and pepper

Preparation:

1. Peel the garlic and cut into small pieces.
2. Squeeze the lemon and pour the juice into a small bowl. Add the garlic and olive oil to the bowl and mix well.
3. Spread the mixture on both sides of the salmon. Season with salt and pepper.
4. Pour some olive oil into the Dutch Oven. Put the salmon in the Dutch Oven and cook for about 20 minutes over low heat from below (approx. 6 briquettes) and medium heat from above (approx. 8-10 briquettes).
5. Cut the olives, sundried tomatoes and tomatoes into small pieces.
6. After 20 minutes add the remaining ingredients to the Dutch Oven. Bake another 5 minutes.
7. Serve and enjoy the finished trout.

BRAISED TUNA WITH MUSHROOMS

Serving:4 - Preparation time: 30 minutes

Ingredients:

- 2 tablespoons olive oil
- 1 tablespoon of tuna fillet with butter for 4 people
- 4 tomatoes, chopped
- 1 cup of white wine
- 2 cups of mushrooms
- 1 onion, chopped
- 2 shallots, chopped
- Salt to taste, pepper to taste

Preparation:

1. Heat the oil and butter over medium-high heat for 30 seconds, then add the shallots and onions and stir.
2. Cover and continue cooking over medium-high heat until translucent, 5-6 minutes. Stir every two minutes to avoid burning.

3. Add chopped tomatoes and mushrooms and sauté until tender. Add the tuna fillets and pour the wine over the fish. Season with salt and pepper.
4. Cover and bake at 180°C for 20 minutes or until tuna is cooked but not dry. Serve on mashed potatoes.

SPAGHETTI WITH SEA FRUITS

Serving:6 - Preparation time: 50 min

Ingredients:

- 500 grams of spaghetti
- 1.5 kg of frozen seafood
- 3 tablespoons olive oil
- 100 ml of white wine
- 1 clove of garlic
- 400 g chopped tomatoes
- Salt and pepper
- ½ bunch of fresh parsley

Preparation:

1. Defrost seafood. Peel and chop the garlic. Wash and finely chop the parsley.
2. Heat the water in the Dutch Oven and cook the noodles until firm and slightly chewy. Drain and set aside.
3. Heat the oil in the Dutch Oven. Fry garlic. Add seafood, sweat briefly, then deglaze with white wine. Allow the white wine to reduce slightly.
4. Add chopped tomatoes and season with salt and pepper. Fold in the noodles and reheat.
5. Serve with fresh parsley and enjoy.

GASPERGOU BOUILLABAISSE

Serving: 4-5 - Prep time: 40 minutes

Ingredients:

- 900 g freshwater drum fillets
- 450 g oysters
- 225 g deveined peeled shrimp
- 1 can crab meat – (170 g)
- 2 tablespoons butter or margarine
- 2 tablespoons olive oil
- 1/4 cup all-purpose flour
- 1 cup chopped onion
- 1/2 cup chopped celery
- 1 clove of garlic - chopped
- 5 cups of water
- 1 can of tomatoes – (500 g)
- 1/2 cup dry white wine
- 2 tablespoons chopped parsley
- 1 tablespoon of lemon juice
- 1 bay leaf
- Salt

- 1/4 tsp saffron
- 1/4 teaspoon cayenne pepper

Preparation:

1. Melt butter in a 4-to-5-liter oven. Add olive oil and stir in flour. Cook and stir thoroughly. Add the onion, celery, and garlic and stir-fry until the vegetables begin to brown. Gradually stir in the water. Cut the tomatoes and add them with the juice.
2. Add the wine, parsley, lemon juice, bay leaf, salt, saffron, cayenne pepper and 1/4 of the fish. Bring to a boil and simmer for 20 minutes. Add the remaining fish and cook another 5 to 8 minutes. Add shellfish and cook 3 to 5 minutes or until seafood is cooked through.

BAKED GRATIN

Serving:8 - Prep time: 1 hour

Ingredients:

- 1 medium onion, chopped
- 1 medium green pepper, seeded and chopped
- 1 cup of butter
- 450 g crab meat
- 4 cups of water
- 450g medium prawns, peeled and deveined
- Scallops
- Flounder fillets
- 3 cups of hot milk
- 1 cup grated cheddar cheese
- 1 tablespoon. Vinegar
- 1/2 tsp. Salt-
- Pinch of pepper
- Hot sauce
- 1/2 cup grated parmesan

Preparation:

1. In a heavy skillet, sauté onion and peppers in 1/2 cup butter until tender. Stir in 1/2 cup flour. Cook over medium-high heat for 10 minutes, stirring frequently. add crab meat; mix well. Press the mixture into the bottom of a lightly greased casserole dish or individual casserole dishes. Put aside.
2. Place the water in a large Dutch oven. Bring to a boil. Add shrimp, scallops and flounder. cook 3 minutes; drain, reserving 1 cup of the cooking liquid. Set aside seafood.
3. Melt remaining butter in a heavy saucepan over low heat. Add the remaining flour and stir until smooth. Then cook for 1 minute, stirring constantly.
4. Gradually add milk and reserved cooking liquid. Cook over medium-high heat, stirring constantly, until mixture is thick and bubbly.
5. Stir in cheddar cheese, vinegar, hot sauce (your choice), salt, pepper. Add seafood; stir gently.
6. Spoons of fish mixture over crab meat; Sprinkle with parmesan. Bake in the oven at 180°C for 30 minutes or until lightly browned.

7. Pour the contents of the frying pan into the Dutch Oven. Add wine and parsley. Cover and cook until potatoes are tender.

PASTA WITH SALMON

Serving:4 - Preparation time: 50 min

Ingredients:

- 500 g tagliatelle
- 1 onion
- 4 salmon fillets
- 4 tablespoons olive oil
- 1 clove of garlic
- 300 ml cream
- 100 ml of tomato passata
- Oregano
- 2 tablespoons of fresh herbs
- Salt and pepper

Preparation:

1. Peel and finely chop the onions and garlic. Roughly dice the salmon.
2. Heat the water in the Dutch Oven and cook the noodles until firm and slightly chewy. Drain and set aside.
3. Heat the oil in the Dutch Oven. Place the onions and garlic in the Dutch Oven and sauté. Add salmon and fry.
4. Then add the cream and tomato passata to the ingredients and season with fresh herbs, oregano, salt and pepper.
5. Fold in the noodles and fry for 2 minutes.
6. Serve and enjoy.

HERB FETTUCCINE WITH SCALLOPS

Serving:4 - Preparation time: 20 minutes

Ingredients:

- 450 g of scallops
- 225g fettucini or linguine
- 1 tablespoon butter
- 1 tablespoon cooking oil
- 3 cloves of garlic; chopped
- 2 carrots; to cut
- 2 cups snow peas
- 3 spring onions; thinly sliced
- 1/2 cup dry white wine
- 1/3 cup of water
- 2 tsp fresh tarragon
- 1 tsp instant chicken broth granules
- 1/4 teaspoon cayenne pepper
- 2 tablespoons cornstarch
- 2 tablespoons cold water
- 1/4 cup parmesan; grated
- Black pepper

Preparation:

1. Thaw scallops (if frozen). Cut each large scallop in half.
2. Cook the noodles in a Dutch oven or large saucepan in lightly salted water according to package directions. Return to pan and add butter.
3. Stir gently to apply then set aside. Heat the oil in a wok or large skillet over medium-high heat. Sauté garlic for 15 seconds. Add carrots and fry for 4 minutes.
4. Add snow peas and spring onions. Stir and fry until vegetables are tender (2-3 minutes).
5. Remove from pan. Chill the pan for a minute. Add the wine and the first portion of water.
6. Add the tarragon, bouillon granules and crushed hot red pepper flakes. Bring to a boil. Add the scallops and reduce the heat. Simmer uncovered until scallops are opaque (1-2 minutes), stirring occasionally.
7. Stir together the cornstarch and the second batch of water. Add to the pan and stir during cooking until thickened.
8. Cook and stir for another 2 minutes. Return the vegetables and pasta to the pan. Stir gently to apply. Sprinkle each serving with grated parmesan and black pepper.

WHITEFISH WITH TOMATOES AND GARLIC

Serving:4 - Preparation time: 20 minutes

Ingredients:

- bunch of coriander; chopped
- 3 cloves of garlic; chopped
- 3 tomatoes; to cut
- 4 fillets of whitefish or sea bass; (150-170g)
- 1/4 cup olive oil
- 1 tsp paprika
- Instant Chicken Broth Granules
- 1/2 tsp ground cumin
- 1/2 tsp ground turmeric
- 1/2 tsp ground pepper
- 3 cups of water

Preparation:

1. Spread the coriander evenly over the bottom of the heavy Dutch Oven.
2. Sprinkle with garlic and spread the tomatoes on top. Then put the fish on top of the tomatoes.
3. Whisk together the oil, paprika, bouillon granules, cumin, turmeric, and pepper in a small bowl. put fish on top.
4. Add enough water to the pot to reach the bottom of the fish. Bring water to a boil over high heat.
5. Cover the pot, reduce the heat to medium and simmer until the fish is cooked, about 10 minutes
6. 6. Using a large spatula, transfer the fish and vegetables to a platter. Pour some of the cooking liquid over it and serve.

CANNELLONI STUFFED WITH SALMON

Serving:4 - Prep time: 40 minutes

Ingredients:

- 12 cannelloni
- 3 salmon fillets
- 2 shallots
- 2 cm ginger
- 400 ml milk
- 200 grams of spinach
- 300 grams of mozzarella
- Nutmeg
- 1 bunch of parsley
- 4 tablespoons of tomato paste
- 1 tablespoon of olive oil
- Salt and pepper

Preparation:

1. Place all ingredients except cannelloni, milk, mozzarella, spinach and cream in a bowl and puree with a hand blender. Pour the mixture into the cannelloni and spread evenly in the Dutch oven.
2. In a separate bowl, add the chopped spinach. Mix milk and cream well. Season with salt, nutmeg and pepper. Then put in the Dutch Oven.
3. Scatter the mozzarella over the cannelloni, then bake, covered, over medium-high heat, top and bottom, until cheese is brown, about 30 minutes. Finished!
4. Serve and enjoy.

ASIAN SHRIMP WITH NOODLES

Serving:2 - Prep time: 40 minutes

Ingredients:

- 300 g king prawns
- 2 tablespoons of soy sauce
- 150 grams of pasta
- 4 cloves of garlic
- 1 chili pepper
- 80 g celery
- 1 red onion
- 150 grams of green beans
- 100 grams of kale
- 200 ml vegetable broth
- 1 tsp ginger
- Sesame oil for frying

Preparation:

1. Peel the garlic clove and the red onion and cut into small pieces. Cut the chili into rings. Cut kale into strips.
2. Put the king prawns in the Dutch oven with 1 tablespoon of soy sauce and sauté briefly.
3. Add the garlic clove, chili pepper, red onion, ginger, celery, green beans and kale to the Dutch Oven with the remaining soy sauce and simmer for about 10 minutes.

4. Then add that and the broth and simmer for another 10 minutes.
5. Serve on a plate with the pasta and enjoy. Enjoy your meal!

SHRIMP GUMBO

Serving: 4-6 - Prep time: 1 hour 15 minutes

Ingredients:

- 2 tablespoons olive oil
- 2 onions, chopped
- 4 garlic cloves, crushed
- 225 g okra, chopped
- 2 cups of peppers, chopped
- 2 cups tomatoes, chopped
- 2 cups mushrooms, chopped
- 1 ham, smoked
- 1 teaspoon of cayenne pepper
- 1 tablespoon hot sauce
- 1/2 teaspoon chili powder
- 450 g shrimp, peeled
- 2-4 cups of hot water, depending on the thickness of the broth
- 4 cups broth of your choice
- Salt and pepper to taste

Preparation:

1. Heat oil on medium for 30 seconds, then add garlic and onions and stir. Cover and continue cooking over medium heat until translucent, 5-6 minutes.
2. Stir every two minutes to avoid burning. Add mushrooms, okra, and tomatoes and sauté for 5 minutes, stirring frequently.
3. Add everything else except shrimp. Stir well, cover and simmer for an hour. Check the liquid - it shouldn't be too soupy. Gumbo should thicken as it cooks.
4. Add shrimp and simmer for 10 minutes just before serving.

DUTCH OVEN SQUID

Serving:4 - Preparation time: 50 min

Ingredients:

- 4 squids
- 500 grams of potatoes
- 200 grams of tomatoes
- 2 tablespoons of fresh herbs
- 2 onions
- 2 cloves of garlic
- Salt and pepper

Preparation:

1. Cook the potatoes in the Dutch oven and cut into small pieces.
2. Wash tomatoes and cut into small pieces.
3. Peel and chop the onion and garlic into small pieces.
4. Spread the potatoes on the bottom of the Dutch Oven and add the other ingredients. Finally, place the squids on top of the other ingredients (the squid arms are facing up).
5. Cover the entire lid with briquettes and cook for about 90 minutes.
6. Serve and enjoy.

SPAGHETTI WITH MUSSELS

Serving:4 -Preparation time:50min

Ingredients:

- 1.5 kg of mussels
- 4 tablespoons olive oil
- 2 cloves of garlic
- 350 g chopped tomatoes
- 50 ml white wine
- Salt and pepper
- some parmesan

Preparation:

1. Peel and thinly slice the garlic.
2. Heat some water in the Dutch Oven. Put the mussels in the water. Remove as soon as they open, separating the flesh from the skin. Put the clam water in a separate container.
3. Heat the oil in the Dutch Oven. Add garlic slices and sauté lightly. Pour the white wine into the Dutch Oven and allow to reduce slightly.
4. Then put the mussel water and the chopped tomatoes in the Dutch Oven and simmer for about 15 minutes.
5. Add the mussels and cook for another 2 minutes. Season with salt and pepper.
6. Serve with spaghetti and parmesan and enjoy.

BAKED SALMON WITH MISS AND SHIITAKE

Serving:4 - 6 - Preparation time: 25 minutes

Ingredients:

- 1 tablespoon of olive oil
- 1 tablespoon grated fresh ginger
- 2 tablespoons of soy sauce
- 1 tablespoon red miss paste
- 2 garlic cloves, finely chopped
- Juice of 1 lime
- 450 g salmon fillets, fresh
- 2 cups shiitake mushrooms, whole
- 1 tablespoon of olive oil

Preparation:

1. Mix 1 tablespoon oil, ginger, garlic, soy sauce, lime juice and miso paste into a marinade. Pour salmon fillets over and marinate for 10 minutes to several hours. In a

Dutch Oven, add 1 tablespoon olive oil and sauté the shiitake mushrooms until cooked through.

2. Place the marinated salmon fillets on the stove and pour over the remaining marinade. Arrange the shiitake mushrooms around the fillet.

3. Fry over high heat (210°C) for 10 minutes until just beginning to brown, then reduce the heat and bake uncovered at 160°C for a further 10 minutes. Serve with rice and salad.

PEPPERED SHRIMP

Serving:4 - Preparation time: 25 minutes

Ingredients:

- 450 grams of butter
- 1/2 cup lemon juice
- 2 teaspoons fresh basil, chopped
- 2 teaspoons of cayenne pepper
- 2 teaspoons fresh oregano, chopped
- 5 garlic cloves, chopped
- 1 bay leaf, crumbled
- 1/2 cup black pepper, finely ground
- Salt
- 4 lb. shelled raw prawns

Preparation:

1. Melt the butter in a large, deep skillet (like a Dutch oven) or cast iron skillet over low heat. Once melted, increase the heat and add the remaining ingredients except the shrimp. Cook, stirring frequently, until a rich mahogany color is achieved, about 10 minutes.

2. Add shrimp, stirring and turning to coat the seasoned butter well. Cook for 10 minutes, or until the shrimp have turned a rich, deep pink.

3. Serve the shrimp in their shells and peel them at the table.

BAKED TROUT IN TOMATOES

Serving:4 - Prep time: 50 minutes

Ingredients:

- Cut 2 trout in half
- 1 large can of tomatoes
- 2 medium onions, sliced and sautéed in margarine
- 1/2 tsp oregano
- 1/2 tsp basil
- 1 bay leaf

Preparation:

1. Place trout and tomatoes in your Dutch Oven.
2. Then add the onions in one layer to cover them.
3. Scatter the oregano and basil over the onions. Add bay leaf. Cover and bake for 45 minutes.

PASTA CASSEROLE WITH SPINACH AND SALMON

Ingredients:

- 300 grams of cream cheese
- 500 ml milk
- 500 grams of pasta
- 300 g salmon fillet
- 500 g frozen spinach
- Salt and pepper
- Nutmeg
- 400 grams of mozzarella
- 1 onion
- 1 clove of garlic
- Some olive oil

Preparation:

1. Peel and finely chop the onion. Peel and chop the garlic. Dice salmon fillet. Cut the mozzarella into slices.
2. Pour olive oil into the Dutch Oven. Add onions and garlic and sauté. Then add the salmon and sauté lightly.
3. Add spinach after 2 minutes. Fry everything for another 5 minutes. Stir occasionally.
4. Add milk, uncooked pasta and cream cheese. If necessary, add some milk. Then season with salt, pepper and nutmeg and simmer gently for 3 minutes.
5. Stir well again. Then spread the mozzarella slices on top and cook over low heat from below and medium heat from above for 30 minutes until the cheese is crispy and the pasta is cooked.
6. Serve and enjoy.

STUFFED SQUID

Serving:4 - Preparation time: 60 min

Ingredients:

- 400 grams of squid
- 4 tablespoons cream cheese
- 4 egg yolks
- 4 tablespoons chopped parsley
- 2 red chili peppers
- 2 tsp chopped dill
- 1 pepper
- Salt and pepper
- 2 lemons

Preparation:

1. Clean the squid and season with salt and pepper.
2. Mix the cream cheese with the egg yolk and add the parsley, chilli, dill and diced peppers.
3. Fill the squid with the mixture and place in the Dutch Oven and bake for about 10 minutes over low heat from below and medium heat from above.
4. Drizzle the finished squid with lemon juice, serve and enjoy.

MUSSELS WITH WHITE WINE SAUCE

Serving: 4-6 - Prep time: 20 minutes

Ingredients:

- 2 tablespoons olive oil
- 4 tablespoons salted butter
- 2 garlic cloves, finely chopped
- 2 shallots, finely chopped
- 2 cups of white wine
- 1 cup fresh cream (optional)
- 1 sprig of fresh tarragon
- 1 cup chopped parsley
- 900g of fresh mussels, washed and soaked for an hour.

Preparation:

1. Sauté the garlic and shallots in olive oil and butter for two minutes. Pour in the wine, add the tarragon and simmer gently for a few minutes.
2. Add the heavy cream if using and mix well. Increase the heat slightly until the mixture is bubbling, then add the mussels and cover the pot.
3. Steam for 7 to 10 minutes or until the shells open. Discard unopened mussels. Arrange in bowls, pour the broth over the shellfish and sprinkle with parsley.
4. Delicious eaten with hot crusty bread for dipping in the broth.

BAKED MAHI

Serving:3 – 4 - Prep time: 40 minutes

Ingredients:

- 1 mahi-mahi or red snapper fillet, about 225g (each)
- 1/4 cup orange juice
- 2 tsp lemon juice
- 3/4 tsp cornstarch
- 1-2 tablespoons of water
- 1 tsp orange marmalade
- 1 tsp lemon zest

Preparation:

1. Preheat the oven to 200 °C. Spray with cooking spray before heating.
2. Arrange the fish fillets in a separate pan. Drizzle with orange and lemon juice and season with salt and pepper.
3. Let rest 10-15 minutes, turning once to marinate. Bake the fish for 12-15 minutes or until the fish flakes easily.
4. Put the fish fillets on a plate, cover and keep warm.
5. Dissolve cornstarch in water. Add jam and lemon zest.
6. Stir over medium-high heat for 3-4 minutes, or until sauce thickens. Serve the sauce over the fish.

SALMON IN SOY SAUCE WITH KIWICH UTNEY

Serving:4 - Preparation time: 25 min

Ingredients:

- 300 grams of rice
- 2 cm ginger
- 1 red chili pepper
- 6 tablespoons sweet soy sauce
- 4 kiwis
- 1 clove of garlic
- 2 spring onions
- 4 pieces of salmon fillet
- 4 tablespoons of water
- Salt
- Olive oil for frying

Preparation:

1. Cook rice according to package directions.
2. Peel and finely dice the kiwis. Peel ginger and grate very finely. Wash and finely chop the chili. Mix everything well in a bowl and set aside.
3. Peel and slice the garlic. Wash the spring onions and cut diagonally into slices.
4. Mix the sweet soy sauce with 4 tablespoons of water. Add the garlic and spring onions to the mixture.
5. Heat the oil in the Dutch Oven. Salt the salmon and fry in the hot oil for 2 to 3 minutes on each side.
6. Add the scallion and soy sauce mixture and simmer until thick. Pour the liquid over the salmon from time to time.
7. Serve salmon with rice and kiwi chutney and enjoy.

PRAWNS IN SAFFRON SAUCE

Serving:4 - Preparation time: 30 min

Ingredients:

- 500 grams of shrimp
- 200 grams of carrots
- 2 cloves of garlic
- 200ml cream
- 100 ml milk
- 1 tsp mustard
- Saffron threads
- Salt and pepper
- Olive oil for frying

Preparation:

1. Peel, devein and wash the shrimp. Wash carrots and cut into fine slices. Peel the garlic and chop in to fine slithers.
2. Put the vegetables and shrimp in the Dutch Oven and fry for about 5 to 10 minutes.
3. Mix the remaining ingredients and add to the shrimp. Simmer for 10 to 15 minutes. Finished!
4. Serve with or without spaghetti and enjoy

CARIBBEAN SHRIMP WITH LIME CHILI AND COCONUT

Serving:4 - 6 - Preparation time: 20 minutes

Ingredients:

- 2 tablespoons olive oil
- 2 tablespoons of butter
- 4 garlic cloves, finely chopped
- 900g freshly peeled prawns of any size
- Juice of 2 limes
- 1 cup coconut cream
- Red chilli flakes
- Ground chili
- 1/2 cup coriander, chopped
- Salt to taste

Preparation:

1. Heat the oil and butter together over medium-high heat for 30 seconds, then add the minced garlic and stir quickly for a minute.
2. Add the peeled shrimp and sear over medium-high heat, stirring, until the shrimp turn pink about every minute (about 7 to 10 minutes).
3. Pour the lime juice, spices and coconut cream over the mixture and stir. Cook for another minute and remove from heat.
4. Season with salt and sprinkle with chopped coriander. Serve with jasmine rice.

SEAFOOD PILAF

Serving: 4 - 6 - Prep time: 40 minutes

Ingredients:

- 2 tablespoons olive oil
- 2 tablespoons of butter
- 2 cups of rice
- 4 cups vegetable or seafood soup
- 1 tomato, chopped
- 4 cloves of garlic, chopped
- 1/2 cup parsley, chopped
- 1 onion
- 6 carnation stems
- Cayenne pepper
- 225 g assorted fresh fish and shellfish

Preparation:

1. Heat the oil and butter over medium-high heat for 30 seconds, then add the garlic, onion, and leeks and stir. Cover and continue cooking over medium heat until translucent, 5-6 minutes.
2. Stir every two minutes to avoid burning. Add rice, stir and cook until no longer runny, about 4 minutes. Add the broth, tomato, garlic, parsley, cayenne pepper and stir. Mix cloves with onions and add to the broth with the other ingredients.

3. Cook over medium-high heat for 20 minutes, stirring occasionally. Add seafood and cook, covered, about 10 minutes longer.
4. Shrimp should be pink and the shells should be open when done.

GREEK SCAMPI

Serving:4 - Prep time: 45 minutes

Ingredients:

- 1 tsp olive oil
- 5 garlic cloves, chopped
- 1.5 kg whole tomatoes, drain, roughly chop
- 1/2 cup Chopped fresh parsley
- 600 g large prawns, peeled
- 110 g feta cheese
- 2 tablespoons fresh lemon juice
- 1/4 teaspoon freshly ground pepper

Preparation:

1. Preheat the oven to 200 °C
2. Heat the oil in a large Dutch oven over medium-high. add garlic; Fry for 30 seconds.
3. Add tomatoes and 1/4 cup parsley. reduce temperature; Simmer 10 min, add shrimp; Boil 5 minutes.
4. Pour the mixture into a baking pan; Sprinkle with cheese. Bake for 10 minutes at 200°C. With 1/4 cup parsley, lemon juice and pepper sprinkle on meat dishes.

CORNISH CHICKENS WITH APRICOT COGNAC AND ALMONDS

Serving:4 - Preparation time: 45 – 60 minutes

Ingredients:

- 2 to 3 tablespoons of olive oil
- 4 Cornish Hens (broilers)
- 2 cups apricot or plum, dried and chopped
- 1/2 cup cognac
- 1/2 cup hot water
- 1/2 cup flaked almonds
- 1 onion, sliced
- 2 tablespoons Herbes de Provence
- Handful of fresh herbs: rosemary, tarragon, thyme salt, pepper to taste

Preparation:

1. Soak the chopped apricots and plums in cognac and hot water, just enough to cover them. Leave to soak for as long as possible, from 30 minutes to overnight. Pour 1 tablespoon of olive oil onto the bottom of the cast iron cooker and spread evenly. Rub each chicken with olive oil, dried herbs, salt and pepper. Put in a pan.
2. Put some fresh herbs in the chicken cavity. Place the soaked fruit mixture around the chickens; Add onion

slices. Scatter the almonds on top. Bake at high heat (220 °C) for 20 minutes.

3. Reduce the heat to 160°C and bake, covered, for an additional 25 to 30 minutes or until the chickens are done. Be sure to stir the fruit and chicken at least once during the cooking process.

4. Serve chicken with cooked fruit and baking juices poured over meat. Gladly served with rice

ZUCCHINI STUFFED WITH MINCED MEAT

Serving:4 - Prep time: 40 minutes

Ingredients:

- 4 zucchini
- 500 grams of minced meat
- 75 g of tomato paste
- 200 grams of chopped tomatoes
- 200 g Parmesan cheese
- 1 pepper
- 1 onion
- Salt, pepper, oregano
- Some olive oil

Preparation:

1. Slightly heat the oil in the Dutch oven. Fry ground beef. Add tomato paste and mix in. Cut the pepper and onion into small pieces and add to the pot.

2. Wash and halve zucchini. Scoop the flesh out of the zucchini.

3. Stuff the minced meat mixture with the vegetables into the hollowed-out zucchini.

4. Place in the Dutch Oven, sprinkle with Parmesan and cook over medium heat for about 20 minutes.

5. Serve and enjoy the zucchini.

CHICKEN HUNTER

Serving: 4-6 - Prep time: 1 hour

Ingredients:

- 2 tablespoons of butter
- 1 chicken, cut into pieces
- 2 cups assorted mushrooms, sliced
- 2 shallots, chopped
- 1 tablespoon of Herbes de Provence
- 1 cup red wine, dry
- Salt to taste

Preparation:

1. Heat butter for 30 seconds, then add chicken pieces. Fry over medium-high heat until brown on both sides, about 20 minutes total. Cover the chicken and let it simmer on a low flame for about 20 minutes.

2. Remove the chicken, leaving the juices and fats in the pot. Add mushrooms and shallots and sauté until

brown. Add red wine, herbs and salt and simmer for 10 minutes.

3. Return the chicken to the pot, mix well, cover and simmer another 10 minutes, or until done

POTATO PAN WITH BACON

Serving:4 - Preparation time: 25 min

Ingredients:

- 8 medium potatoes
- 300 grams of bacon
- 1 large onion
- 1 pepper
- 4 eggs
- Olive oil for frying
- parsley, thyme
- Salt and pepper

Preparation:

1. Boil the potatoes and then cut them into 1 cm thick slices. dice bacon. Peel and chop the onion. Wash the peppers, deseed, remove the stalk and cut into small cubes.

2. Heat the oil in the pan. Fry onions and peppers. Add potatoes and bacon and sauté. Season to taste with salt, pepper, thyme and parsley.

3. Beat the eggs, add to the remaining ingredients and cook well with the lid closed and low heat from below and high heat from above.

4. Arrange on plates and enjoy. Enjoy your meal!

ROASTED PORK LOIN WITH AUTUMN APPLES AND CIDER

Serving: 4-6 - Prep time: 1 hour 30 minutes

Ingredients:

- 2 tablespoons olive oil
- 1 tablespoon salted butter
- 2 onions, chopped in rounds
- 1 pork loin
- 4 apples, quartered
- 1 cup dry, hard (alcoholic) apple cider
- Salt to taste, pepper to taste

Preparation:

1. Pour the olive oil into the Dutch Oven and spread evenly. Add butter, melt over medium heat and sauté onions until golden brown. Rub your pork loin with olive oil, salt and pepper.

2. Place in the center of the pan. Spread your side dish (apples and onions) down the back. Pour 1 cup apple cider into the pan. Cover and cook slowly at 170 °C for 90 minutes.

3. The meat should be tender enough to pull apart with a fork. salt and pepper to taste.

BUCKWHEAT BEEF PILAF

Serving:8 - Prep time: 1 hour 50 minutes

Ingredients:

- 1/3 cup olive oil
- 8 tablespoons unsalted butter
- 1 large onion diced
- 450 - 650 g beef fillet cut into pieces
- 3 large carrots
- 2.5 cups of buckwheat groats
- 4 1/4 cups cold filtered water + 1 cup hot water
- 2 tsp salt and black pepper or to taste
- 1 tsp cumin to taste
- 1 whole clove of garlic unpeeled

Preparation:

1. Place a large saucepan or Dutch oven on stovetop over medium/high heat and add 1/3 cup olive oil and 4 tablespoons butter. Add onion and sauté, stirring occasionally, until tender (about 5 minutes).
2. Add diced beef and sauté for 5 minutes, turning once (beef will not cook through). Add the carrots and stir for another minute.
3. Add 4 1/4 cups cold water and season with 1 tsp cumin, 2 tsp salt and 1/4 tsp pepper or to taste. Bring to a boil, then reduce heat to low, cover and cook for 1 hour.
4. Meanwhile (about 10 minutes before the timer runs out) heat a large nonstick skillet over medium/high and melt 4 tablespoons butter. Add 2 1/2 cups buckwheat and toast until golden brown. Pour the buckwheat into the saucepan in an even layer and carefully pour in enough hot water to cover the buckwheat (feel free to add 1 cup of hot water).
5. Cut the garlic clove in half parallel to the base to reveal the cloves and place over the buckwheat, pressing lightly into the buckwheat. Cook, uncovered, over medium-high heat until most of the surface liquid has boiled off (10 minutes).
6. Poke 8-10 holes in the buckwheat to allow steam to escape to the surface. Then cover with a lid, reduce the heat to low and let the pot sit for another 30 minutes. Remove the garlic and stir gently.

CHICKEN FAJITA ALFREDO

Serving:5 - Prep time: 35 minutes

Ingredients:

- 225 g cellentani or spiral pasta
- 225 g sliced fresh mushrooms
- 1 yellow summer squash, sliced
- 2 teaspoons olive oil
- 2 garlic cloves, chopped
- 1 serving leftover chilli chicken fajitas, roughly chopped
- 2 cans of diced tomatoes with basil, oregano and garlic, not drained
- 3/4 cup alfredo sauce

- 3/4 teaspoon dried oregano

Preparation:

1. Cook noodles according to package directions.
2. Fry the mushrooms in a casserole and sauté in oil until tender. add garlic; Fry 1 minute longer. Stir in fajitas, tomatoes, alfredo sauce, and oregano.
3. Bring to a boil. Reduce heat; Cover and simmer for 5-10 minutes, stirring occasionally. drain pasta; add to the fajita mixture and add.

BEEF GOULASH WITH FRESH HERBS

Serving: 4-6 - Prep time: 2 hours

Ingredients:

- 2 tablespoons olive oil
- 6 garlic cloves, quartered and 1 onion, chopped
- 900 gr. Beef goulash pieces
- 1 large leek, chopped
- 2 carrots, chopped
- 2 cups mushrooms, chopped
- 2 cups tomatoes, chopped
- 4 potatoes, peeled and quartered
- 2 tablespoons dried herbs de Provence
- Salt and pepper to taste
- Chopped parsley to refine
- 1 cup red wine or 1/4 cup sherry
- 4 cups beef broth or vegetable broth
- Extra hot water on demand

Preparation:

1. Heat oil over medium-high heat for 30 seconds, then add minced garlic and onion and sauté until translucent. Stir every two minutes to avoid burning. Add pieces of meat and lightly brown, mixing frequently.

2. Add your chopped veggies in the following order, stirring between each addition: mushrooms, tomatoes, carrots, potatoes. Add broth and wine, then fresh herbs. Make sure the meat and vegetables are covered with enough liquid. If more is needed, add hot water as needed.

3. This liquid should evaporate a little. The mixture should not be too soupy, but not too dry either. Simmer slowly, 90 minutes to 2 hours. Meat is very tender when done. Be sure to remove any large sticks from the fresh herbs. Salt to taste before serving. Add parsley.

CABBAGE ROLLS WITH MINCED MEAT

Serving:4 - Preparation time: 35 min

Ingredients:

- 4 large cabbage leaves
- 400 grams of minced meat
- 100 g herbal cream cheese
- Salt and pepper

Preparation:

1. Mix the ground beef with the cream cheese and season with salt and pepper.
2. Place the ground beef mixture on the cabbage leaves and roll up. Secure with two kitchen strings.
3. Cook cabbage rolls on top and bottom over medium-high heat for 30 minutes. remove threads. Finished!
4. Serve and enjoy

MINCED MEAT AND POTATO GRATIN

Serving:4 - Prep time: 80 minutes

Ingredients:

- 500 grams of potatoes
- 500 grams of cauliflower
- 300 grams of minced meat
- 200 grams of cheese
- 1 onion
- 2 cups cream
- Salt and pepper

Preparation:

1. Boil the potatoes in a saucepan and then cut into small slices. Wash cauliflower and cook in boiling water for about 5 minutes.
2. Put the minced meat in the Dutch Oven with olive oil and fry. Season with salt and pepper.
3. Peel the onion, cut into small pieces and also place in the Dutch Oven. Add cream and stir well. Take out and set aside.
4. Line the bottom of the Dutch Oven with potato slices, season with salt and pepper and place the ground beef mixture and cauliflower over the potatoes. Finally a layer of cheese on top.
5. Cook the dish in the Dutch Oven for about 60 minutes over low heat from below and medium heat from above.
6. Serve and enjoy.

CHOPPED CHICKEN

Serving:4 - Preparation time: 35 min

Ingredients:

- 800 g chicken breast
- 400 ml cream
- 600 grams of mushrooms
- 150 ml white wine (dry)
- 1 cucumber
- 1 tablespoon of dill
- Some lemon juice
- Paprika powder
- Olive oil for frying
- Salt and pepper

Preparation:

1. Wash the cucumber and cut into very fine slices. Sprinkle with salt and let stand 5 minutes. Then drain. Add the dill, 100 ml cream, lemon juice and pepper and mix well.
2. Cut the chicken breast into pieces. Clean the mushrooms and cut them in slices.
3. Heat the oil in the Dutch Oven. Fry the mushrooms, remove and set aside.
4. Add a little more oil to the Dutch Oven. Fry the chicken breast. Season with salt, pepper and paprika and deglaze with white wine. Let the white wine boil down.
5. Add the mushrooms and the remaining cream and let everything simmer together for about 10 minutes.
6. Serve with the cucumber salad and enjoy.

CHICKEN THIGHS WITH GARLIC GINGER CARAMEL

Serving:3 – 4 - Prep time: 1 hour

Ingredients:

- 1.3 kg chicken thighs
- Kosher salt
- 2 tablespoons vegetable oil
- 8 peeled cloves of garlic
- 1/2 cup of water
- 1/3 cup light brown sugar
- 1/4 cup rice vinegar
- 2 slices of peeled ginger
- 1 cup chicken broth
- 1/4 cup soy sauce
- 2 shallots, thinly sliced

Preparation:

1. Season the chicken pieces on both sides with Kosher salt.
2. Heat oil in a large, heavy, wide-bottomed saucepan, such as B. a Dutch Oven, heat over medium heat.
3. Cook the chicken in batches, about 8 minutes per side, until crisp. Place the pieces on a plate.
4. Add the garlic to the saucepan and cook, stirring constantly, for about 2 minutes. Transfer the garlic to the plate with the chicken.
5. Turn off the heat and pour the fat from the pan.
6. Place the pan back on the stove and set the temperature to medium-high. Add the water and brown sugar and cook until thickened, about 5 minutes.
7. Add the vinegar and stir until the granulated sugar has dissolved again.
8. Add ginger, chicken broth and soy sauce. Add the chicken, skin-side up, along with the garlic. Bring the mixture to a boil. Reduce the heat and cook until the chicken is fully cooked, about 25 minutes. Transfer the chicken to a plate.
9. Bring the sauce to a boil and cook for 8 to 10 minutes. Place the chicken back in the Dutch Oven and brush with the sauce. Sprinkle with the spring onions.

10. Add peas and parsley. Cook for another 10 minutes and serve

CHICKEN AND RICE

Serving: 4-6 - Prep time: 2 hours

Ingredients:

- 2 tablespoons olive oil
- 1 chicken, cut into pieces
- 2 cups of rice
- 12 cups of hot water or broth
- 2 carrots, chopped
- 1 leek, chopped
- 1 onion, chopped
- Cayenne pepper
- Nutmeg
- Salt to taste

Preparation:

1. Heat oil over medium-high heat for 30 seconds, then add chicken pieces and sear, browning on each side. Add all the vegetables and continue to sauté, stirring well and often.
2. Add rice, sauté for a few minutes, then add hot water and spices. Cover and simmer for 2 hours, until thick and chicken is tender. Salt to taste.

TENDER FRIED CHICKEN

Serving: 4-6 - Prep time: 35 minutes

Ingredients:

- Oil for frying
- 3 chicken thighs
- 3 chicken thighs Buttermilk to coat chicken in a bowl Place flour in a shallow bowl
- 2 eggs, beaten, in a shallow bowl panko or breadcrumbs in a shallow bowl
- Salt and pepper to taste
- Chili pepper to taste
- 1 tablespoon of Herbes de Provence

Preparation:

1. Marinate chicken in buttermilk overnight. Heat oil for frying. Turn chicken in flour. Dip in egg batter. Dip in panko mixed with spices.
2. Add hot oil and fry until brown on each side. Remove and place on a paper towel. Continue frying in small batches so as not to overcrowd the chicken.
3. Reduce the heat and return the chicken pieces to the pan and sear a second time to finish cooking.

BEEF ROULADES WITH BACON

Serving:4 - Preparation time: 120 minutes

Ingredients:

- 4 beef roulades
- 4 slices of bacon
- 4 slices of cheese
- 4 pickles
- 2 onions
- 1 tablespoon of mustard
- 2 tablespoons of tomato paste
- 500 ml of tomato passata
- Salt and pepper
- Thyme
- Oregano
- 200 ml of red wine
- Paprika powder
- 2 tablespoons olive oil

Preparation:

1. Quarter the cucumbers, peel the onions and cut into rings.
2. Roll out the roulades, press flat again, spread with mustard and top with cucumber, part of the onion, cheese and bacon. Season with salt and pepper. Roll up and secure with skewers.
3. Place the roulades in the Dutch oven together with the oil and fry on all sides. Take out and set aside.
4. Place the remaining onions in the Dutch Oven and sauté. Place the tomato paste, tomato passata and red wine in the Dutch Oven. Season with salt, pepper, thyme, paprika powder and oregano.
5. Add the roulades to the sauce and let simmer for about 90 minutes with the lid closed.
6. Serve and enjoy.

POTATO GRATIN WITH HAM

Serving:6 - Preparation time: 100 min

Ingredients:

- 1.5 kg of potatoes
- 200ml cream
- 200 ml milk
- 400 g diced ham
- 500 g Emmental cheese
- 1 tablespoon nutmeg
- Salt and pepper
- 4 onions

Preparation:

1. Heat the water in the Dutch Oven. Boil potatoes. Remove, peel and slice.
2. Peel and chop onions.
3. Layer the potato slices, ham, cheese and onions in the Dutch Oven. Season everything with pepper, salt and nutmeg.
4. Then pour milk and cream over it. Finally a layer of cheese on top.
5. Bake on low heat from below and high heat from above for about an hour.

6. Serve and enjoy.

SPAGHETTI BOLOGNESE

Serving:4 - Preparation time: 150 min

Ingredients:

- 1 clove of garlic
- 1 onion
- 4 tablespoons olive oil
- 2 carrots
- 150 ml of red wine
- 500 grams of minced meat
- 100 ml milk
- 400 g chopped tomatoes
- 2 tablespoons of tomato paste
- Salt and pepper
- Oregano
- Paprika powder

Preparation:

1. Peel and finely chop the garlic and onion. Peel and dice the carrots.
2. Heat the oil in the Dutch oven. Fry onions and garlic. Add the carrots and minced meat and sauté.
3. Taste, laze with red wine. Let the red wine boil down. Add the tomato paste and season with salt, pepper and paprika powder.
4. Add milk and chopped tomatoes. Season the sauce with oregano. Let everything simmer for about 2 hours with the lid closed over low heat.
5. Serve with pasta and enjoy.
1.

CHICKEN CACCIATORE WITH PEPPERS TOMATOES AND ONIONS

Serving: 4 - 6 - Prep Time: 1 hour 10 minutes

Ingredients:

- 3 to 4 pounds (about 1814 g) chicken thighs
- Kosher salt and freshly ground black pepper
- 3 tablespoons (45 ml) olive oil
- 225g medium yellow onion, thinly sliced
- 225g red peppers, stemmed, seeded and thinly sliced
- 5 medium garlic cloves, thinly sliced
- 3/4 cup (175 ml) dry white wine
- 795g whole tomatoes, peeled, drained and manually plus 1/2 cup (120ml) reserved canned juice
- 2 sprigs of fresh rosemary, sage or thyme
- 1 bay leaf
- Chopped parsley for garnish (optional)

Preparation:

1. Preheat the oven to 175°C. Season the chicken with salt and pepper.

2. In a Dutch oven or large, straight skillet, bring the oil to a simmer over medium-high heat. Add chicken and cook, turning occasionally, until browned throughout, about 6 minutes per side. After cooking, place the chicken on a platter and set aside. Add the onion, peppers, and garlic and cook, stirring and scraping any browned bits, until tender, about 8 minutes.
3. Add wine and bring to a boil. Add tomatoes and reserved juices, along with sprigs of herbs and bay leaves. Continue to simmer and season with salt and pepper. Pour chicken and accumulated juices into liquid and vegetables. Place in the oven and cook, uncovered, until the chicken is fully cooked through and tender (about 30 minutes) or until the sauce has thickened. Serve immediately and garnish with chopped parsley, if you like. Remove the pot from the oven and let cool for 10 minutes before serving.

CHICKEN NOODLES WITH TOMATO SAUCE

Serving:6 - Preparation time: 30 minutes

Ingredients:

- 340 g linguini or fettuccine
- 450g medium chicken breast, sliced
- Salt and black pepper to taste, 2 tablespoons of olive oil
- 6 Roma tomatoes, diced (plus more for garnish if desired)
- 1/4 cup spring onions, finely chopped
- 1/4 tsp hot chilli flakes, 1 clove of crushed garlic
- 2 tablespoons chopped fresh basil plus more for serving
- 4 tablespoons unsalted butter
- 1 cup of dry white wine
- 1/2 cup whipping cream and parmesan to serve

Preparation:

1. Cook the noodles in salted water with 1 tablespoon of olive oil until al dente and slightly al dente according to the package insert. Wash, drain and set aside. Wash the chicken and season both sides with salt and pepper. Heat a large deep skillet or Dutch oven with 2 tablespoons oil over medium-high heat. Add the chicken and sear the first side until golden (5 minutes), turn, cover and sear an additional 5 minutes or until done. Remove from the pan and let rest for 10 minutes.
2. In the same skillet over medium/high heat, add diced tomatoes, spring onions, 1/4 teaspoon chili flakes, 2 tablespoons chopped basil, crushed garlic cloves, and 4 tablespoons butter. Season with 1/8 tsp black pepper or to taste. Add 1 cup of wine, stirring occasionally, until mixture is smooth and most of the wine has evaporated.
3. When there is only 1/4 cup liquid left, stir in 1/2 cup heavy cream and 1/2 tsp salt or season to taste. Add the chicken back in and taste. Heat gently for 2 minutes, then mix the pasta with the sauce. Serve with parmesan, chopped fresh parsley and more diced tomatoes for extra freshness.

BRAISED PORK WITH CHILIS

Serving: 4-6 - Prep time: 2-3 hours

Ingredients:

- 2 tablespoons olive oil
- 900 gr. pork loin
- 6 garlic cloves, crushed
- 2 habanero chilies, chopped
- 2 onions, sliced
- 1 teaspoon of salt
- 1/4 teaspoon chili powder
- 2 cups tomatoes, chopped

1. Preparation:

1. Pour 1 tablespoon of olive oil on the bottom of the Dutch Oven. Take the remaining olive oil and rub the pork loin with oil, salt and chilli powder. Place in the center of the pot.
2. Sprinkle with chopped onions, chilies and tomatoes. Cover and bake on low, 140-160°C, 2 or 3 hours, until pork pulls apart easily with a fork.

HERBED FRIED CHICKEN WITH CARROTS, GREEN BEANS AND POTATOES

Serving: 4 - 6 - Prep time: 1 hour 20 minutes

Ingredients:

- 2 tablespoons olive oil
- 1 whole chicken
- 1 leek, quartered
- 2 carrots, quartered
- 2 cups fresh green beans, whole
- 2 cups mushrooms, whole
- 4 potatoes, quartered
- 2 tablespoons salt of herbs de Provence to taste
- Pepper to taste

Preparation:

1. Rub the chicken with 1 tbsp olive oil, salt, pepper and 1 tbsp Herbes de Provence. Place in the center of the pot. Bake uncovered over very high heat (about 450F) for 20 to 25 minutes or until golden brown. Take out of the oven.
2. Arrange the vegetables around the chicken and drizzle with olive oil. Sprinkle with the remaining herbs de Provence and put back in the oven. Reduce heat to 160°C and sauté an additional 40 to 60 minutes or until chicken is tender.
3. Make sure to mix the veggies and cut the chicken in half once. When the chicken is nicely browned, remove from the oven and cover with either a lid or foil and allow to rest for 10 minutes before serving. Be careful not to overcook the chicken.

CHICKEN CACCIATORE

Serving:4 - Prep time: 45 minutes

Ingredients:

- 8 chicken thighs
- 1 tsp salt
- 1 tsp freshly ground black pepper
- 3 tablespoons olive oil
- 1 large red pepper, chopped
- 1 red onion, chopped
- 225 g mushrooms, sliced
- 3 garlic cloves, finely chopped
- 3/4 cup dry white wine, (170) ml
- 800 g chopped tomatoes with juice
- 3 sprigs of fresh thyme
- 2 bay leaves

Preparation:

1. Preheat the oven to 175°C. Season the chicken thighs on both sides with salt and pepper.
2. Add some olive oil to a Dutch oven and sauté over medium heat for about 4-5 minutes on each side to sear the chicken. Then remove from the pan.
3. Heat some more olive oil in your Dutch Oven and sauté onions, peppers and garlic for about 4 minutes.
4. Add the white wine, tomatoes, bay leaves and thyme to the vegetables and heat until the sauce is simmering
5. Now add the mushrooms, skin side up, to the sauce along with the chicken pieces and bake for about 35-40 minutes or until the chicken is fully cooked through in the oven. Taste and serve hot.

CHOPPED MUSHROOM LASAGNA

Serving:4 - Preparation time: 60 min

Ingredients:

- 400 g lasagne sheets
- 200 g grated Gouda cheese
- 3 onions
- 2 cloves of garlic
- 250 grams of mushrooms
- 200ml cream
- 2 tsp light instant sauce
- 125 ml white wine
- 400 g mixed minced meat
- 500 ml of tomato passata
- 4 tablespoons of oil
- 3 teaspoons Herbes de Provence
- 3 tablespoons ketchup
- Herbs of Provence
- Salt and pepper

Preparation:

1. Thoroughly wash and slice the mushrooms. Wash and finely chop the onions and garlic.

1. 2. For the light sauce: Sauté a third of the chopped onions and garlic. Then add cream, light instant sauce, paprika and mushrooms and simmer in the Dutch oven over medium heat for approx. 5 minutes.
2. 3. For the red sauce: heat the oil in the Dutch oven. Fry the ground beef and the remaining onions until the meat is brown. Add the tomato passata, herbs de Provence, ketchup and white wine and mix well. Season with salt and pepper. Simmer for 20 minutes over medium heat.
3. 4. Layer in the Dutch oven: first red sauce, then lasagne sheets, then light sauce, then cheese, then lasagne sheets, then red sauce again and so on. Bake with the lid closed for about 30 minutes, over low heat from below and medium heat from above. Serve and enjoy. Enjoy your meal!

BEEF BRISKET, FIRM AND SLIGHTLY CHEWY

Serving:8 - Prep time: 3 hours

Ingredients:

- 1 fresh brisket (1.5 kg)
- 1 teaspoon of salt
- black pepper
- 2 tablespoons of vegetable oil
- 2 cups of water
- 1 can (225 g) tomato sauce
- 1 small onion, chopped
- 2 tablespoons of red wine vinegar
- 1 tablespoon of chili powder
- 1 teaspoon dried oregano
- Cumin
- Garlic powder
- Salt
- 1/8 to 1/4 teaspoon ground red pepper
- black pepper
- 3 medium red peppers, cut into strips
- 2 cups sliced carrots

Preparation:

1. Season the beef with salt and pepper. Heat oil in a casserole; Both sides until the beef is seared. Meanwhile, mix the next 11 ingredients. Pour over the meat.
2. Cover and bake at 180°C for 2 hours. Add peppers and carrots; Bake 1 hour longer or until meat is tender. Take the meat out of the pan. Let stand 15 minutes before slicing. Bring to a boil to thicken the juice. Fry, uncovered, 13-15 minutes or until thickened, stirring occasionally.

CREAMY CHICKEN WITH RICE

Serving: 8-10 - Preparation time: 30 minutes

Ingredients:

- 1/4 cup olive oil
- 4 tablespoons unsalted butter

- 1 medium onion, finely diced
- 2 large carrots grated or cut into matchsticks
- 225g boneless, skinless chicken thighs, trimmed and cut into pieces
- 2 tsp salt
- 1/4 teaspoon freshly ground black pepper
- 2 bay leaves optional
- 1 cup dry white wine such as Chardonnay
- 5 cups hot low-sodium chicken broth
- 2 cups of medium-grain rice such as jasmine rice
- 1 clove of garlic
- 1/3 cup fresh Italian parsley, finely chopped
- 1/2 cup grated parmesan cheese, plus more for serving

Preparation:

1. In a Dutch oven or heavy-duty saucepan with a tight lid, add 1/4 cup olive oil and 2 tablespoons unsalted butter over medium/high heat. Once the butter is melted and hot, stir in the diced onion, grated carrot, and 1 teaspoon salt. Fry until tender and golden brown (8-10 mins).
2. Add sliced, chopped chicken thighs, 2 bay leaves, another tsp salt, and 1/4 tsp black pepper. Fry, stirring occasionally, until chicken is golden brown on all sides (5 minutes).
3. Increase the temperature and add 1 cup of white wine. Reduce the wine and scrape the bottom until most of the wine has evaporated.
4. Add the hot chicken broth and stir in the rice.
5. Cut off the end of a whole garlic bulb without separating the cloves (leaving the root end intact) to reveal the garlic cloves. Place the whole head, cut side down, in the center of your rice. Bring to a boil, then reduce heat, cover and simmer until rice is fully cooked (15 minutes).
6. Reduce the heat, remove the garlic clove and quickly stir in the remaining 2 Tbsp butter until fully incorporated. Finally, stir in the chopped parsley and 1/2 cup Parmesan cheese.
7. It should be creamy. Serve immediately or keep the lid warm until ready to serve. Garnish with fresh parsley to serve.
8. Bring to a boil, then reduce heat, cover and simmer until rice is fully cooked and liquid is absorbed (15-18 minutes). Give the rice a quick stir and serve with dill or parsley.

CHICKEN DUMPLINGS

Serving:6 - Preparation time: 20 minutes

Ingredients:

- 3 celery ribs, chopped
- 2 medium carrots, sliced
- 3 cans (400ml each) low sodium chicken broth
- 3 cups diced cooked chicken breast
- 1/2 teaspoon poultry seasoning
- 1/8 teaspoon pepper
- 3 cups low-fat cookie/baking mix

- 2/3 cup non-fat milk

Preparation:

1. In a Dutch oven coated with cooking spray, cook celery and carrots over medium-high heat, stirring, about 5 minutes. Stir in the broth, chicken, and spices. bring to a boil; Reduce heat until everything comes to a gentle boil.
1. For dumplings, mix the biscuit mixture and milk until a soft dough forms. Reduce heat; cover and cook until a toothpick inserted into the dumpling comes out clean (do not lift the lid for the first 10 minutes), 10-15 minutes.

VEAL MUSSELS

Serving:4 - Preparation time: 10 minutes

Ingredients:

- 2 tablespoons olive oil
- 2 tablespoons of butter
- 4 veal cutlets, thinly sliced or turkey cutlets
- 1/2 cup flour, in a shallow bowl
- 2 eggs, beaten, in a shallow bowl
- Bread 1/2 cup, in a shallow bowl
- Lemon, cut into quarters
- Salt

Preparation:

1. Dredge the veal escalope in flour. Dip in beaten egg. Dip in the breading so each cutlet is completely coated on both sides.
2. Heat the oil and butter over medium-high heat for 30 seconds, then add the breaded veal chops. Fry for about 10 minutes, turning halfway through. Both sides should be browned.
2. Serve with lemon wedges and press onto the schnitzel just before eating. salt and pepper to taste.

VEGETABLE CASSEROLE WITH CHICKEN

Serving:4 - Preparation time: 35 min

Ingredients:

- 700 g chicken fillet
- 2 zucchini
- 2 onions
- 2 yellow peppers
- 2 spring onions
- 500 ml of tomato passata
- 200g herbal quark
- 3 tablespoons of tomato paste
- 1 clove of garlic
- 200 g Parmesan cheese
- 1 tablespoon of olive oil
- Salt, pepper, oregano

Preparation:

3. Fry the chicken fillet in the Dutch oven with a little olive oil on both sides and season with salt and pepper.
4. Wash vegetables and cut into small pieces and cubes. Then pour all the vegetables over the chicken.
5. Place tomato passata in a small container and season with salt, pepper and oregano. Then mix in the herb quark. Put everything together in the Dutch Oven.
6. Cook over low heat from below and high heat from above for 25 minutes.
7. Serve and enjoy the finished dish.

SALSA VERDE CHICKEN

Serving:6-8 - Preparation time: 30 minutes

Ingredients:

- 1.3 kg boneless skinless chicken breast or thighs
- 1 medium onion, sliced
- 4 crushed garlic cloves
- 1 jar of Salsa Verde, 24 oz (0.91 kg)
- 78.33 g chicken bone broth
- 65.5 g of tomato paste
- 2 tablespoons extra virgin olive oil
- 1 tablespoon of paprika
- 2 teaspoons ground cumin
- 2 teaspoons ground coriander
- Sea-salt
- black pepper

Preparation:

1. Preheat the oven to 160°C (or use a slow cooker).
2. Place all ingredients in an enamelled Dutch Oven or other large, heavy, ovenproof saucepan and stir to coat the chicken in the sauce.
3. Cover and place in the oven for 3 hours, or until the chicken is tender and pulls apart easily.
4. Place the pot in the oven for an additional 30 minutes to 1 hour to allow the liquid to thicken into a thick sauce.
5. Remove chicken from Dutch Oven (save sauce) and allow to cool slightly before shredding with 2 forks or fork and spoon.
6. Add the shredded meat to the reserved sauce.

RIBS BRAISED WITH RED WINE AND SOY

Serving:1 – 2 - Preparation time: 20 minutes

Ingredients:

- 110g boneless beef spare ribs, cut into chunks
- Kosher salt
- 2 TBSP. Plus 1 tsp. Grape seed oil or olive oil
- 1 large onion, chopped
- 8 garlic cloves, crushed
- 1 x 5 cm piece of ginger, peeled and sliced
- 2 cups of dry red wine
- ½ cup Marin (sweet Japanese rice wine)
- ⅓ cup soy sauce

- ¼ cup (packaged) light brown sugar
- 225 g radish or radish peeled, cut into pieces
- 1 large egg, beaten to mix
- Shilgochu or Gochugaru (coarse Korean pepper flakes), sliced shallots and boiled rice (for serving)

Preparation:

1. Season the ribs with salt. Heat 2 tbsp. Heat oil in a small saucepan over medium-high flame. Cook the ribs in 2 batches, turning them occasionally and reducing the heat if necessary to avoid burning them. Put on a plate.
2. Add the onion, garlic, and ginger to the same saucepan and cook, stirring frequently, until tender and lightly browned, about 6-8 minutes.
3. Add wine; bring to a boil. Reduce heat and simmer until liquid is reduced by half (8-10 minutes). Add mirin, soy sauce, brown sugar and 2 cups water.
4. Return the ribs to the pot and bring the liquid to a boil. Partially cover the pot and cook, reducing the heat to ensure a very gentle simmer, adding a splash of water as needed, until the ribs are very tender.
5. When the sauce is thick enough, let the meat sit for 3 to 3.5 hours. Add the radish.
6. 1 TEASPOON. Pour oil into a large non-stick skillet. Add the egg and tilt the pan and fry the egg for about 1 minute. Enter it
7. Cutting board and cut it into thin slices.
8. Refine with egg, Shilgochu and spring onions. Serve with rice.

ROAST BEEF ON SUNDAYS

Serving: 4-6 - Prep time: 1 hour 20 minutes

Ingredients:

- 2 tablespoons olive oil
- 900 gr. — 1.3 kg of roast beef
- 2 tablespoons Herbes de Provence
- 6 cloves of garlic
- 3 slices of bacon, divide
- Salt and pepper
- 4 cups potatoes, carrots and beets, quartered

Preparation:

1. Rub the roast with oil, salt and pepper.
2. Place the herbs de Provence in the roast and pierce them with a knife to make slits. Lay the bacon slices over the roast.
3. Place in the center of the pot and surround with vegetables. Bake at 400°F for 20 minutes to toast, then reduce the heat to 350°F. Cook at 20 minutes per 450 grams.
4. Stir the vegetables several times. Ready to serve when the beef is still pink inside. Remove from heat, cover with lid or foil and let rest 10 minutes before serving.

DUTCH OVEN LEG OF LAMB WITH POTATOES

Serving:8 - Preparation time: 3h 30 min

Ingredients:

- 2 cloves of garlic
- 1.5 kg leg of lamb
- 200 ml chicken broth
- 100 ml of white wine
- 2 tablespoons olive oil
- 15 medium potatoes
- 3 tablespoons rosemary
- 1 tablespoon of thyme
- 60 grams of green olives
- 60 grams of black olives
- Salt and pepper

Preparation:

1. Peel and thinly slice the garlic cloves. Wash and halve the potatoes.
2. Prick the lamb from many sides with a knife, rub with garlic and rosemary and season with salt and pepper.
3. Heat the oil in the Dutch oven and brown the leg of lamb on all sides over a medium heat.
4. Add the wine and cook with the lid closed and low heat from above and below for about 2 ½ hours.
5. Add the potatoes and cook for a further 30 minutes with the lid on, until the potatoes are tender.
6. Once the meat is cooked, add the olives and let stand 5 minutes. The lamb with olives is ready.
7. Serve and enjoy.

OSSOBUCO ROMEO AND JULIET

Serving:4 - Prep time: 2 hours

Ingredients:

- 1 tablespoon of olive oil
- 4 cloves of garlic, chopped
- 1 onion, chopped 1 leek, chopped
- 4 tomatoes, chopped
- 2 cups mushrooms, chopped
- Osso Bucco - 2 or 3 large pieces
- 1/2 cup flour, in a shallow bowl
- 2 tablespoons Herbes de Provence
- 1/2 cup Chianti or 1/4 cup Madeira
- Salt to taste Pepper to taste

Preparation:

1. Add olive oil to the cast iron stove. Dredge meat in flour. Fry over high heat until brown on both sides.
2. Add greens, garlic, onion and leek. Add 1 cup of red wine. Sprinkle with salt, pepper and dried herbs. If you use fresh herbs, put them on meat.
3. Cover and cook slowly at 135 °C for 2 hours. Meat should break down easily when fully cooked.

MEXICAN STYLE RIBS

Serving:10 - Preparation time: 24h

Ingredients:

- 3 kg ribs
- 8 tablespoons BBQ sauce
- 200 g cheddar cheese
- 500 grams of white beans
- 400 g kidney beans
- 3 onions
- 200ml ketchup
- 100 ml chopped tomatoes
- 300ml BBQ sauce
- Salt and pepper

Preparation:

1. Brush ribs with 8 tablespoons BBQ sauce. Leave overnight.
2. Peel and roughly chop the onions.
3. Add all ingredients to the Dutch Oven except for the ribs and cheese and mix well. Then place the ribs on top. And keep pouring the sauce over it.
4. Cook over low heat from below (approx. 6 briquettes) and high heat from above (approx. 14 briquettes) for approx. 60 minutes. Then add the cheese and cook for another 40 minutes.
5. Carefully remove the ribs from the Dutch Oven and lightly sear in a separate pot.
6. Serve with the sauce and enjoy

FILLED WRAPS FROM THE DUTCH OVEN

Serving:6 - Prep time: 40 minutes

Ingredients:

- 6 wraps
- 500 g mixed minced meat
- 1 onion
- 1 red pepper
- 250 g grated mozzarella
- 2 tomatoes
- 6 eggs
- 1 tsp paprika powder
- 4 lettuce leaves
- 1 can of corn
- 1 can of kidney beans
- 1 may have chopped tomatoes
- 3 jalapenos
- 1 clove of garlic
- Salt and pepper
- Olive oil for frying

Preparation:

1. Peel and finely chop the onions and garlic. Wash the peppers and jalapeños, remove the stalk, deseed and cut into small pieces. Wash the tomatoes, remove the stalk and cut into small pieces. Drain kidney beans and corn. Wash lettuce leaves.
2. Heat the oil in the Dutch oven. Fry onions and garlic. Add ground beef and sauté until brown. Then add the peppers, corn, chopped tomatoes and kidney beans and simmer for 5 minutes. Season with paprika, salt and pepper. Remove from the Dutch Oven and set aside.
3. Reheat the oil in the Dutch Oven and add the eggs. Season with salt and pepper and stir well. Remove the scrambled eggs from the Dutch Oven and set aside. Lay out the wraps and fill with the minced meat mixture, lettuce, tomatoes, jalapeños, some cheese and egg and roll up and brush with a little olive oil. Reheat the oil in the Dutch Oven, place the filled wraps in the Dutch Oven and sprinkle with the remaining cheese.
4. After about 10 minutes over low heat from the bottom and medium heat from the top, the wraps will be hot and the cheese will have melted. The wraps are done. Serve and enjoy.

BAVARIAN POT ROAST

Serving:6 - Prep time: 1 hour 20 minutes

Ingredients:

- 1 boneless pot roast beef (approx. 1.3 kg)
- 2 tablespoons canola oil
- 1-1/4 cups of water
- 3/4 cup beer or beef broth
- 1 can (225 g) tomato sauce
- 1/2 cup chopped onion
- 1 tablespoon of sugar
- 1 tablespoon of vinegar
- Teaspoon of salt
- 1 teaspoon ground cinnamon
- 1 bay leaf
- Pepper
- 1/2 teaspoon ground ginger
- Corn starch and water, optional

Preparation:

1. Fry the oil in a Dutch oven. Mix water, beer, tomato sauce, onion, sugar, vinegar, salt, cinnamon, bay leaf, pepper and ginger. Pour over the meat and bring to a boil. reduce temperature; cover and simmer until meat is tender, about 2 – 3 hours.
2. Remove flesh. Discard bay leaf. If desired, thicken juices with cornstarch and water.

GOLDEN TURMERIC CHICKEN

Serving: 4-6 - Prep time: 1 hour 30 minutes

Ingredients:

- 1 to 2 tablespoons coconut oil, lightly melted
- 1 whole chicken, cut into pieces
- 1 to 2 tablespoons of turmeric
- Salt to taste
- 4 sweet potatoes, quartered
- 2 onions, quartered

Preparation:

1. Rub the chicken pieces with melted coconut oil. Using your hands, generously sprinkle the chicken pieces with turmeric and salt and rub the seasoning into the meat and skin.
2. Spread over the chicken pieces in a pan with the sweet potatoes and onions. Cover and bake slowly at 150 °C for approx. 90 minutes. Meat is tender and easily falls off the bone when fully cooked. Delicious served over rice.

BEAN CASSOULET

Serving:8 - Prep time: 35 minutes

Ingredients:

- 5 tablespoons olive oil
- 8 skinless, boneless chicken thighs (800 g)
- 1 packet (400g) cooked Italian chicken sausage pieces, sliced.
- 4 shallots, finely chopped
- 2 teaspoons chopped fresh rosemary or 1/2 teaspoon dried rosemary, crushed
- 2 teaspoons chopped fresh thyme or 1/2 teaspoon dried thyme
- 1 can (800 g) diced roasted tomatoes, drained
- 1 can (450 g) baked beans
- 1 cup chicken broth
- 1/2 cup fresh or frozen cranberries
- 3-day-old croissants, diced (about 6 cups)
- 1/2 teaspoon lemon pepper spice
- 2 tablespoons chopped fresh parsley

Preparation:

1. Preheat the oven to 200°. In a Dutch oven, heat 2 tablespoons oil over medium-high heat. Brown the chicken thighs in batches on both sides. Remove from pan and add sausage. Cook and stir until lightly fried. Take out of the pan.
2. In the same pan, heat 1 tablespoon oil over medium-high heat. Add shallots, rosemary and thyme; Cook and stir until shallots are tender, 1-2 minutes. Stir in the tomatoes, beans, broth, and cranberries. Return the chicken and sausage to the pan. Bring to a boil. Bake, covered, until chicken is tender, 20-25 minutes.

3. Mix croissant pieces with remaining oil; Sprinkle with lemon pepper. Spread over the chicken mixture. Bake uncovered until croissants are golden brown, 12-15 minutes. Sprinkle with parsley

FRENCH CHICKEN WITH ONIONS

Serving:2 - Prep time: 35 minutes

Ingredients:

- 3 tablespoons unsalted butter
- 900 g onion (sliced)
- 2 garlic cloves (chopped)
- 1 teaspoon fresh thyme leaves (chopped)
- 2 tablespoons of flour
- 2 cups low-sodium or unsalted beef broth
- 1 tablespoon olive oil
- 450 g bone-in chicken thighs
- 2 teaspoons balsamic vinegar
- 2 tablespoons Dijon mustard
- 1 cup Gruyere (grated)
- Salt and ground black pepper

Preparation:

1. In a large Dutch oven or ovenproof skillet, melt the butter over medium-high heat. Add the onions and cook until a deep golden brown color is achieved, about 1 hour, stirring every 5 - 10 minutes. Season lightly with salt.
2. Preheat the oven to 180°C.
3. Add the garlic, thyme and flour to the onions. Stir and cook for a minute. Add half of the broth. Deg, rot the pan. Bring to a boil and simmer for 5 minutes.
4. Meanwhile, season the chicken thighs with salt and pepper. In another large skillet over medium heat add the oil. Add the chicken, skin-side down, and sear until golden brown, 3-4 minutes. Turn and fry for another 3-4 minutes.
5. Return to the onions and add the remaining soup, balsamic vinegar and mustard. Bring to a boil and let simmer for about 5 minutes. Season with salt and pepper.
6. Put the chicken in the onions. Cover with a lid or foil. Bake in the oven for 20 minutes. Set the oven to 220°C. Scatter the cheese over the chicken and onions. Return to the oven until cheese is melted, about 3-4 minutes. Remove from the oven and let rest for 5 minutes. Serve with baguette. Cook uncovered in the oven for a few minutes, or until the chicken is fully cooked.
7. Season to taste and serve hot.

VEAL MARENGO

Serving: 4-6 - Prep time: 40 minutes

Ingredients:

- 2 tablespoons olive oil
- 2 tablespoons butter veal for 4 people, cut into chunks

- 1 onion, chopped
- 4 cloves of garlic, chopped
- 1 cup white wine
- 1 cup tomato sauce
- 2 cups mushrooms, sliced
- 1 tablespoon Herbes de Provence
- Salt to taste Pepper to taste

Preparation:

1. Heat the oil and butter over medium-high heat for 30 seconds, then add the garlic and onions and stir. Cover and continue cooking over medium heat until translucent, 5-6 minutes.
2. Stir every two minutes to avoid burning. Add the veal and sear over high heat, which will brown the meat.
3. Add wine, tomato sauce, mushrooms and herbs, salt and pepper. Cover and simmer on low heat for 40 minutes.

41. BARBECUE PORK

Serving:12 - Prep time: 4 hours

Ingredients:

- 1 Boneless Pork Shoulder Roast (3kg – 4kg)
- 1 teaspoon garlic powder
- Salt
- 1/2 teaspoon freshly ground pepper
- 6 chipotle peppers in clay sauce, finely chopped (about 1/3 cup)
- 1 large sweet onion, halved and sliced
- 2 tablespoons brown sugar
- 2 cans of Dr. Pepper
- 1 cup barbecue sauce
- French fries, rustic herb pastries, and savory coleslaw, optional

Preparation:

1. Preheat the oven to 325°. Sprinkle roast with garlic powder, salt and pepper; Rub with chipotle peppers. Put in a dutch oven. Refine with sweet onions; sprinkle with brown sugar. give dr Pepper in the roast. Bake, covered, until meat is tender, 4 to 4 1/2 hours.
2. Take out the roast. Cool down a bit. Strain the juices and add the onions. Skim fat from juices.
3. Shred the pork with 2 forks. Return the juices, onions and pork to the Dutch oven. stir in barbecue sauce; Heat over medium heat, stirring occasionally. Serve with fries and biscuits and coleslaw if desired.

CHICKEN TETRAZZINI

Serving:8 - Preparation time: 1 hour 5 minutes

Ingredients:

- 340 g thin spaghetti or linguine
- 560g shredded roast chicken or chicken breast

- 450 g mushrooms, thickly sliced
- 1 medium onion, finely chopped
- 3 cloves of garlic chopped
- 2 olive oil
- For the cream sauce
- 4 tablespoons unsalted butter
- 40 g all-purpose flour
- 600 ml low sodium chicken broth
- 1 tablespoon lemon juice
- 360ml milk & cream
- 1 teaspoon sea salt or to taste
- 0.25 tsp black pepper, freshly ground
- 15g chopped parsley plus more for garnish
- 170 g grated mozzarella

Preparation:

1. Preheat the oven to 180°C. In a large saucepan of salted water, cook the pasta according to package directions until firm and slightly tough, then wash until no longer boiling, drain and set aside.
2. Cut 4 cups of chicken from a roast chicken, cut into bite-sized pieces and set aside.
3. Set a large Dutch oven or saucepan to medium/high. Add 2 tablespoons oil, then add sliced mushrooms and sauté 3 minutes or until tender. Add diced onions and cook until onions are soft and golden brown, 5-7 mins. Add minced garlic and sauté another 1-2 minutes until fragrant. Place on cutting board with chicken.
4. In the same skillet, melt 4 Tbsp butter and stir in 1/3 cup flour until lightly golden (1 1/2 min).
5. Add 1/2 cup chicken broth, 1 tbsp lemon juice, 1 tsp salt, 1/4 tsp pepper and stir until smooth. Add 1 1/2 cups milk and heavy cream. Bring to a boil and season with sauce, salt and pepper.
6. Return the chicken, mushrooms, onions, and pasta to the saucepan, then sprinkle over 1/4 cup chopped fresh parsley and stir. Sprinkle the top generously with grated mozzarella, cover and bake at 180°C for 30 minutes, then remove the lid and bake for a further 15 minutes.

LAMB KÖFTE (MEATBALLS)

Serving:4 - Preparation time: 20 minutes

Ingredients:

- 1 tablespoon of olive oil
- 4 garlic cloves, finely chopped
- 450 gr. lamb mince
- 1/4 cup sautéed pine nuts
- 1 cup parsley, finely chopped
- 1/4 cup of currants
- 1/4 cup chopped mint, fresh or 1 tablespoon dried
- 1/4 teaspoon cayenne pepper
- Dash cardamom, ground salt to taste
- Pepper to taste
- 2 cups chopped tomato yogurt to taste
- 1 teaspoon of lemon juice
- dash sumac

Preparation:

1. Mix all ingredients (except olive oil, tomatoes, lemon juice, sumac and yogurt) by hand in a bowl. Shape into golf ball sized balls and then slightly lengthen them into the shape of tiny soccer balls by rubbing them back and forth between your palms.

2. Pour olive oil into the Dutch Oven. Place lamb balls or kofte in a layer underneath. Do not overlap or stack. Sear the lamb balls over high heat and sear on each side. Make sure they are evenly browned all over. Don't fully cook.

3. Don't burn! Turn the heat down and add the chopped tomatoes. Mix well. Cover and simmer gently for 15 to 20 minutes. Make sure the meat doesn't dry out. Serve with yogurt mixed with 1 teaspoon lemon juice and a pinch of sumac.

RED WINE BRAISED RIBS (NO SOY)

Serving:6 - Prep time: 2 hours 30 minutes

Ingredients:

- 4 lb. beef short ribs 2-3 cm thick
- kosher salt
- Pepper
- 3 tablespoons cooking oil
- 1 small onion, roughly chopped
- 6 carrots peeled and cut
- 6 garlic cloves diced
- 2 tablespoons of tomato paste
- 2 cups of dry red wine
- 3 cups beef broth
- 2 sprigs of fresh thyme
- 2 sprigs of fresh rosemary
- Parsley for refinement

Preparation:

1. Preheat the oven to 180°C. Season the ribs generously with salt and pepper

2. In a large Dutch oven or heavy saucepan, heat the oil over medium-high heat. Sear the ribs on all sides and place on a plate. Add onions and carrots to cook, stirring occasionally, about 10 minutes. Add garlic and cook another minute. Then add the tomato paste and cook for another 5 minutes.

3. Deglaze the pot with red wine, then add the beef broth and bring to a boil. Turn the heat down and put the ribs back in. Add the rosemary and thyme to the pot. Cover with a lid and cook for 2 hours, then reduce the heat to 160°C and cook for a further hour. Remove the pot from the oven and let cool for 10 minutes before serving.

BEEFBALLS IN TOMATO SAUCE

Serving: 4-6 - Preparation time: 30 minutes

Ingredients:

- 1 tablespoon of olive oil
- 6 garlic cloves, finely chopped
- 450 gr. ground beef
- Herbs of Provence
- 1 cup chopped parsley
- 2 tablespoons of tomato paste
- 1/2 cup dry breadcrumbs
- Pinch of chilli powder
- Salt to taste
- Pepper to taste
- 2 cups tomatoes, chopped
- 1 cup tomato sauce
- 1 cup broth
- 1/2 cup red wine

Preparation:

1. Set aside 2 minced garlic cloves for later. Mix the remaining garlic, meat, herbs, parsley, 2 tablespoons tomato paste, breadcrumbs and spices in a bowl.
2. Form into golf ball sized meatballs. Pour olive oil into the Dutch Oven. Heat oil over medium-high heat for 30 seconds, then add meatballs and sear evenly on all sides.
3. Not fully cooked. Add tomato sauce mixed with remaining garlic, beef or vegetable stock and chopped tomatoes and red wine, cover and cook over low heat for 20 minutes. Season with salt and pepper. Serve it with pasta or any other way you like to eat it.

VENISON MEDALLIONS IN SOUR CHERRY SAUCE

Serving:4 - Prep time: 90 minutes

Ingredients:

- 8 deer medallions
- 125 ml burgundy
- 200 g sour cherries
- 1 tbsp sour cherry jelly
- Oil for frying
- 500 g ground game bones
- 1 bunch of greens
- 5 juniper berries
- 500ml of water
- Salt and pepper

Preparation:

1. For the broth: Put the venison bones, soup greens, juniper berries, water, salt and pepper in the Dutch Oven and simmer over a medium heat for about 1 hour.
2. Take out after the hour. Then pass through a sieve back into the Dutch Oven and boil down to 1/8 liter of liquid. Remove from the Dutch Oven and set aside.
3. Season the venison medallions with salt and pepper and fry in a little oil in the Dutch oven for 3 to 4 minutes on both sides. Remove from the Dutch oven and keep warm.
4. Deglaze the roast stock with Burgundy and game stock and let it boil down for about 10 minutes.

5. Stir in the jelly and season with salt and pepper. Warm the pitted sour cherries in the sauce and serve with the venison medallions.
6. Serve and enjoy.

KASSEL ON SAUERKRAUT

Serving:4 - Preparation time: 2 h 30 min

Ingredients:

- 1.5 kg of pork neck
- 800 grams of sauerkraut
- 1 bay leaf
- 2 onions
- 750ml of water
- 3 juniper berries
- 2 tablespoons dark sauce thickener
- Salt and pepper
- Oil for frying

Preparation:

1. Peel and roughly chop the onions. Fry the Kasseler on all sides in the Dutch oven over high heat. Add the sauerkraut and simmer over low heat from above and below for about 1 hour.
2. Add the onions, water, bay leaf, juniper berries, salt and pepper and cook with the lid on for 1 hour.
3. Skim off the roast stock and mix well with the dark sauce in a separate saucepan, bring to the boil and allow the sauce to thicken.
4. Remove bay leaf and juniper berries.
5. Cut the Kasseler into slices and arrange on a plate with the sauerkraut and the sauce.

SPANISH POTATO PAN

Serving:4 - Prep Time:50min

Ingredients:

- 400g chorizo
- 6 potatoes
- 2 cloves of garlic
- 2 peppers
- 2 chili peppers
- 2 onions
- 2 tomatoes
- 100 ml of white wine
- 200 ml meat broth
- 4 tablespoons olive oil
- Salt and pepper
- some sugar

Preparation:

1. Peel the garlic clove and onion and cut into small pieces. Wash the chili pepper, bell pepper and tomato and cut into small pieces.

2. Heat the olive oil in the Dutch Oven. Fry the onion, garlic, chili pepper and paprika.
3. Cut the chorizo and potatoes into small pieces and add to the pot.
4. After a few minutes, deglaze with wine and beef broth. Cook. Season with salt, pepper and sugar.
5. Simmer over medium heat with the lid on for about 20 minutes.
6. Serve and enjoy the finished dish.

VEAL ESCALOPE WITH MUSHROOMS

Serving:4 - Preparation time: 15 minutes

Ingredients:

- 2 tablespoons olive oil
- 1 tablespoon of butter
- 4 veal chops
- 2 cups mushrooms, sliced
- 2 shallots, chopped
- 1/2 cup white wine
- 2 tablespoons of tomato paste
- 1/2 cup broth or hot water
- Salt to taste

Preparation:

1. Heat the oil and butter over medium-high heat for 30 seconds, then add the shallots and stir. Cover and continue cooking over medium heat until translucent, 5-6 minutes.
2. Stir every two minutes to avoid burning. Add mushrooms and sauté until nicely browned. Add the schnitzel and sauté for 5 minutes, turning once.
3. Mix tomato paste with hot water or broth and wine. Pour into the pot, cover and simmer for another 5 minutes. Salt to taste.

DUCK WITH CHERRIES AND PORT WINE

Serving: 4-6 - Prep time: 1 hour 30 minutes

Ingredients:

- 1 tablespoon of olive oil
- 4 duck breasts or legs
- 1 tablespoon of Herbes de Provence
- 2 cups fresh cherries, pitted
- 1 tablespoon of butter
- 2 shallots, chopped
- 1 cup connection
- 1 teaspoon honey salt to taste
- Pepper to taste

Preparation:

1. Pour olive oil into the Dutch Oven. Sear the duck pieces over high heat until brown but not cooked through. Fry on all sides

2. Remove duck from pot, but leave melted duck fat behind. Add the shallots and butter and sauté until brown. Add port wine, honey and salt to saucepan with shallots and cooked duck fat; mix well and simmer for a few minutes.
3. Add cherries and duck. Cover and simmer for 20 minutes. When duck is cooked but still slightly pink, remove from heat and set aside 10 minutes before serving.
4. Slice the duck breast and arrange on the plate covered with the fruit sauce.

LAMB FILLET WITH CHERRY SAUCE

Serving:2 - Prep time: 45 minutes

Ingredients:

- 500 g lamb fillets
- 2 sprigs of rosemary
- 3 cloves of garlic
- 1 piece of ginger
- 10 cherries
- Salt and pepper
- 1 tsp soy sauce
- 1 tsp honey
- 2 tablespoons of balsamic vinegar
- Olive oil for frying

Preparation:

1. Put the lamb fillet in the Dutch oven with the ginger, the chopped garlic cloves, the sprigs of rosemary and some olive oil and fry.
2. After a few minutes add balsamic vinegar and season with salt, pepper and soy sauce. Add honey and mix well. Simmer for 10 minutes.
3. Then add the cherries and simmer for another 5 to 10 minutes.
4. Arrange on two plates and serve. Enjoy your meal!

CREAM OF CHICKEN CURRY

Serving: 4-6 - Prep time: 35 minutes

Ingredients:

- 2 tablespoons olive oil
- 2 tablespoons of butter
- 4 chicken breasts, cut into small pieces
- 2 cups mushrooms, sliced
- 1 onion, sliced
- 2 cups peas, fresh or frozen
- 2 carrots, sliced
- 2 cups cream
- 1/2 cup broth
- 2 tablespoons curry powder salt to taste

Preparation:

1. Heat oil and butter over medium-high heat for 30 seconds, then add onions and stir. Add mushrooms and sauté lightly. Add chicken pieces and continue frying.
2. Reduce heat, add carrots, peas, curry powder, stock and cream, mix well and simmer until carrots are tender and chicken is tender, 10 to 15 minutes.
3. Salt to taste. Serve over rice.

SPAGHETTI CARBONARA

Serving:6 - Preparation time: 20 min

Ingredients:

- 500 grams of spaghetti
- 400 grams of bacon
- 2 tablespoons olive oil
- 4 eggs
- 200 ml milk
- 100 g of grated parmesan
- Black pepper

Preparation:

1. Heat the water in the Dutch Oven and cook the noodles until firm and slightly chewy. Drain (reserving some pasta water) and set aside.
2. Meanwhile, in a separate container, mix together the parmesan, eggs and milk.
3. Dice the bacon. Heat the oil in the Dutch oven and fry the bacon. Add the pasta, then add the mixture from the container and some of the pasta water.
4. Mix everything well and fry for about 5 minutes. Season with black pepper.
5. Serve and enjoy

ROAST BEEF

Serving:8 - Prep time: 2 hours 30 minutes

Ingredients:

- 1 tablespoon canola oil
- 1 roast beef (approx. 1.5 kg)
- 1 clove of garlic, chopped
- 2 teaspoons dried basil
- 1 teaspoon of salt
- 1 teaspoon dried rosemary, crushed
- Pepper
- 1 medium onion, chopped
- 1 teaspoon beef broth granules
- 1 cup of brewed coffee
- 3/4 cup of water
- Sauce:
- 1/4 cup all-purpose flour
- 1/4 cup cold water

Preparation:

1. In a Dutch oven, heat oil over medium heat; Fry on all sides. Take out of the pan. Mix garlic and spices; sprinkle over the roast.
2. Add onion of the same variety; boil at medium temperature and stir gently; Stir in broth, coffee, and 3/4 cup water. Add the roast; bring to a boil. Reduce heat; Cover and simmer until meat is tender, about 2 1/2 hours.
3. Remove the roast from the pan and reserve the pan juices. Leave on 10 minutes before cutting. Mix flour and cold water until smooth. Stir into the cooking juices. Bring to a boil while stirring constantly. Cook and stir 1-2 minutes until thickened. Serve with roast.

CABBAGE ROLLS

Serving:4 - Prep time: 35 minutes

Ingredients:

- 450 g lean ground beef (90% lean)
- 1 clove of garlic, chopped
- 1 small head cabbage, chopped
- 2 1/2 cups of water
- 2/3 cup uncooked long grain rice
- 1 tablespoon hot sauce
- 1 teaspoon of onion powder
- 1 teaspoon of dried basil
- 1/4 teaspoon cayenne pepper
- Pepper
- 1 tin (800 g) of tomato passata
- Salt
- Grated parmesan, optional

Preparation:

1. In a Dutch oven, cook beef and garlic over medium-high heat until meat is no longer pink.
2. Stir in the next 8 ingredients. Bring to a boil and reduce the heat; Cover and simmer until rice is tender, 25-30 minutes.
3. Stir in tomatoes and salt; Sprinkle with cheese if you like.

ENCHANTED GROUSE

Serving:6 - Prep Time:

Ingredients:

- 2 tablespoons olive oil
- 2 tablespoons salted butter
- 4 garlic cloves, finely chopped
- 1 whole chicken cut into pieces
- 2 cups assorted wild mushrooms, thinly sliced
- 1 cup cream
- 1/2 cup flour, placed in a shallow bowl
- 1 tablespoon of Herbes de Provence
- 1/4 cup cognac or brandy or 1/2 cup white wine
- Salt and pepper to taste
- 1/2 cup chopped parsley for garnish

- Mashed potatoes or boiled egg noodles
- Corn starch and water, optional

Preparation:

1. Dredge chicken pieces in flour. Place olive oil and butter in cast iron stove. Heat oil and butter over medium-high heat for 30 seconds, then add chicken pieces dredged in flour.
2. Fry over high heat, flip and fry the other side. Removed. Leave the leftovers in the pot, add the chopped garlic and sauté with the mushrooms until brown. Put the chicken pieces back into the pot.
3. Wine and cream, herbs and cognac and mix. Simmer over low heat until chicken is tender, about 20 to 30 minutes. Season with salt and pepper.
4. Sprinkle with freshly chopped parsley and serve over mashed potatoes or egg noodles

SPICY MEAT MEETS SWEET RICE

Serving:4 - Preparation time: 35 min

Ingredients:

- 500 grams of minced meat
- 1 egg
- 1 ½ tablespoons soy sauce
- 250 ml vegetable broth
- 1 tablespoon of tomato paste
- 1 pinch of Sambal Oelek
- 1 hot pepper
- 3 carrots
- 75 grams of raisins
- 50 g slivers of almonds
- 200 grams of rice
- 400ml of water
- 1 pinch of cinnamon
- ½ tsp coriander
- Salt and pepper
- Sesame oil for frying

Preparation:

1. Mix the meat with the egg, salt, pepper, cayenne pepper and ½ tbsp soy sauce and form small balls. Heat the oil in the Dutch Oven lid and fry the balls in it for about 10 minutes, turning them constantly.
2. Then remove the roast, deglaze with the vegetable stock and bring to the boil. Add 1 tablespoon soy sauce, tomato paste and sambal oelek. Season again and return the meatballs to the sauce. Cut the peppers into rings and sprinkle over the meatballs.
3. For the rice: Heat the oil in the Dutch oven and sauté the carrots, almond slivers and rice until translucent. Add raisins, cinnamon, coriander, 1 tsp salt and water. Bring everything to a boil and then cook over low heat for 15 to 20 minutes.
4. Serve the rice with the sauce and enjoy

RABBIT WITH WILD FOREST MUSHROOMS

Serving:4 - Preparation time: 30 minutes

Ingredients:

- 2 tablespoons olive oil
- 1 tablespoon butter (optional)
- 2 garlic cloves, chopped
- 1 cup parsley, chopped
- 1 cup cream
- 1 cup broth or choice
- 1/2 cup brandy, cognac or whiskey
- 1 sprig each of fresh tarragon and thyme
- 1 whole rabbit, cut into quarters
- 2 cups wild mushrooms (like chanterelles)
- 2 cups chestnuts, peeled and halved
- Salt to taste

Preparation:

1. Add olive oil (and butter if using) to the bottom of the Dutch Oven. Heat oil/butter over medium-high heat for 30 seconds, then add garlic and stir.
2. Add rabbit pieces and quickly sear for a few minutes, browning each side. Reduce the heat and add the mushrooms, sauté until brown.
3. Add broth, alcohol, salt, fresh herbs, cream and chestnuts.
4. Simmer for 20 minutes or until rabbit is cooked through and tender. Sprinkle with chopped parsley over the rice before serving.

CHICKEN WITH CHESTNUTS AND CREAM

Servings: 4-6 - Preparation time: 15 minutes

Ingredients:

- 2 tablespoons olive oil
- 1 onion, chopped
- 1 clove of garlic, chopped
- 3 boneless chicken breasts, quartered
- 2 cups chestnuts, pre-cooked and peeled
- 2 cups brown mushrooms, whole
- 2 cups cream
- 2 cups chicken broth
- Dash cognac or brandy
- A pinch of nutmeg salt to taste

Preparation:

1. Heat oil on medium for 30 seconds, then add garlic, onion and mushrooms and sauté for 10 minutes.
2. Add chicken pieces and continue to sauté, stirring frequently, about 10 minutes. Add the cream, broth, brandy and chestnuts and simmer for 10 minutes.
3. Add nutmeg and salt before serving.

POSOLE

Serving:5 - Prep time: 1 hour

Ingredients:

- 900 g pork stew, cut into cubes
- 1 large onion, chopped
- 2 tablespoons canola oil
- 2 garlic cloves, chopped
- 3 cups beef broth
- 2 doses (225 g) are drained
- 2 cans (110g) chopped green chillies
- 1 to 2 jalapeños, seeded and chopped, optional
- Salt
- 1/2 teaspoon ground cumin
- 1/2 teaspoon dried oregano
- Pepper
- 1/4 teaspoon cayenne pepper
- 1/2 cup chopped fresh coriander
- Tortilla strips, optional

Preparation:

1. Cook noodles according to package directions.
2. Fry the mushrooms in a casserole and sauté in oil until tender. add garlic; Fry 1 minute longer.
3. Stir in fajitas, tomatoes, alfredo sauce and oregano. Bring to a boil. Reduce heat; Cover and simmer for 5-10 minutes, stirring occasionally. drain pasta; add to the fajita mixture and add.

BEEF STEW

Serving:8 - Prep time: 2 hours

Ingredients:

- 170 g bacon, cut into strips 1/4 wide
- Fry in 2 tablespoons of olive oil
- 900 g beef stew (or beef feed cut into pieces)
- 2 1/sea salt or to taste
- 1 black pepper
- 1/4 cup all-purpose flour
- 2 cups of good dry red wine
- 450 g mushrooms, thickly sliced
- 4 carrots, peeled and cut into 5mm pieces
- 1 medium yellow onion, diced
- 4 garlic cloves chopped
- 1 tablespoon tomato paste
- 4 cups low-sodium beef broth
- 2 bay leaves
- 1/2 tsp dried thyme
- 450 g small potatoes, halved or quartered

Preparation:

1. In a large ovenproof saucepan, sear the bacon over medium-high heat until golden brown and releasing fat. In a separate bowl remove the bacon.
2. While the bacon is cooking, place the beef in a large mixing bowl and season with 1/2 tablespoon salt and 1 teaspoon black pepper. Sprinkle the beef with 1/4 cup flour and mix to evenly coat the beef.
3. Place the beef in 2 batches in the hot bacon fat and cook on medium/high until the beef is brown (3

minutes per side). Add olive oil if needed. Add the roasted beef with bacon to the bowl.

4. Pour 2 cups of wine into the saucepan, bring to a boil and scrape the bottom to degrease the saucepan. Add the sliced mushrooms and simmer over medium heat for about 10 minutes.
5. Meanwhile, heat a large non-stick skillet on medium/high and add 2 tbsp olive oil. Add sliced carrots, diced onion and 4 minced garlic cloves and sauté for 4 minutes. Add 1 tbsp tomato paste and sauté for another minute. Put the vegetables in the soup pot.
6. Add 4 cups beef broth, 2 bay leaves, 1/2 tsp dried thyme, 1 tsp salt, and 1/2 tsp pepper. Place the beef and bacon in the pot and add the potatoes. Stir to mix, making sure the potatoes are submerged in liquid.
7. Bake at 170°C for 1 hour and 45 minutes. Add the salt and reduce the heat to medium. Cook until the shallots are translucent.

COTTAGE CAKE

Serving:6 - Preparation time: 70 min

Ingredients:

- 450 grams of minced meat
- 2 carrots
- 2 onions
- 1 tablespoon flour
- ½ tsp cinnamon
- 300 g of grated cheese
- 25 grams of butter
- ½ tsp oregano
- 1 tablespoon of tomato paste
- 275 ml beef broth
- 800 grams of potatoes
- Salt and pepper
- Oil for frying

Preparation:

1. Wash and peel potatoes. Peel and small dice the onions and carrots. Bring water to a boil over high heat. Boil the potatoes until soft, drain the water and set the potatoes aside.
2. Fry the onions in some oil. Then add the meat and carrots and fry until the meat is brown, about 5 minutes. Add the flour, oregano, tomato paste, and beef stock and simmer over medium heat for about 20 minutes.
3. Meanwhile, mash the potatoes and stir in the butter.
4. Stir the meat mixture well again. Then spread the mashed potatoes evenly over the mixture. Finally sprinkle the grated cheese on top.
5. Bake with the lid closed over low heat from below and medium heat from above for approx. 30 minutes.
6. Serve and enjoy.

GREEK PEPPERS WITH STUFFING

Serving:4 - Prep time: 45 minutes

Ingredients:

- 300 g organic minced meat
- 1 egg
- 1 bunch of spring onions
- 2 cloves of garlic
- ½ tsp oregano
- 300 ml vegetable broth
- 100 g feta cheese
- 6 tablespoons of yogurt
- 200 grams of rice
- 4 red peppers
- Salt and pepper
- Sesame oil for frying

Preparation:

1. Cook rice according to package directions.
2. Clean and wash the spring onions and cut into fine rings. Peel and finely chop the garlic clove. Crumble feta.
3. Heat the oil in the Dutch Oven. Sauté the spring onions and garlic until translucent. Then add the minced meat and fry until crumbly. Season with oregano, pepper and salt.
4. Add the rice, sheep's cheese, yoghurt and egg and mix well. Remove the Dutch Oven from the embers and set aside.
5. Halve the peppers lengthwise, wash, deseed and remove the stalk. Fill with rice, vegetable mass. Then put it back into the empty Dutch Oven.
6. Pour in the vegetable broth and cook everything for about 30 minutes over medium heat from above and below.
7. Serve and enjoy.

DUTCH SEASONED PASTA

Serving:4 - Preparation time: 20 min

Ingredients:

- 400 g of fusilli pasta
- 300 g coarse meatloaf
- 2 large onions
- Some pasta water
- 1 tube of tomato paste
- Lots of Maggi
- Salt and pepper
- Oil for frying

Preparation:

1. Cook pasta until firm and slightly chewy.
2. Roughly dice the meatloaf. Peel onions and dice small.
3. Heat the oil in the Dutch Oven and sauté the onions and meatloaf from below over high heat.
4. Add tomato paste and liquefy with some pasta water. Season to taste with salt, pepper and Maggi.
5. Fold the noodles into the sauce and heat up and down over a low heat for about 5 minutes with the lid closed.
6. Serve and enjoy.

STUFFED CASSEROLE WITH GREEN PEPPER

Serving:10 - Preparation time: 15 minutes

Ingredients:

- 4 cups cooked instant brown rice
- 450g extra lean ground beef
- 3-4 large green peppers, diced
- 1/2 cup diced onion
- 820 g diced tomatoes, drained
- 400 g corn, drained
- 1 cup ketchup
- 280 grams of mushrooms
- 1/2 tsp minced garlic
- 2 cups low-fat shredded cheddar cheese

Preparation:

1. Brown the ground beef and onion in a large stock pot or Dutch oven and drain. You can also use a pan.
2. Boil chopped green peppers in water until tender (10-15 minutes). You can also microwave them for about 5 minutes. Cook rice in a separate pot.
3. Combine cooked rice, green peppers, ground beef, and remaining ingredients (except cheese) in a saucepan, Dutch oven, or casserole dish.
4. Refine with grated cheese. Bake at 180°C for 12-15 minutes or until cheese is melted.
5. Then heat to 250°C and fry for 1-2 minutes until cheese is lightly browned and bubbly. Serve hot.

LOIN MAHARANI

Serving:4 - Preparation time: 60 min

Ingredients:

- 1 loin
- ½ pineapple (fresh)
- 100 ml cream
- 50 ml milk
- 100 ml pineapple juice
- 1 tsp thyme
- 1 tsp rosemary
- 1 teaspoon curry
- 1 onion
- 2 tablespoons of barbecue sauce
- 1 tablespoon Worcestershire sauce
- Olive oil for frying
- Salt and pepper

Preparation:

1. Peel and chop the pineapple. Peel and chop the onion.
2. Season the fillet with salt, pepper, thyme and rosemary and place in the Dutch oven with the olive oil. Fry briefly and then cook over medium heat from above and below for about 30 minutes. Remove and keep warm in aluminum foil.
3. Put the remaining ingredients in the Dutch Oven and simmer for 10 minutes. Finished!

4. Serve both together with rice and enjoy.

BRAISED LAMB

Ingredients:

- 1 kg leg of lamb
- 3 cloves of garlic
- 5 carrots
- 3 onions
- 2 sprigs of rosemary
- 1 sprig of thyme
- 600 ml vegetable broth
- 200 g tomato passata
- 2 tablespoons olive oil
- Salt and pepper

Preparation:

1. Peel garlic and onion. Finely chop the onion and press the garlic. Chop rosemary. Peel carrots and cut into small pieces.
2. Rub the leg of lamb with salt, pepper, olive oil and rosemary. Place in the Dutch Oven and roast evenly.
3. Remove. Place the carrots, onions and garlic in the Dutch Oven. Place the lamb shank on the vegetables. Pour the vegetable broth, tomato passata and sprig of thyme over the vegetables.
4. Cook with the lid closed and medium heat for about 90 minutes.
5. Thinly slice the leg of lamb and serve with the sauce and potatoes and enjoy.

ARROZ WITH CHICKEN

Serving:4 - Prep time: 1 hour 10 minutes

Ingredients:

- 1 whole chicken cut into pieces
- 1/2 large onion, diced
- 2 garlic cloves, crushed or grated
- 1 pepper, diced
- 1 may have diced tomatoes
- 1 tablespoon of tomato paste
- 2 tablespoons fresh parsley chopped
- 1 1/2 cup chicken broth
- 1 cup fresh or frozen peas (thawed)
- 1 1/2 cups Uncle Ben's original rice
- 1/2 teaspoon of paprika
- 1/2 teaspoon turmeric
- 3 tablespoons olive oil

Preparation:

1. Fry the chicken pieces, skin-side down, in olive oil for 6-8 minutes until golden brown. Turn and cook for another 3-5 minutes. Take out and set aside.
2. Sauté the onion and sauté the peppers with additional olive oil, if needed, for 2-3 minutes until tender.

3. Add the rice and garlic and stir-fry for about 30 seconds.
4. Add tomato paste and stir. Add diced tomatoes, chicken broth, turmeric and paprika. Mix well.
5. Place the chicken skins in the pot, side up. Bring to a boil and bring the heat to a boil. Cover the pot and cook for 40-50 minutes. Add peas and parsley. Cook for another 10 minutes and serve.

LAMB FILLET WITH YOGHURT

Serving:4 - Preparation time: 35 min

Ingredients:

- 600 g lamb fillet
- 2 onions
- 1 clove of garlic
- 20 cherry tomatoes
- 2 peppers
- 4 tablespoons olive oil
- 400 ml vegetable broth
- 3 tablespoons lemon juice
- 200 grams of yoghurt
- Salt and pepper

Preparation:

1. Peel and finely chop the onions and garlic. Wash tomatoes and peppers and cut into small pieces.
2. Heat the olive oil in the Dutch Oven. The lamb fillet from both sides about 4 to 5 minutes. Take out and keep warm.
3. Add the onions, garlic, tomatoes and peppers to the pot and sauté. Deglaze with vegetable stock and lemon juice

and let simmer for about 5 minutes. Season with salt and pepper.
4. Put the lamb fillets back into the Dutch Oven and cook for another 2 minutes.
5. Decorate the lamb fillets with the yoghurt, serve and enjoy.

BEEF FILLET WITH SPICY CURRANTS

Serving:3 - Preparation time: 35 min

Ingredients:

- 700 g beef fillet
- 200 ml of blackcurrant juice
- 1 chili pepper
- 1 piece of ginger
- 2 tsp honey
- Sea salt and pepper
- 1 clove of garlic
- Olive oil for frying

Preparation:

1. Place the fillet of beef in the Dutch oven and sear on both sides.
2. Mix the currant juice with the honey and add the chopped chili pepper, the piece of ginger and the clove of garlic. Season with sea salt and pepper.
3. After a few minutes, strain the sauce and discard any leftover bits. Add to the beef fillet and simmer for about 15 minutes.
4. Serve hot immediately and enjoy.
5. Bon appetit!

SWISS RÖSTI

Serving:8 - Preparation time: 25 min

Ingredients:

- 1 kg of potatoes
- 250 g of raclette cheese
- 3 tablespoons olive oil
- 250 ml cream
- Salt and pepper

Preparation:

1. Peel and coarsely grate the potatoes. Place in a sieve and squeeze out the liquid.
2. Dice the cheese and mix into the potatoes. Season with salt and pepper.
3. Add 2 to 3 tablespoons of oil to the Dutch Oven. Then place the piles of potatoes and cheese in the Dutch Oven. Put some cream on each stack. Bake on medium-high heat for 15 to 20 minutes until golden brown on top and bottom.

POTATO OMELET

Serving:6 - Preparation time: 25 min

Ingredients:

- 1.5 kg of potatoes
- 4 large onions
- 4 tablespoons olive oil
- 12 eggs
- Salt and pepper

Preparation:

1. Peel, wash and thinly slice the potatoes. Peel and chop the onions.
2. Heat 7 tbsp olive oil in the Dutch Oven. Cook the potatoes and onions in it over medium heat for 25 minutes. Season with salt and pepper.
3. Whisk eggs in a bowl, salt and pepper. Add the cooled potatoes and onions and mix well.
4. Heat the remaining oil and add the egg mixture to the Dutch Oven. With the lid closed and low heat from below and medium heat from above, let the eggs set for about 10-15 minutes.
5. The potato omelette is ready. Serve and enjoy. Good Appetite.

VEGETARIAN BLACK BEANS & SWEET POTATO CHILI

Serving:4 -Prep time: 45 minutes

Ingredients:

- 1 tablespoon of olive oil
- 1 onion
- 1 teaspoon of cumin
- 1 red pepper
- 1 poblano chili
- 2 chipotle peppers
- 2 tablespoons adobo sauce
- 2 cups vegetable broth (to make sure you use broth to thin the soup as needed)
- 800 g diced tomatoes
- 3 canned beans are fine)
- 2 sweet potatoes (medium, diced and roasted)
- 1 avocado
- chopped coriander
- Lime
- grated cheddar cheese

Preparation:

1. Make sure the beans and sweet potatoes are cooked before beginning. Prepare the peppers by slicing them in half, removing the seeds, and then slicing them into 1 inch (2.5 cm) pieces. Roughly chop the chipotle peppers.
2. Heat the olive oil in a large saucepan or Dutch oven over medium-high heat. Add the onion and cook until softened, about 5 minutes.
3. Add the cumin and cook for about 1 minute, then add the peppers (save the adobo sauce until the end) and cook the vegetables for another 5 minutes.
4. Then add the vegetable broth, diced tomatoes and black beans. Continue to simmer until the beans and tomatoes are warmed through and tender and most of the liquid has evaporated.
5. Finally, stir in the sweet potatoes and adobo sauce and simmer for about 3 minutes. If needed, add additional vegetable broth to thin the chili. It should be thick but fakeable.
6. Serve in soup bowls with a spoon. Garnish with diced avocado, chopped cilantro, a hearty sprinkle of cheddar cheese and a squeeze of lime juice.

RAVIOLI IN ARTICHOKE AND RADICCHIO SAUCE

Serving:4 - Prep Time:50min

Ingredients:

- 500 grams of ravioli
- 200 g artichoke hearts
- 200 grams of radicchio
- 4 tablespoons olive oil
- 1 clove of garlic
- 2 onions
- 2 tablespoons of butter
- 200 ml of white wine
- 50 g Parmesan cheese

- 100 ml cream
- Salt and pepper
- Fresh basil

Preparation:

1. Peel and finely chop the garlic and onions. Cut radicchio and artichoke hearts into thin strips.
2. Heat the water in the Dutch Oven and cook the noodles until firm and slightly chewy. Drain and set aside.
3. Heat the oil in the Dutch Oven. Fry garlic and onion. Then put radicchio and artichoke hearts in the Dutch Oven and roast for 5 minutes.
4. Deglaze with white wine and allow to reduce slightly. Add cream and butter. Season with salt and pepper. Fold in the noodles and reheat.
5. Serve with fresh basil and parmesan and enjoy

BAKED GNOCCHI WITH VEGETABLES

Serving:4 - Prep time: 35 minutes

Ingredients:

- 1 red onion (large, 2 cups, chopped)
- 2 zucchini (small-medium, 2 and 1/2 cups, called crescents)
- 110 g mushrooms (halved or quartered depending on size)
- 1 red bell pepper (large, 1 heaping cup, chopped)
- 400 g potato gnocchi (frozen, uncooked and do not thaw)
- 3 tablespoons olive oil
- 1/2 tbsp dried basil (dried oregano, dried parsley, garlic powder)
- 1/2 teaspoon onion powder (dried thyme, sweet paprika)
- 1/8 teaspoon red pepper flakes (optional)
- fine sea salt
- ground pepper
- freshly grated parmesan
- Sauce (optional: coriander or marinara sauce)

Preparation:

1. Preheat the oven to 210°C. Cut the red onion into chunks, halve the zucchini, then halve again to get half a moon, half or quarter of the mushrooms (a quarter large and a quarter smaller depending on size), and chop the red pepper into chunks.
2. Add all of the chopped veggies to a large skillet or 2 half skillets. Put the gnocchi in the pan. Drizzle olive oil over everything, then add all the spices: dried basil, dried oregano, dried parsley, garlic powder, onion powder, dried thyme, sweet paprika, red pepper flakes (if desired), and salt and pepper to taste. Mix well and then spread in an even layer to avoid overlapping vegetables/gnocchi.
3. Bake for a few minutes, then remove, flip and stir to keep everything in an even layer.

4. Then return to the oven for an additional 10-15 minutes or until the vegetables are cooked to your preference (about 10 minutes). Take out of the oven.
5. Grate parmesan cheese directly on top. Serve hot. Drizzle over the herb-cilantro sauce, if you like.

AUBERGINE, TOMATO AND CHICKPEA STEW

Serving:4 - Prep time: 45 minutes

Ingredients:

- 4 peppers
- 4 cups of quinoa
- 2 tablespoons olive oil
- 2 garlic cloves (chopped)
- 1 cup black beans
- 1 cup of corn
- 1 cup of tomato sauce (Italian)
- 1 cup grated cheese

Preparation:

1. Preheat the oven to 180°C. Cook the quinoa according to package directions if it's not already cooked. Cut off the tops of the peppers and wash the insides, being careful to remove any seeds. Dry thoroughly and place in a glass bowl.
2. Heat the olive oil in a large pan. The onions on medium
3. Let the temperature smell. Add the garlic and cook for another minute. Then add quinoa, black beans, corn and tomato sauce. Stir over low heat until warm and well blended.
4. Stuff each pepper with 1 cup of the quinoa mixture, then top each pepper with 1/4 cup cheese. Next, pour about 1/4 cup of water at the bottom of the casserole dish to soften the peppers as they cook.
5. Cover with foil and bake at 180°C for 30 minutes. Finally, remove the foil and bake the dish for another 15 minutes to allow the cheese to melt and brown. Serve warm.

MEXICAN RICE CASSEROLE

Serving:5 - Preparation time: 15 minutes

Ingredients:

- 1 red onion (small, diced)
- 1 tablespoon of olive oil
- 1 teaspoon of chili powder and salt
- 1 teaspoon of smoked paprika
- 1 teaspoon dried oregano
- 1 red bell pepper (seeded and diced)
- 110 g diced green chilies (drained or 1 jalapeño, diced)
- 1 cup corn kernels and 2 teaspoons cumin
- 400 g black beans (drained)
- 340 g salsa (or enchilada sauce)
- 1/2 cup rice (brown rice)
- 1/2 cup grated cheese (optional)
- 1/4 cup shredded cheddar cheese

- fresh coriander and spring onions and 1 avocado

Preparation:

1. First, heat the oil in a large skillet over medium-high heat. Add the onion and cook for 3 minutes, then add the spices (cumin to the oregano) and stir. Cook for another 2-3 minutes. Then add the red peppers and green chillies and stir. Cook an additional 2-3 minutes, then add the drained beans, corn, salsa, and rice. Mix well.
2. Turn on the oven for grilling and pour the mixture into the pan with the grated cheese. Place pan in oven and cook until cheese is golden and bubbly, about 3-4 minutes.
3. Serve warm with diced spring onions, cilantro and avocado. Cook until lentils are tender, 25-35 minutes, stirring occasionally to keep lentils from sticking to bottom of pan. Fold in the spinach and cook until wilted, 3 minutes. Serve with coconut rice.

VEGETARIAN LENTIL CURRY

Serving:4 - Prep time: 90 minutes

Ingredients:

- 400 grams of tofu
- 2 onions
- 2 cloves of garlic
- 400 ml coconut milk
- 200 g of red lentils
- 3 teaspoons hot curry powder
- Salt and pepper
- 2 tablespoons olive oil

Preparation:

1. Cut the tofu into small cubes. Peel and finely chop onions and garlic cloves.
2. Heat the olive oil in the Dutch Oven. Fry onions and garlic. Add lentils, curry, salt and pepper.
3. Add coconut milk and simmer for about 5 minutes.
4. Add tofu and simmer for another 5 minutes.
5. Serve and enjoy the finished lentil curry.

SHRIMP SKEWER

Serving:4 - Preparation time: 20 min

Ingredients:

- 400 grams of shrimp
- 2 teaspoons lemon juice
- 2 cloves of garlic
- Salt and pepper
- 2 onions
- 2 tablespoons olive oil
- Wooden skewers

Preparation:

1. Peel the onion and cut into 2 cm cubes. Place the garlic in a garlic press and squeeze. wash shrimp.
2. Heat the olive oil in the Dutch Oven. Sauté prawns and onions until translucent.
3. Skewer the shrimp and onion alternately on the wood.
4. Brush the skewers with lemon juice and garlic and place in the Dutch Oven for a further 10 minutes over low heat and with the lid closed.
5. Serve and enjoy.

CHICKPEA ROSTI

Serving:4 - Prep time: 40 minutes

Ingredients:

- 600 g chickpeas (jar)
- 2 onions
- 8 grams of ginger
- 2 chili peppers
- 3 tsp black cumin
- 3 tsp cumin
- 4 tablespoons coconut oil
- 4 tablespoons spelled flour
- some flour
- ½ tsp baking powder
- 8 tablespoons of water
- 2 tablespoons coriander
- 2 cloves of garlic
- Salt and pepper

Preparation:

1. Prepare the chickpeas according to the product description. Peel onion and garlic clove and cut into small pieces. Heat coconut oil in the Dutch Oven. Add onions, garlic, cumin and black cumin and sauté. Removed.
2. Put the chickpeas, chili pepper, some flour and baking powder in a bowl and mix well. Add all the herbs, onion mixture and water and mix well again. Place the entire mixture in a blender and puree. Season with salt and pepper.
3. Pour the coconut oil back into the Dutch Oven, heat, then use a ladle to spoon the mixture into the saucepan in individual heaps. Fry each side for about 2 minutes. Put aside.
4. When all the patties are baked, place them in the Dutch oven from above and below with the lid closed and low heat for about 10 minutes. Finished! Serve and enjoy

OLIVE HASH BROWNS

Serving:4 - Preparation time: 1 day 40 minutes

Ingredients:

- 1 kg of potatoes
- 100 grams of green olives
- 1 large onion
- 50 g Parmesan cheese
- Salt and pepper
- 2 tablespoons olive oil

Preparation:

1. Boil the potatoes in their skins until almost done and leave to soak overnight. Then peel and coarsely grate the potatoes.
2. Peel and finely dice the onion. Pit the olives and cut into fine rings.
3. Place all ingredients in a bowl and mix well. Season with salt and pepper.
4. Then spread evenly in the Dutch oven and bake over medium heat from below and on top for approx. 30 minutes until golden brown.
5. Let cool and cut into small pieces.
6. Serve and enjoy.

SWEET CURRY

Serving:4 - Preparation time: 30 min

Ingredients:

- 2 onions
- 4 bananas
- 2 tbsp curry powder
- 400 ml coconut milk
- 1 tsp turmeric
- 1 tsp mustard seeds
- 1 tsp coconut oil
- Salt, pepper, chili powder

Preparation:

1. Peel bananas and cut into small pieces. Peel onion and cut into small pieces.
2. Heat coconut oil in the Dutch Oven. Fry onions. Add the bananas and fry them too.
3. Add mustard seeds and coconut milk and mix well. Season with salt, pepper, chilli powder and turmeric.
4. Simmer over low heat with the lid closed for about 10 minutes.
5. Serve the finished dish with rice or potatoes and enjoy.

POTATO SPAGHETTI

Serving:4 - Preparation time: 60 min

Ingredients:

- 750 grams of potatoes

- 4 onions
- 150 g beef jerky
- 1 bunch of chives
- 3 fresh egg yolks
- some butter
- Salt and pepper

Preparation:

1. Peel, wash and dice the potatoes and cook in a Dutch oven with a little salted water. Drain and press hot through a potato ricer.
2. Peel the onions and dice them together with the beef jerky. Put both in the Dutch Oven with a little butter and fry lightly. Take out and add to the potato mixture. Mix well and season with salt and pepper.
3. Then add the finely chopped chives and the 3 egg yolks to the potato mixture and work all the ingredients into a smooth dough. Leave to rest for 30 minutes.
4. Form finger-thick sausages from the dough. Heat the butter in the Dutch oven and fry the sparrows in batches until golden brown on all sides.

BRUSCHETTA WITH ARTICHOKES

Serving:4 - Prep time: 90 minutes

Ingredients:

- 8 slices of ciabatta bread
- 8 tomatoes
- 3 tablespoons olive oil
- 3 tablespoons of balsamic vinegar
- 1 tablespoon of sugar
- 2 cloves of garlic
- 100 g artichokes, chopped
- Salt, pepper and parsley

Preparation:

1. Place the ciabatta slices in the Dutch Oven and roast for 1 minute on both sides. Take out and keep warm.
2. Preheat the oven to 200°.
3. Cut the tomatoes into small slices and place in the Dutch Oven. Place the artichokes between the tomatoes.
4. Place the salt, pepper, oil and balsamic vinegar in a small bowl and mix well. Then pour the tomato mixture over it.
5. Cook for 15 to 20 minutes over medium heat from the top and bottom of the Dutch Oven.
6. Place the tomatoes on the ciabatta, decorate with parsley, serve and enjoy.

FRUTTI DI MARE

Serving:4 - Preparation time: 20 min

Ingredients:

- 200 g salmon fillet
- 200 g fish fillet
- 8 king prawns
- 400 grams of mussels
- 400 grams of tomatoes
- 2 cloves of garlic
- 250 ml fish stock
- 250 ml white wine
- 2 tablespoons lemon juice
- 3 tablespoons olive oil
- Salt and pepper

Preparation:

1. Peel the garlic and cut into small pieces with the tomatoes. Cut the fish fillets into small pieces. Peel and devein the prawns.
2. Heat the Dutch Oven with some water. Add mussels until they open. Throw closed clams in the trash and set open clams aside.
3. Heat the olive oil in the Dutch oven and add the garlic, tomatoes, fish stock and white wine.
4. Put all types of fish in the Dutch Oven and let stand for 5 minutes. Add clams. Season with salt, pepper and lemon juice and mix well.
5. Serve and enjoy the finished dish.

VEGETARIAN OVEN FAJITAS

Serving:2 - Preparation time: 20 minutes

Ingredients:

- 1 yellow pepper (cut into strips)
- 1 red pepper (cut into strips)
- 1 zucchini (small, cut into strips)
- 1 small onion (sliced)
- 400 g Portobello mushrooms (sliced)
- 1 tablespoon of olive oil
- Garlic powder
- 1/2 teaspoon cumin
- 1/2 teaspoon chili powder
- 1/2 teaspoon onion powder
- Salt (or to taste!)
- Pepper (or to taste!)
- 1/8 teaspoon cayenne pepper (a pinch)
- Cooking spray
- 4 whole wheat tortillas
- Lime
- Salsa
- Coriander
- Cheese
- Sour cream

Preparation:

1. Preheat the oven to 220 °C and line a baking tray with foil.
2. Spray the pan with cooking spray. Mix the vegetables with the olive oil and all the spices. Spread the seasoned vegetable mixture in the pan.
3. Cook for 20 minutes. Finally rub the salad with some Parmesan and drizzle some olive oil over the tomatoes if you like.

PUMPKIN FRIES

Serving:4 - Preparation time: 25 minutes

Ingredients:

- 1 kg Hokkaido pumpkin
- 6 tablespoons olive oil
- 2 tsp paprika powder
- 2 teaspoons curry
- Salt and pepper

Preparation:

1. Halve the pumpkin, remove the seeds and cut the flesh into small chips.
2. Prepare a large bowl, put the fries in it and add the olive oil and spices and mix well.
3. Place the pumpkin strips in the Dutch Oven and bake for approx. 15 minutes at medium heat from below and high heat from above.
4. Serve and enjoy the finished pumpkin fries.

SALMON QUICHE WITH PEPPERS

Serving:4 - Prep time: 45 minutes

Ingredients:

- 100 g low-fat quark
- 3 tablespoons sesame oil
- 1 egg yolk
- 3 eggs
- 2 teaspoons of baking soda
- 200 g
- Wholemeal spelled flour
- 2 peppers
- 4 tablespoons of water
- 1 small zucchini
- 1 clove of garlic
- 2 tablespoons fresh thyme
- 250 g salmon fillet
- 100 ml milk
- Salt and pepper

Preparation:

1. Chop the garlic, slice the zucchini and cut the peppers into strips. Cut the salmon into bite-sized pieces.
2. Mix together the quark, oil, egg yolk, water and ½ tsp salt. Then add flour and baking powder and mix well.

3. Spread the batter on the bottom of the Dutch Oven. Grease a little beforehand. Prick the base several times with a fork.
4. Whisk together the eggs, milk, garlic, half the thyme and season with salt and pepper.
5. Spread the salmon and vegetables on the dough and pour the egg milk over it.
6. Bake in the Dutch oven with the lid closed (medium heat from below and above for approx. 35 minutes).
7. Serve sprinkled with thyme and enjoy.

AROMATIC SPINACH

Serving:4 - Prep time: 45 minutes

Ingredients:

- 800 g organic spinach
- 8 grams of ginger
- 2 cloves of garlic
- 2 onions
- 2 teaspoons coriander
- 2 tsp turmeric
- 2 tsp cumin
- 3 tablespoons olive oil
- 80ml of water
- Salt and chili powder

Preparation:

1. Peel the onion, garlic and ginger and cut into small pieces.
2. Heat the oil in the Dutch oven. Add onion, garlic and ginger and sauté.
3. After two minutes, add coriander, cumin, turmeric and sauté for another two minutes.
4. Add spinach and water and mix everything together.
5. Simmer over low heat with the lid closed for another 15 minutes. Season with salt and chili powder.
6. Serve and enjoy the finished dish.

RATATOUILLE

Serving:4 - Preparation time: 30 minutes

Ingredients:

- 4 onions
- 2 cloves of garlic
- 4 red peppers
- 4 zucchini
- 4 tomatoes
- 3 tablespoons olive oil
- 200 ml vegetable broth
- Salt, pepper, rosemary

Preparation:

1. Wash, peel and chop the onions and garlic into small pieces. Wash zucchini, peppers and tomatoes and cut into small slices.

2. Heat the olive oil in the Dutch Oven and fry the ingredients for 5 to 10 minutes.
3. Add vegetable stock and season with salt and pepper. Let everything simmer for another 10 minutes.
4. Garnish with rosemary and enjoy.

BAKED POTATOES

Serving:4 - Preparation time: 60 min

Ingredients:

- 4 large potatoes
- 2 tablespoons of thyme
- 2 tablespoons olive oil
- 150 grams of cottage cheese
- 4 tablespoons of milk
- 5 tablespoons mixed herbs
- Salt and pepper
- Parsley to decorate

Preparation:

1. Wash potatoes and prick lightly on several sides.
2. Tear four squares of aluminum foil to wrap the potatoes.
3. Brush aluminum foil with oil. Place the potatoes on the aluminum foil and season with salt and pepper. Then wrap well.
4. Place in the Dutch Oven and bake for approx. 45 to 55 minutes over medium heat from below and high heat from above. To check, poke a fork in the potato and see if it's soft.
5. For the herb quark: Mix the milk, quark, mixed herbs, pepper and salt well.
6. Cut the potatoes open slightly and add the herb quark to the potatoes. Decorate with parsley.
7. Serve and enjoy.

POTATO POT

Serving:4 - Prep time: 40 minutes

Ingredients:

- 600 grams of potatoes
- 3 turnip greens
- 3 onions
- 8 grams of ginger
- 4 tablespoons almond butter
- 1 liter of vegetable broth
- 2 tbsp coconut oil
- 2 chili peppers
- 2 tsp cumin
- 2 tsp turmeric
- 2 teaspoons coriander
- 2 cloves of garlic
- Salt and pepper
- Curry powder

Preparation:

1. Peel the onion and ginger and cut into small pieces.
2. Heat coconut oil in the Dutch Oven. Fry onions and ginger in it.
3. Peel the potatoes and kohlrabi and cut into small pieces. Also put in the Dutch Oven and fry. Season with salt, pepper, curry powder, turmeric, coriander, almond butter and cumin.
4. Cut the chilli into small pieces, add them as well and mix well.
5. Pour the vegetable broth over the mixture and simmer, with the lid on, over medium heat for about 10 to 15 minutes.
6. Serve and enjoy the finished dish.

VEGETARIAN STUFFED EGGPLANT

Serving:4 - Preparation time: 70 min

Ingredients:

- 4 eggplants
- 4 onions
- 4 cloves of garlic
- 8 small tomatoes
- 1 tablespoon olive oil
- Salt and pepper

Preparation:

1. Wash the aubergines, cut in half lengthways and scoop out the inside with a spoon.
2. Prepare a bowl of cold salted water and add the eggplant for about 30 minutes.
3. Peel and finely chop the onions and garlic. Cut tomatoes into small pieces.
4. Place the garlic, onions and tomatoes in a small bowl and season with salt and pepper.
5. Put the tomato filling in the eggplants.
6. Heat up the Dutch Oven. Add the aubergines, drizzle with olive oil and bake for about 20 minutes over a low heat from below and high heat from above.
7. Serve and enjoy the finished dish.

MASALA

Serving:4 - Preparation time: 20 min

Ingredients:

- 400 g Hokkaido pumpkin
- 500 grams of chickpeas
- 2 cans of chopped tomatoes
- 2 onions
- 4 tablespoons olive oil
- 6 tablespoons of masala
- 600ml of water
- 2 cloves of garlic
- Herbal salt and pepper
- ½ bunch parsley

Preparation:

1. Wash pumpkin and cut into small pieces. Drain and drain the chickpeas. Peel onion and cut into small pieces.
2. Heat the olive oil in the Dutch Oven. Add all ingredients and sweat.
3. Put the chopped tomatoes and the water in the Dutch Oven. Add all other ingredients and stir.
4. Simmer on medium heat for about 10 minutes.
5. Arrange the finished masala on plates and enjoy.

HOT VIOLA DA GAMBA

Serving:4 - Preparation time: 30 min

Ingredients:

- 24 shrimp
- 3 chili peppers
- 2 cloves of garlic
- 8 tablespoons olive oil
- 6 tablespoons lemon juice
- Salt and pepper

Preparation:

1. Peel the garlic and cut into small pieces. Cut the chili into rings.
2. Heat the Dutch Oven with two tablespoons of olive oil and sauté the shrimp. Add the remaining oil and the chillies. Season with salt and pepper.
3. Drizzle the finished shrimp with lemon juice.
4. Serve and enjoy.

VEGETARIAN CHILI

Serving:8 - Prep time: 35 minutes

Ingredients:

- 2 medium yellow onions
- 6 cloves of garlic
- 2 tablespoons olive oil
- 400 g canned beans, drained
- 2 x 800g cans of diced tomatoes
- 2 × 110g cans of roasted green chillies
- 1 cup bulgur wheat (gluten free)
- 1 cup frozen corn and 1/3 cup chili powder
- 3 tablespoons dried oregano
- 2 teaspoons garlic powder
- 2 teaspoons kosher salt and 1/4 teaspoon black pepper
- 1 tablespoon maple syrup or honey
- 1/8 teaspoon chipotle powder
- Hot sauce, sour cream, cheese, cilantro or chives for finishing (garnish with vegan nacho cheese for vegans)

Preparation:

1. Cut the onions and finely chop the garlic. In a large saucepan or Dutch oven, heat the olive oil over medium-high heat. Add the onions and sauté until

tender, about 5 minutes, stirring occasionally. Add the garlic and fry for about 1 minute.

2. Add remaining Ingredients: beans, tomatoes with juice, green chiles, bulgur wheat, frozen corn, chili powder, oregano, garlic powder, kosher salt, black pepper, maple syrup or honey, and chipotle powder. Mix to combine. Add a little water if needed to make sure everything is covered (we added about 1 cup).

3. Bring to a boil, then simmer for 20 to 30 minutes until the bulgur is tender. Taste and add more spices if you like. Flavor with hot sauce and serve with sour cream, grated cheese and cilantro or chives.

SPINACH MUFFINS

Serving:4 - Prep time: 40 minutes

Ingredients:

- 600 g spinach (fresh)
- 8 eggs
- 300 grams of mozzarella
- 500 grams of mushrooms
- 250ml of water
- 2 tablespoons of milk
- 2 tablespoons of sour cream
- Salt and pepper
- Olive oil for frying

Preparation:

1. Clean and slice the mushrooms. Clean the spinach.
2. Heat the oil in the Dutch oven and sauté the mushroom slices for about 8 minutes until soft. Put aside.
3. Add the water and spinach to the saucepan and simmer for about 4 minutes.
4. In a large bowl, mix eggs, mushrooms, cheese, spinach, sour cream, and milk. Season with salt and pepper.
5. Pour the batter into muffin cases. Heat up the Dutch Oven. Place the muffin cases in the pot and bake with the lid closed (medium heat from top and bottom) for about 20 to 25 minutes.
6. Serve and enjoy.

MEDITERRANEAN GNOCCHI

Serving:4 - Preparation time: 30 min

Ingredients:

- 1 kg of gnocchi
- 2 onions
- 2 cloves of garlic
- 2 zucchini
- 100 g sun-dried tomatoes
- 3 tablespoons olive oil
- Salt and pepper

Preparation:

1. Peel and chop the onion, garlic and courgettes into small pieces.
2. Heat the water in the Dutch Oven and cook the gnocchi according to the package instructions until firm and slightly tough. Drain and set aside (keep warm).
3. Heat the olive oil in the Dutch Oven. Fry onion and garlic. Put the zucchini in the pot and sauté.
4. Add gnocchi and sun-dried tomatoes and mix well. Season with salt and pepper and stir well.
5. Serve and enjoy the finished dish.

COCONUT CAULIFLOWER CURRY

Serving:4 - Prep time: 50 minutes

Ingredients:

- 2 tablespoons of vegetable oil
- 1 onion (small, diced)
- 1 jalapeño (seeded and chopped)
- 1 tablespoon fresh ginger (grated)
- 1/4 cup red curry paste
- 400 g full-fat coconut milk
- 400 g diced tomatoes
- 1 head cauliflower
- kosher salt
- freshly ground black pepper

Preparation:

1. In a large saucepan or Dutch oven, heat the oil over medium-high heat. Add the onion and jalapeño and cook until soft, about 3 minutes.
2. Add the ginger and cook, stirring, until fragrant, about 1 minute. Stir in curry paste and cook 1 minute.
3. Stir in coconut milk and tomatoes with juice. Add the cauliflower and 1/2 cup water. Season with salt and pepper.
4. Bring to a boil, then reduce heat and simmer until cauliflower is just tender, 10 to 15 minutes.

FENNEL PASTA

Serving:4 - Preparation time: 50 min

Ingredients:

- 500 grams of spaghetti
- 1 bulb of fennel
- 3 tablespoons olive oil
- 2 cloves of garlic
- Parmesan cheese
- 2 onions
- 2 tablespoons of pine nuts
- 300 ml vegetable broth
- Salt and pepper

Preparation:

1. Heat 1 water in Dutch Oven and cook the noodles until firm and slightly chewy. Drain and set aside.

2. Peel and finely chop 2 onions and garlic.
3. Pour water back into the Dutch Oven and cook the fennel until firm and slightly al dente. Cut the fennel into small pieces.
4. Heat 4 oil in the Dutch Oven. Sweat the onions and garlic lightly. Add all the other ingredients to the Dutch Oven except for the pasta and parmesan and simmer over medium heat for 10 minutes. Season with salt and pepper.
5. Fold the pasta into the sauce and cook for another 3 minutes.
6. Garnish with Parmesan and serve and enjoy.

TOMATO AND POTATO GRATIN

Serving:4 - Preparation time: 50 min

Ingredients:

- 500 grams of potatoes
- 100 ml milk
- 1 cream
- 1 clove of garlic
- 200 g grated Emmental cheese
- 6 tomatoes
- Thyme
- Salt and pepper

Preparation:

1. Peel the potatoes, wash and cut into very thin slices. Peel and finely press the garlic. Wash the tomatoes, remove the stalk and cut into slices.
2. Mix the milk, cream, garlic clove, pepper, salt and thyme well.
3. Layer the potatoes and tomatoes alternately in the Dutch Oven. Then pour the sauce over the tomatoes and potatoes. Finally sprinkle the cheese on top.
4. With the lid closed, cook over low heat from below and medium heat from above until potatoes are tender, about 40 minutes.
5. Serve and enjoy.

VEGETARIAN LASAGNE

Serving:4 - Preparation time: 50 min

Ingredients:

- 500 g lasagne sheets
- 300 g tomato passata
- 1 can of kidney beans
- 1 can of corn
- 1 packet of feta
- 1 tablespoon of olive oil
- 3 tablespoons of tomato paste
- 2 peppers
- 2 onions
- 400 grams of mozzarella
- Salt and pepper
- Some paprika powder

Preparation:

1. Wash, deseed and dice the peppers. Cut the onions. Cut the mozzarella into slices. Crumble feta.
2. Put some oil in the Dutch Oven. Put the onions and kidney beans in the Dutch Oven over medium heat and sweat briefly. Add the corn, peppers, tomato passata and tomato paste and simmer for 5 minutes. Season with salt, pepper and paprika.
3. Set aside all but a small portion of the sauce. Place a layer of lasagne sheets on top of the remaining sauce in the pot. Then layer alternately as follows: gravy, feta, lasagne sheets, gravy, feta, lasagne sheets until sauce is empty and forms final layer.
4. Finally, distribute the mozzarella slices evenly over the sauce.
5. Simmer with the lid closed (cover with approx. 4 to 6 briquettes) for approx. 20 minutes. Serve and enjoy.

SWEET POTATO PAN

Serving:4 - Preparation time: 50 min

Ingredients:

- 4 large sweet potatoes
- 2 cloves of garlic
- 8 grams of ginger
- 1 lemon
- 3 tablespoons olive oil
- 3 onions
- 60 g chopped almonds
- 2 tablespoons brown cane sugar
- 2 tsp chili powder
- 2 tsp cumin
- 2 tsp cardamom
- 2 tsp curry powder
- 2 tsp turmeric
- 600 ml vegetable broth
- Salt and pepper

Preparation:

1. Peel and chop the onions, garlic and ginger into small pieces. Peel sweet potatoes and cut into small pieces. Wash and finely chop the spinach leaves.
2. Heat the oil in the Dutch oven. Fry onions, garlic and ginger.
3. Add sweet potatoes and sauté over medium heat for about 5 minutes. Season with chilli, cumin, curry, turmeric and cane sugar.
4. Add the vegetable broth, mix well and cook over low heat with the lid on for about 10 minutes.
5. Add the spinach and mix well again. Season with lemon juice, salt, pepper and cardamom.
6. Serve the finished dish, decorate with the chopped almonds and enjoy.

CHILI CORN

Serving:4 - Preparation time: 10 minutes

Ingredients:

- 4 peeled corn cobs
- 2 tablespoons of butter
- 1/2 teaspoon chili powder
- 1/2 teaspoon grated lime zest
- Salt
- 1/4 teaspoon freshly ground black pepper

Preparation:

1. Place the corn in a microwave-safe bowl. cover bowl.
2. In a small microwave-safe bowl, add butter. Microwave for 15 seconds or until butter melts. Stir in the chilli powder, lime zest, salt and pepper. Spread the butter mixture evenly over the cooked corn.
3. Now cook the nachos and wait for the cheese to melt. Place the pan in a heat-safe place and allow the nachos to cool for a few minutes.

CRISPY CHEESE POTATOES

Serving:4 - Preparation time: 50 min

Ingredients:

- 12 medium potatoes
- 3 tablespoons olive oil
- 1 tablespoon rosemary
- 200 g of grated parmesan
- 1 tablespoon curry powder
- Salt and pepper

Preparation:

1. Wash the potatoes thoroughly, cut into quarters and place in a bowl. Add oil, pepper, salt and curry powder and mix well.
2. Place the potatoes, skin side down, in the lightly oiled Dutch Oven.
3. Bake at low heat from below and high heat from above for about 20 minutes. Then sprinkle the parmesan on top and bake for another 20 minutes until the cheese has melted. When the potato wedges are soft on the inside and golden brown at the corners, they're done.
4. Serve and enjoy

BEETROOT RISOTTO

Serving:4 - Preparation time: 50 min

Ingredients:

- 400 g beetroot
- 200 g risotto rice
- 700 ml vegetable broth
- 2 tablespoons olive oil
- 2 onions

- 2 cloves of garlic
- Salt and pepper

Preparation:

1. Cook beets with water in the Dutch Oven. Take out and set aside.
2. Slightly heat the olive oil in the saucepan. Chop and sauté the onion and garlic.
3. Add the rice and pour in the vegetable broth.
4. Cook with the lid closed and low heat from below for 30 minutes.
5. Wash and peel the beetroot, place in a bowl and puree with a hand blender.
6. Put the finished cream in the Dutch Oven and lightly fry everything with the lid open.
7. Serve and enjoy.

MUSHROOMS WITH PEPPER AND TOMATO FILLING

Serving:4 - Preparation time: 25 min

Ingredients:

- 500 grams of mushrooms
- 2 tablespoons herbs
- 100 grams of tomatoes
- 100 grams of peppers
- Salt and pepper

Preparation:

1. Clean the mushrooms and remove the stalk.
2. Wash tomatoes and peppers, chop finely and mix with herbs. Season with salt and pepper.
3. Fill the mushrooms with the mixture and bake in the Dutch oven at medium heat from above and below for about 20 minutes until the mushrooms are cooked.
4. Serve and enjoy

SPANISH TORTILLA

Serving:4 - Prep time: 40 minutes

Ingredients:

- 10 potatoes
- 4 tablespoons olive oil
- 10 eggs
- 2 onions
- Salt and pepper

Preparation:

1. Wash potatoes, peel and cut into small slices.
2. Bring salted water to a boil in the Dutch Oven and let the potatoes cook for about 5 minutes. Put aside.
3. Peel the onion and cut into small pieces.
4. Heat the olive oil in the Dutch Oven. Fry onions. Add potatoes and fry until golden brown. Season with salt and pepper and mix well.

5. Whisk the eggs, place in the Dutch Oven and cook with the lid on over low heat from above and below. Season again with salt and pepper. Finished!
6. Serve and enjoy the tortilla.

RISI BISI

Serving:4 - Preparation time: 30 min

Ingredients:

- 20 grams of butter
- 1 onion
- 200 grams of rice
- 400 ml vegetable broth
- 250 g frozen peas
- Salt and pepper

Preparation:

1. Finely chop the onions and add to the Dutch Oven together with the butter. Add the rice and vegetable stock and season with salt and pepper.
2. Cook for about 20 minutes over low heat from below and medium heat from above. After 15 minutes, mix in the peas. Season again with salt and pepper. Cook for another 5 minutes. Finished!
3. Serve and enjoy

REIBEKUCHEN

Serving:4 -Preparation time: 25 min

Ingredients:

- 10 medium potatoes
- 3 onions
- Olive oil
- Salt and pepper

Preparation:

1. Peel the potatoes and onions and puree them in a blender.
2. Pour the mixture into a strainer to allow the liquid to drain.
3. Then put in a bowl and add salt to taste and mix well.
4. Heat the oil in the Dutch oven and pour the mixture into the oil in tablespoon-sized portions and flatten slightly. Small round flatbreads are made in the Dutch oven.
5. Fry the donuts on both sides until golden brown.
6. Serve with applesauce or crème fraîche and salmon and enjoy.

SCHUPFNUDELN WITH RED SAUCE

Serving:4 -Preparation time: 50 min

Ingredients:

- 750 grams of pasta

- 3 tablespoons olive oil
- 10 basil leaves
- 4 tomatoes
- 2 mozzarella cheeses
- 4 tablespoons of tomato paste
- 200ml of water
- Salt and pepper
- Thyme
- Rosemary

Preparation:

1. Wash and dice tomatoes. Dice mozzarella. Wash and roughly chop the basil.
2. Heat the oil in the Dutch oven. Fry the Schupfnudeln crispy. Add tomato paste and water. Season with salt, pepper, rosemary and thyme.
3. Add tomato pieces and mozzarella pieces and sauté for two minutes.
4. Serve with basil and enjoy.

STRUDEL WITH VEGETABLES

Serving:4 -Prep time: 90 minutes

Ingredients:

- 400 ml vegetable broth
- 160g lentils
- 2 zucchini
- 1 lemon
- 8 yufka dough sheets
- 2 tablespoons olive oil
- 2 red peppers
- 2 eggs
- 2 tsp tomato paste
- 2 tablespoons butter
- Salt and pepper

Preparation:

1. Put the vegetable stock and lentils in the Dutch Oven and cook for about 15 minutes. Take out and set aside.
2. Peel and chop the garlic, courgettes and peppers into small pieces. Squeeze the lemon and put the juice in a small bowl.
3. Heat the olive oil in the Dutch Oven. Fry the garlic, zucchini and peppers. Season with salt, pepper and lemon juice. Add lentils and mix well. Put aside.
4. Lay out the yufka leaves and brush with butter.
5. Spread half of the lentils on the pastry sheets and roll up the pastry sheets lengthwise.
6. Bake the yufka pastry sheets in the Dutch oven at medium heat on top and low heat on bottom for about 30 minutes.
7. Serve and enjoy the finished strudel.

BLACK BEANS, EGG AND VEGETABLES

Serving:4 -Preparation time: 20 minutes

Ingredients:

- 400g green salsa
- 1/4 cup cilantro (bulk packed)
- 1/2 red peppers
- 1/2 yellow pepper (or green)
- 1/2 red onion
- 3 1/2 tablespoons olive oil
- 1/2 teaspoon ground cumin
- 1/2 teaspoon ground coriander
- 1 cup canned black beans (drained)
- 3/4 tsp black pepper
- 6 large eggs
- black pepper
- 170 g mixed Mexican cheese (grated)
- 12 corn tortillas
- Diced avocado
- Sour cream

Preparation:

1. Preheat the oven to 180°C.
2. Pour about 1/2 cup salsa verde in the bottom of a casserole dish. Put aside.
3. Finely chop the coriander and set aside. Finely dice the peppers and onion.
4. Bring to a boil, then reduce heat and simmer until cauliflower is tender, 10 to 15 minutes.

BAKED ZUCCHINI

Serving:4 -Preparation time: 25 min

Ingredients:

- 4 zucchini
- 250 grams of mozzarella
- 4 tablespoons parmesan
- Olive oil
- Salt and pepper

Preparation:

1. Wash zucchini, cut in half and cut lengthwise.
2. Brush zucchini with oil and place in aluminum foil.
3. Place the mozzarella and parmesan in the aluminum foil over the courgettes. Season with salt and pepper.
4. Close the aluminum foil and place in the Dutch Oven from above and below at medium heat for 10 minutes.
5. Serve and enjoy the finished dish.

PASTA WITH GORGONZOLA

Serving:6 -Preparation time: 50 min

Ingredients:

- 200 grams of Gorgonzola

- 4 tablespoons olive oil
- 2 cloves of garlic
- 100 ml of white wine
- 200 g Parmesan cheese
- 400 ml cream
- Salt and pepper
- Oregano

Preparation:

1. Peel and chop the garlic. Cut the gorgonzola into small pieces.
2. Heat the oil in the Dutch oven. Fry garlic. Deg, lounging with white wine. After 5 minutes add the cream and season with salt and pepper.
3. Add the gorgonzola and parmesan and simmer for about 15 minutes until the cheese has melted. Stir occasionally. Season to taste with salt, pepper and oregano.
4. Serve with pasta and enjoy.

PASTA WITH CHEESE SAUCE

Serving:4 -Preparation time: 50 min

Ingredients:

- 3 tablespoons olive oil
- 400g Various types of cheese (e.g. Gorgonzola, Parmesan, Fontina, Emmental)
- 2 cloves of garlic
- 200 ml vegetable broth
- 100 ml cream
- 100 ml milk
- Salt and pepper
- Nutmeg

Preparation:

1. Peel and chop the garlic. Cut cheese into pieces.
2. Heat the oil in the Dutch oven. Fry garlic. Add the cream, milk and vegetable stock and simmer gently.
3. After 5 minutes add the cheese. Let cook for 10 minutes. Stir occasionally until cheese is melted. Season with salt, pepper and nutmeg.
4. Serve with spaghetti and enjoy.

SWEET POTATO

Serving:4 -Prep Time:

Ingredients:

- 4 sweet potatoes
- 20 grams of butter
- 20 grams of brown sugar
- 50 ml orange juice
- ½ tsp cinnamon
- 1 tsp lemon juice
- 1 tsp lemon zest

Preparation:

1. Peel, wash and slice the sweet potatoes.
2. Melt the butter in the Dutch oven.
3. Mix the orange juice, sugar, lemon juice and cinnamon well.
4. Put the sweet potatoes in the Dutch Oven and pour the sauce over them.
5. Cover and cook in the Dutch Oven for approx. 30 minutes over low heat from below and medium heat from above. Then sprinkle lemon zest on top, bake on high heat for another 20 until sweet potatoes are slightly crispy.
6. Serve and enjoy.

RAISIN CURRY

Serving:4 -Preparation time: 30 min

Ingredients:

- 2 tablespoons of clarified butter
- 400 ml coconut milk
- 100 g walnut kernels
- 2 cm ginger
- 100 grams of raisins
- 2 teaspoons lemon juice
- 2 teaspoons turmeric
- 2 teaspoons curry powder
- 1 tsp cumin
- 1 tsp cinnamon
- 1 red chili pepper
- 2 teaspoons of brown sugar
- Salt and pepper

Preparation:

1. Peel the ginger and chili and cut into small pieces.
2. Heat the ghee in the Dutch oven and roast the chili, ginger, cumin, cinnamon and turmeric for about 2 minutes.
3. Add raisins, walnuts and sugar. Then add coconut milk and mix well.
4. Add the lemon juice, curry powder, salt, pepper and sugar and season.
5. Simmer on low heat for about 10 minutes.
6. Serve the finished dish with rice and enjoy.

SPICY ALMOND CARROTS

Serving:4 -Preparation time: 15 min

Ingredients:

- 600 grams of carrots
- 1 onion
- 2 cm ginger
- 150 ml almond milk
- 2 teaspoons vegetable broth
- 2 tsp coconut oil
- 10 coriander leaves
- Salt

Preparation:

1. Peel the carrots and cut into strips about 1 cm thick. Peel and finely chop the onions and ginger.
2. Heat the oil in the Dutch oven, sauté the onions and ginger in it. Add the carrot strips and sauté for about 5 minutes.
3. Whisk together the almond milk and vegetable stock and pour into the pan.
4. Simmer until the carrots have reached the desired consistency. Season with coriander and salt.
5. Serve and enjoy.

SMALL SALMON SNACK

Serving:4 -Preparation time: 20 min

Ingredients:

- 500 g fresh salmon fillet
- 4 tablespoons ground almonds
- 2 tsp paprika powder
- Some lemon juice
- 3 tablespoons olive oil
- salt and pepper

Preparation:

1. Put oil in the Dutch Oven. Fry salmon. Season with salt and pepper.
2. Sprinkle over the ground almonds and paprika and continue to sauté.
3. Cut the salmon into small pieces, drizzle with lemon juice and serve.

SOUPS & STEWS

BEEF GOULASH

Serving:4 -Prep time: 4 hours 20 minutes

Ingredients:

- 1 kg beef goulash
- 4 onions
- 2 bay leaves
- ½ celery
- 2 cloves of garlic
- 200 ml of red wine
- 2 tablespoons of tomato paste
- 2 carrots
- 300 ml beef broth
- 1 teaspoon of juniper berries
- 1 carnation
- Salt and pepper
- Paprika powder
- 2 tablespoons canola oil

Preparation:

1. Dice the beef. Peel and finely chop the onions and garlic. Cut the carrots and celery into pieces. Put the oil in the Dutch Oven and sear the meat well. Then remove and set aside.
2. Put the garlic and onions in the Dutch Oven and sauté. Then add the remaining vegetables and sauté until the vegetables are dark. Deglaze with red wine and let it boil down.
3. Add tomato paste and meat and mix well. Fold in the spices and pour in the broth.
4. Simmer for about 4 hours over low heat with the lid closed. The meat will then fall apart on its own. With noodles. Serve with dumplings, potatoes, bread or rice and enjoy.

STEW FOR STRENGTH AND WARMTH

Serving:4 -Preparation time:2h

Ingredients:

- 300 g of Spanish salami
- 300 grams of bacon
- 2 onions
- ½ celery
- 1 tsp paprika powder
- 100 ml orange juice
- 1 bay leaf
- 2 tablespoons olive oil
- 1 can of tomato passata
- 60 grams of tomato paste
- 500ml of water
- 100 g red lentils
- 1 can of kidney beans
- 1 can of chickpeas

- 1 clove of garlic
- 1 pepper

Preparation:

1. Cut the salami into pieces. dice bacon. Peel onion and garlic and chop finely. Peel and chop celery. Drain beans and chickpeas.
1. 1st 2.   Heat the oil in the Dutch oven. Fry the salami and garlic. Add onions, peppers and tomato paste and sauté. Season with salt, pepper and paprika.
2. Add the remaining ingredients and simmer, with the lid closed, over medium heat for about 90 minutes.
3. Serve with brown bread and enjoy.

CARROT AND POTATO STEW

Serving:4 -Preparation time: 50 min

Ingredients:

- 600 grams of carrots
- 6 potatoes
- 1 onion
- 2 tablespoons olive oil
- 300 grams of minced meat
- 400 ml beef broth
- Curries
- Salt and pepper

Preparation:

1. Peel and dice carrots and potatoes. Peel and coarsely chop the onions.
1. 1st 2.   Put the minced meat in the Dutch oven with the olive oil and fry until crumbly. Put aside.
2. Put all the ingredients except the minced meat in the Dutch Oven and cook the vegetables until soft.
3. Pour off the liquid and roughly mash the vegetables. Then add the minced meat and season with salt, pepper and curry powder. Warm up again.
4. Serve and enjoy.

LENTIL STEW WITH BACON

Serving:4 -Preparation time:3h

Ingredients:

- 400 grams of lentils
- 2 onions
- 1 carrot
- ½ leek
- ½ celery
- 2 tablespoons of balsamic vinegar
- ½ bunch parsley
- 4 potatoes
- 1 bay leaf

- 300 g smoked bacon
- 1 liter of water
- Salt and pepper

Preparation:

1. Soak lentils overnight.
1. 1st 2. Peel and chop the onions. Peel and dice the carrot and potatoes. Cut the leek into rings. dice bacon. Peel and finely chop the celery. Finely chop the parsley.
2. Put all the ingredients in the Dutch Oven except for the potatoes and the parsley. Simmer for about 1 hour over low heat from below and medium heat from above.
3. Add the potatoes and parsley and simmer for another hour. Stir in the balsamic vinegar and season with salt and pepper if needed.
4. Serve and enjoy.

ZUCCHINI SOUP WITH SAUSAGES

Serving:4 -Preparation time: 30 min

Ingredients:

- 6 medium zucchini
- 4 sausages
- 1 liter chicken broth
- 150 ml cream
- 4 slices of white bread
- dill
- Paprika powder
- Salt and pepper
- Butter for frying

Preparation:

1. Wash zucchini, remove stalk and cut into small pieces. Dice the white bread slices and cut the bockwurst into pieces.
1. 1st 2. Simmer the zucchini pieces in the broth over low heat for about 20 minutes. Add cream and season with paprika powder, dill, pepper and salt. Puree the whole thing.
2. Finally, add the pieces of sausage to the soup.
3. Slices of white bread roasted in butter go very well with the soup. To do this, heat the butter in the Dutch oven and fry the pieces of white bread on all sides.
4. Serve the soup with the pieces of white bread and enjoy.

MEATY CHEESE SOUP

Serving:6 -Preparation time: 50 min

Ingredients:

- 500 g minced pork
- 125 g beef jerky
- 2 onions
- 3 leeks
- 1 can of corn
- 1 can of tomato passata

- 1 cup cream
- 250 grams of mushrooms
- 2 points (1.14 liters). herbal melted cheese
- 1 bouillon cube
- 1 liter of water
- Paprika powder
- Salt and pepper
- Oil for frying

Preparation:

1. Peel and dice the onion. Dice the beef jerky. Wash and slice the leek. Wash and quarter the mushrooms. Drain corn.
2. Heat the oil in the Dutch oven. Fry the onions, minced meat, leek and beef jerky.
3. Then add the tomato passata, water and bouillon cube and simmer for 30 minutes with the lid closed and low heat from below.
4. Finally add the cream, cheese and mushrooms and bring to the boil. Season with salt, pepper and paprika.
5. Serve and enjoy.

SPICY CHICKEN SOUP

Serving:4 -Prep time: 55 min

Ingredients:

- 400 g chicken breast
- 220 ml coconut milk
- 500ml of water
- 2 tablespoons clarified butter
- 2 onions
- 2 cloves of garlic
- 2 chili peppers
- 8 grams of ginger
- 2 tsp lemon juice
- 2 tsp curry powder
- Salt and pepper

Preparation:

1. Peel and chop the garlic, onion, ginger and chili into small pieces.
1. 1st 2. Heat the Dutch Oven with ghee and fry the chicken breast. Add the garlic, onion, ginger and chili pepper and sauté as well.
2. Add water and simmer, with the lid closed, over low heat for about 25 minutes.
3. Remove the chicken breasts from the Dutch Oven, cut into small pieces and return to the pot. Season with salt, pepper, curry powder and lemon juice and mix well.
4. Serve and enjoy the finished soup.

STRONG BEAN SOUP

Serve:4 -Prep time:1d

Ingredients:

- 300 g borlotti beans
- 100 g of small pasta
- 1 liter of vegetable broth
- 2 onions
- 2 carrots
- 2 tablespoons of tomato paste
- 2 pieces of bacon rind
- 1 clove of garlic
- some parmesan
- 2 tablespoons of red wine
- Olive oil
- Salt and pepper

Preparation:

1. Soak beans in water overnight and save bean water for later. Mix the vegetable broth from bean water, vegetable broth powder and water.
1. 1st 2. Peel the onion and garlic clove and cut into small pieces with the carrot.
2. Heat the olive oil in the Dutch Oven. Add onions, carrots and garlic and sauté. Deglaze with red wine.
3. Add beans and simmer over low heat from below.
4. Add tomato paste and bacon rind and sauté. Then pour the vegetable stock into the Dutch Oven. Season with salt and pepper.
5. Simmer with the lid closed and low heat from below for about an hour.
6. Serve the finished soup decorated with Parmesan and enjoy.

POTATO STEW WITH SAUSAGE

Serving:4 -Prep time: 90 minutes

Ingredients:

- 10 potatoes
- 1 bunch of soup vegetables
- 2 bay leaves
- Salt and pepper
- 4 sausages
- 1 liter of vegetable broth
- 2 carrots
- Nutmeg

Preparation:

1. Peel and dice potatoes and carrots. Wash and chop the soup vegetables. quarter sausages.
1. 1st 2. Put all the ingredients together in the Dutch Oven and cook for about 1 hour. Season with salt, pepper and nutmeg.
2. Before serving, remove the bay leaves. Finished!

SPICY MEAT SOUP

Serving:6 -Preparation time: 150 min

Ingredients:

- 500 g turkey
- 3 onions
- 1 teaspoon of vegetable stock powder
- 500 grams of mushrooms
- 2 peppers
- 1 can of tomato passata
- ½ can of pineapple
- 300 g peas (frozen)
- 250ml salsa
- 200 ml curry ketchup
- 500 ml milk
- 500 ml cream
- Some water
- 2 tablespoons olive oil

Preparation:

1. Rinse and dice the meat. Clean the peppers and mushrooms and cut into large cubes.
1. 1st 2. Heat the oil in the Dutch oven and fry the meat with the peppers. Season with salt, pepper and bouillon powder.
2. Add the remaining ingredients to the Dutch Oven except for the water and mix well.
3. Pour enough water into the pot to cover the mixture.
4. Simmer over medium heat from below and high heat from above for about 1 ½ to 2 hours.
5. Serve and enjoy.

PEA AND POTATO STEW

Serving:4 -Preparation time: 25 min

Ingredients:

- 400 g green peas
- 400 grams of potatoes
- 1 onion
- 4 carrots
- 1.5 liters of water
- 1 tsp coconut oil
- Salt and pepper
- Nutmeg

Preparation:

1. Peel carrots and potatoes, wash and cut into small pieces. Peel and chop the onion.
2. Place the peas and water in the Dutch Oven and bring to a boil.
3. Add the potatoes, onions and carrots and bring to the boil. Season with salt, pepper and nutmeg.
4. Add coconut oil, briefly remove from the embers and puree everything with a hand blender.
5. Then back on the embers and let the soup boil again.
6. Serve in deep plates and enjoy.

NORWEGIAN BEAN STEW

Serving:4 -Preparation time: 120 minutes

Ingredients:

- 500 grams of brown beans
- 750 ml vegetable stock
- 2 tablespoons of honey
- 1 onion
- 2 tablespoons olive oil
- 1 tablespoon of white wine vinegar
- Salt and pepper

Preparation:

1. Soak the beans in the vegetable broth the day before and let them soak overnight.
2. Peel and chop the onions. Heat the oil in the Dutch oven and sauté the onions.
3. Put the beans with the vegetable broth in the Dutch Oven and simmer for 2 hours with the lid closed.
4. Season with honey, vinegar, salt and pepper.
5. Serve and enjoy.

PUMPKIN SOUP WITH POTATOES

Serving:4 -Prep time: 40 minutes

Ingredients:

- Hokkaido pumpkin
- 6 potatoes
- 3 onions
- 1 clove of garlic
- 750 ml vegetable stock
- 2 cm piece of ginger
- 1 tsp salt
- Pepper
- 1 tablespoon curry powder
- Some cream

Preparation:

1. Wash and roughly chop the pumpkin. Wash, peel and coarsely dice the potatoes. Peel and roughly chop the onions and garlic. Peel and chop ginger.
2. Bring the vegetable stock to a boil in the Dutch Oven over medium-high heat. Add the potatoes, squash, onions, ginger, and garlic and simmer, uncovered, until potatoes are tender, about 30 minutes.
3. Then puree all the ingredients and season with salt, pepper and curry powder. Refine with a little cream if you like.
4. Serve and enjoy.

LENTIL SOUP WITH POTATOES

Serving:4 -Preparation time: 70 min

Ingredients:

- 400 grams of lentils
- 4 medium potatoes
- 4 carrots
- 1.5 l vegetable broth

Preparation:

1. Peel potatoes and carrots, wash and cut into small cubes.
2. Pour the vegetable stock into the Dutch Oven and bring to the boil.
3. Add potatoes, carrots and lentils and simmer for 60 minutes with closed lid and medium heat.
4. Arrange on deep plates and enjoy.

SUGAR PEAS PEPPERMINT SOUP

Serving:4 -Preparation time: 20 min

Ingredients:

- 4 shallots
- 20 g organic butter
- 400 g frozen organic peas
- 750 ml vegetable stock
- 200 ml organic cream
- 2 tablespoons of linseed oil
- Salt and pepper
- Peppermint for garnish

Preparation:

1. Dice shallots. Heat the butter in the Dutch oven and sauté the shallots until translucent.
2. Add the peas and sauté.
3. Boil the vegetable broth, add to the peas and simmer for 5 minutes.
4. Puree the pea stock and pass through a fine sieve. Season with salt and pepper.
5. Finally, cut the peppermint leaves into fine strips and add to the soup.
6. Whip the cream until stiff and pull it through the hot soup.
7. Serve and enjoy.

TOMATO SOUP WITH COCONUT

Serving:4 -Preparation time: 20 min

Ingredients:

- 4 spring onions
- 400ml tomatoes, strained
- 250 ml coconut milk
- 150 ml vegetable broth
- 2 tablespoons freshly squeezed orange juice
- 1 clove of garlic
- 2 pinches of Sambal Oelek
- 3 pinches of cumin
- Salt and cayenne pepper
- Coconut oil for frying

Preparation:

1. Wash the spring onions and cut into fine rings. Peel and press the garlic.
2. Heat the oil in the Dutch oven and sauté the spring onions and garlic for about 3 minutes until translucent.
3. Add tomatoes, coconut milk, vegetable stock and orange juice and mix well.
4. Let everything simmer on low heat for 5 to 6 minutes. Season with salt, cumin, cayenne pepper and sambal oelek and taste.
5. Serve and enjoy

CURRY SOUP WITH CAULIFLOWER

Serving:4 -Preparation time: 25 min

Ingredients:

- 600 grams of cauliflower
- 5 cm ginger
- 1 tablespoon of cumin
- 1 tsp curry powder
- 900 ml vegetable broth
- 2 tablespoons coriander greens
- 200 g organic yoghurt
- 2 tablespoons lemon juice
- Salt and pepper
- Coconut oil for frying

Preparation:

1. Cut the cabbage into pieces, finely chop the ginger.
2. Put coconut oil in the Dutch Oven and briefly roast the cumin.
3. Add the cabbage, ginger, vegetable stock and curry powder and simmer, covered, until the cabbage is tender, about 15 minutes.
4. After everything has cooled down a bit, add the yoghurt, puree and season with lemon juice, salt and pepper.
5. Garnish with chopped cilantro, serve and enjoy.

POTATO AND PEAR SOUP

Serving:4 -Preparation time: 50 min

Ingredients:

- 4 pears
- ½ celery
- 4 potatoes
- 2 onions
- 2 tablespoons canola oil
- 1.5 l vegetable broth
- 100 g of crème fraîche
- 1 tsp oregano
- Some lemon juice
- Pepper and salt
- Muska

Preparation:

1. Peel and roughly dice the potatoes. Peel and chop the onions. Roughly dice the celery. Wash and dice the pear.
2. Heat the oil in the Dutch oven. Sweat onions. Then add the potatoes and celery and sauté.
3. Then add the pear pieces, sauté briefly and then deglaze with vegetable stock. Simmer everything together for about 30 minutes.
4. Stir in the crème fraîche and season with oregano, nutmeg, salt, pepper and lemon juice.
5. Serve and enjoy.

CHEESE LEEK SOUP

Serving:4 -Preparation time: 50 min

Ingredients:

- 300 g Emmental cheese
- 4 spring onions
- 1 liter of vegetable broth
- ¼ Hokkaido pumpkin
- 250 ml milk
- 70 grams of butter
- 70 grams of flour

Preparation:

1. Cut the spring onions into rings. Finely grate the pumpkin.
2. Heat the butter in the Dutch Oven. Add spring onions. Then slowly add the flour and mix well. Gradually add the milk and continue to stir well so that a creamy mass is formed.
3. Add broth and bring to a boil. Add the pumpkin shavings and simmer uncovered for about 15 minutes. Stir in cheese and cook and stir until melted.
4. Serve and enjoy.

FRUITY RED CABBAGE SOUP

Serving:4 -Preparation time: 50 min

Ingredients:

- 500 g red cabbage (fresh)
- 2 onions
- 6 potatoes
- 3 tablespoons olive oil
- 1 liter of vegetable broth
- 100 ml white wine (dry)
- 2 oranges
- 1 cm ginger
- 1 tablespoon of raspberry vinegar
- 3 apples
- 1 tablespoon maple syrup
- Salt and pepper

Preparation:

1. Halve the red cabbage, remove the stalk and cut into thin strips. Peel and finely chop the onions and ginger. Peel and dice the potatoes. Peel 1 orange and cut into pieces. Squeeze 1 orange. Wash and roughly chop the apples.
2. Heat the oil in the Dutch oven. Fry onions and ginger. Add the potatoes and red cabbage and sauté for about 5 minutes.
3. Deglaze with white wine and let it boil down. Then add the vegetable stock, raspberry vinegar, maple syrup, salt and pepper and simmer with the lid closed for about 30 minutes.
4. Add orange juice and apples and simmer for another 10 minutes.
5. Serve with orange slices and enjoy.

GREEN SOUP

Serving:4 -Preparation time: 50 min

Ingredients:

- 1 onion
- 1 clove of garlic
- 150 g spinach leaves
- 1 ½ bunch wild garlic
- 1 tablespoon of olive oil
- 500 ml vegetable broth
- 400 ml milk
- 150 g of grated parmesan
- Salt and pepper
- Nutmeg

Preparation:

1. Peel and finely chop the onions and garlic. Wash wild garlic and cut into fine strips. Wash and finely chop 5 spinach leaves and 2 wild garlic leaves.
2. Cook the remaining spinach in the Dutch oven in salted water for about 5 minutes. Put aside.
3. Heat the oil in the Dutch Oven. Fry onions and garlic. Add the cooked spinach and deglaze with milk and vegetable broth. Add 120g Parmesan and the strips of wild garlic to the broth.
4. Puree everything with a blender. Finished!
5. Use the remaining Parmesan, the remaining spinach and the remaining wild garlic to decorate.
6. Serve and enjoy.

FRESH TOMATO SOUP

Serving:4 -Preparation time: 20 min

Ingredients:

- 1 can of tomato passata
- 1 may have chopped tomatoes
- 1 can of kidney beans
- 1 clove of garlic
- 1 can of corn
- 1 onion

- 500 ml vegetable broth
- 100 g of crème fraîche
- 2 tablespoons olive oil
- Paprika powder
- Salt and pepper

Preparation:

1. Peel and finely chop the onion and garlic.
2. Heat the oil in the Dutch Oven and sauté the onions and garlic. Deglaze with the two cans of tomatoes and the vegetable broth.
3. Add corn and kidney beans. Then stir in the crème fraîche. Season to taste and simmer with the lid on for about 10 minutes.
4. Serve and enjoy.

STRONG POWER SOUP

Serving:4 -Prep time: 80 minutes

Ingredients:

- 6 turnips
- 4 carrots
- 2 onions
- 4 tomatoes
- 4 celery
- 300 grams of yoghurt
- 500 ml vegetable broth
- 2 tablespoons canola oil
- 2 tablespoons of white wine vinegar
- Salt and pepper

Preparation:

1. Peel and chop onions. Peel and dice the carrots. Wash tomatoes and celery and cut into pieces. Wash beetroot and cut into small pieces.
2. Heat the oil in the Dutch oven. Add onions and sauté. Place the remaining vegetables in the Dutch Oven and fry.
3. Deglaze with vegetable broth and white wine vinegar and let everything simmer for about 40 minutes. Season with salt and pepper.
4. Fold in the yoghurt. The soup is ready.
5. Serve and enjoy.

RED SOUP

Serving:4 -Preparation time: 35 min

Ingredients:

- 500 g beetroot
- 2 cm ginger
- 2 potatoes
- 2 tsp lemon juice
- 2 tsp olive oil
- 1 tsp turmeric
- 1 tsp coriander powder

- 600ml of water
- Salt and pepper

Preparation:

1. Wash potatoes and beetroot and cut into small pieces.
2. Heat a Dutch Oven with oil and add ginger, turmeric and coriander and sauté.
3. After about 1 minute add the potatoes and beets and let simmer. Simmer for 20 minutes over medium heat with the lid closed. Season to taste with lemon juice and salt.
4. Puree the entire mixture with an immersion blender.
5. Serve and enjoy the finished soup.

CHEESE SOUP WITH POTATOES AND CORN

Serving:6 -Preparation time: 50 min

Ingredients:

- 2 tablespoons canola oil
- 500 grams of potatoes
- 750 ml milk
- 2 cans of corn
- 180 g grated mozzarella
- 1 tablespoon flour
- 2 onions
- 500 g of crème fraîche
- Salt, pepper, nutmeg
- Mixed herbs

Preparation:

1. Peel and chop onions. Peel and dice the potatoes.
2. Heat the oil in the Dutch oven. Sweat onions. Dust the potatoes with flour and place in the Dutch Oven.
3. Carefully stir in the milk and season with salt, pepper and nutmeg. Cook.
4. Then add the corn, cheese, herbs and crème fraîche and simmer for about 20 minutes.
5. The soup is ready when the cheese has melted and the potatoes are cooked.
6. Serve and enjoy.

MANGO AND CARROT SOUP

Serving:4 -Preparation time: 30 min

Ingredients:

- 1 mango
- 500 g mini carrots
- 1 tablespoon of olive oil
- 200ml of water
- Herbal salt and pepper
- 2 tablespoons of balsamic vinegar
- 2 onions

Preparation:

1. Peel the mango and cut into small pieces. Wash the mini carrots and cut into small pieces.

2. Peel the onion and cut into small pieces. Place in the Dutch Oven with a little olive oil and fry.
3. After 2 minutes add water, carrots and mango pieces.
4. After another 2 minutes add the remaining ingredients, season and simmer for 10 minutes.
5. Serve and enjoy the finished soup.

POTATO SOUP WITH SPINACH

Serving:4 -Preparation time: 25 min

Ingredients:

- 600 g spinach leaves
- 200 grams of potatoes
- 1 liter of vegetable broth
- 200 ml coconut milk
- 1 tsp curry powder
- 2 teaspoons lemon juice
- Salt and pepper

Preparation:

1. Wash spinach. Peel the potatoes, cut into small pieces and cook in boiling water in the Dutch oven. Put aside.
2. Heat coconut oil in the Dutch Oven. Add the spinach and potatoes and sauté.
3. Add vegetable broth and bring to the boil.
4. Mix everything well with a mixer until a creamy mass is formed.
5. Add coconut milk and season with curry powder, salt, pepper and lemon juice and mix well.
6. Serve and enjoy the finished soup.

VEGETABLE SOUP

Serving:4 -Preparation time: 50 min

Ingredients:

- 2 tsp marjoram
- 600 ml vegetable broth
- 1 turnip greens
- 50 g Parmesan cheese
- 2 spring onions
- 4 carrots
- 4 potatoes
- 200 g cherry tomatoes
- 1 tablespoon of olive oil
- Salt and pepper

Preparation:

1. Wash vegetables and potatoes and cut into small pieces.
2. Pour some olive oil into the Dutch Oven. Add vegetables and sauté.
3. Pour in vegetable stock and season with marjoram, salt and pepper.
4. Allow the soup to simmer for a few minutes, decorate with Parmesan and serve and enjoy.

PUMPKIN SOUP WITH COCONUT NUANCE

Serving:4 -Preparation time: 35 min

Ingredients:

- 2 shallots
- 1 clove of garlic
- 1 Hokkaido pumpkin
- 2 carrots
- 60 ml orange juice
- 2 cm ginger
- 300 ml vegetable broth
- 250 ml coconut milk
- 1 tsp curry powder
- Some coconut oil
- Salt and pepper
- Nutmeg

Preparation:

1. Peel and finely chop the shallots, ginger and garlic. Wash and chop the Hokkaido pumpkin. Peel and finely chop the carrots and ginger.
2. Put the ginger, garlic and shallots in the Dutch Oven and sauté in a little oil. Add the pumpkin and carrot and sauté.
3. Season to taste, laze with vegetable broth and coconut milk and simmer over low heat for about 25 minutes.
4. Add orange juice.
5. Then puree everything with a blender. Season with salt, pepper, curry powder and nutmeg.
6. Serve and enjoy.

POTATO PEA SOUP

Serving:4 -Preparation time: 20 min

Ingredients:

- 300 g green peas
- 300 grams of potatoes
- 1 onion
- 2 carrots
- 750 ml vegetable stock
- 1 tsp olive oil
- Salt and pepper

Preparation:

1. Wash, peel and cut the carrots, onions and potatoes into small pieces.
2. Bring the peas to a boil in the Dutch oven together with the vegetable stock.
3. Add the potatoes and other vegetables. Bring everything to a boil over medium heat and season.
4. Add olive oil and puree everything with a hand blender. Boil again.
5. Serve and enjoy.

SALAD SOUP

Serving:4 -Preparation time: 60 min

Ingredients:

- 150 grams of dandelion
- 300 g arugula
- 2 onions
- 2 cloves of garlic
- 4 potatoes
- 1 tsp olive oil
- 600 ml vegetable broth
- Salt and pepper

Preparation:

1. Wash and finely chop the dandelion and rocket. Wash potatoes and cut into small pieces. Peel onion and garlic clove and cut into small pieces.
2. Sweat the onions, garlic and potatoes in a pan with a little oil.
3. Add all other ingredients and simmer for 15 minutes with the lid closed over low heat.
4. Remove and puree with a hand blender. Season with salt and pepper. Finished!
5. Alternatively, when there's no outlet outside, it can be enjoyed as a single-ingredient broth.

VEGAN STEW WITH RED LENTILS, SPINACH AND POTATOES

Serving:6 -Prep time: 40 minutes

Ingredients:

- 270 g red lentils (you can use green or brown lentils)
- 1 yellow onion – diced
- 6 garlic cloves - chopped
- 2 carrots - cut into rings
- 400g roasted canned tomatoes - diced
- 2 red peppers – roasted & chopped
- 1 tablespoon smoked paprika
- 90 g baby spinach (kale, chard, dandelion)
- liters of water (or vegetable broth) + more than necessary
- 8 sprigs of thyme
- 340g golden potatoes - diced
- 1 pinch of sea salt + more to taste

Preparation:

1. Heat a 6 quart saucepan or Dutch oven over medium-high. Add olive oil and minced meat, cook for a few minutes.

LASAGNA SOUP

Serving:6 -Preparation time: 25 minutes

Ingredients:

- 8 uncooked lasagna noodles (broken into bite-sized pieces)
- 450 g mildly ground Italian sausage
- 1 1/2 cups diced white onion
- 4 garlic cloves chopped
- 650g Campbell's Family Size Tomato Soup {1 can}
- 400 g Petite diced tomatoes {1 can}
- 3 teaspoons of peppers
- 2 teaspoons basil
- Salt
- 1 teaspoon of freshly ground pepper
- 340 ml condensed milk {1 can}
- 2 tablespoons olive oil
- 170 g grated mozzarella cheese
- 170 g grated parmesan
- 1 tablespoon chopped parsley for garnish {optional}

Preparation:

1. Preheat the Dutch Oven to medium. After the Dutch Oven has warmed up, add Italian sausage and roast. Remove the Italian sausage from the oven and drain the fat. Add the olive oil, onions and garlic to the casserole and sauté until the onions are translucent.
2. Add the tomato soup, diced tomatoes, condensed milk, boiled sausage, lasagna noodles, paprika, basil and pepper and stir well. Bring the soup to a boil while stirring constantly. Once the soup begins to boil, simmer for 3 minutes, stirring frequently, reduce the heat to medium-low and simmer for 25 minutes, stirring regularly. Serve the soup in bowls and garnish with mozzarella and parmesan. Refine with parsley.

CABBAGE ROLL SOUP

Serving:8 -Prep time: 40 minutes

Ingredients:

- 800 g diced tomatoes
- 450g 90% lean ground beef
- 450 g chopped kale (about 5 cups)
- 5 cups beef broth
- 1 cup rice cauliflower
- 1/2 cup diced onions
- 1/2 cup diced carrots
- 1 tablespoon of olive oil
- 1 teaspoon of dried oregano + 1 salt
- 1 teaspoon dried thyme
- 2 tablespoons freshly chopped parsley

Preparation:

1. If you are roasting the peppers, prepare them by heating a cast-iron skillet over medium-high. Fry the peppers

until done. Place in a bowl, cover and let cool. Cut the peppers into pieces and set aside until ready to use.
2. Heat a heavy saucepan over medium-high heat. Add a dash of water (or a dash of olive oil) along with the diced onions, a pinch of sea salt, and the carrots. Cook for about 5 minutes until the onion is done. Add the bay leaf, thyme and garlic and stir well. Mix in the lentils, roasted peppers, smoked paprika, and canned tomatoes. Pour into the water.
3. 3. Bring the stew to a boil and season with sea salt. Add the diced potatoes and cook together until the potatoes and lentils are cooked through, about 15 minutes. Remove the bay leaves and thyme stems and add the spinach. Cover with the lid and allow to collapse in the heat of the steam. Serve hot with fresh herbs, chilli flakes and a piece of crusty homemade bread.

CREAMY MAC AND CHEESE CHICKEN SOUP

Serving:8 -Prep time: 45 minutes

Ingredients:

- 1 1/2 cup macaroni
- 700 g boneless skinless chicken breast, diced
- Kosher salt
- Freshly ground black pepper
- 4 tbsp. Unsalted Butter
- 1 small onion, chopped
- 1 small red pepper, chopped
- 1/3 cup all-purpose flour, spooned and leveled
- 4 cups chicken broth
- 4 cups whole milk
- 2 teaspoons of Dijon mustard
- 1 small head of broccoli, cut into small florets (about 4 cups)
- 225 g extra sharp cheddar cheese, grated (approx. 2 cups)
- Sliced fresh chives to refine

Preparation:

1. Cook noodles according to package directions; put aside. Season chicken with salt and pepper. Melt 1 tablespoon butter in a large saucepan or Dutch oven over medium-high heat. Add the chicken and cook until golden, 6 to 9 minutes, stirring occasionally. Place the chicken on a plate.
2. Reduce temperature to medium. Add the onion, bell pepper, and the remaining 3 tablespoons of butter to the saucepan. Cook, stirring occasionally, until tender, 3 to 5 minutes. Add flour and cook, stirring constantly, for 1 minute. Slowly stir in the broth, then add the milk and mustard. Simmer until thickened, about 7 to 8 minutes. Stir in broccoli and chicken. Simmer 4 to 6 minutes, until the broccoli is tender and the soup has thickened. Remove from the stove and let stand 1 minute. Stir in cooked pasta and slowly stir in cheese until melted. Season with salt and pepper. Refine with chives.

CHICKEN MEATBALLS AND VEGETABLE NOODLE SOUP

Serving:8 -Prep time: 1 hour 10 minutes

Ingredients:

- 2 TBSP. olive oil
- 1 small onion and 3 cloves of garlic, chopped
- 1/4 cup dry white wine and 1 tablespoon. red wine vinegar
- 2 sprigs of fresh thyme
- 8 cups chicken broth
- 450 g ground chicken breast
- 1/4 cup plain dry breadcrumbs
- 1 large egg
- 2 TBSP. Grated parmesan and more to serve
- 2 TBSP. Chopped fresh parsley
- 2 TBSP. Chopped fresh basil and more for garnish
- Kosher salt and ground black pepper
- 6 cups assorted vegetable noodles (like zucchini, yellow squash, carrots, or butternut squash)
- 300 g cherry tomatoes, halved

Preparation:

1. Heat the oil in a large saucepan or Dutch oven over medium-high. Add the onion and garlic and saute until golden brown, stirring occasionally, 4 to 6 minutes. Add wine and thyme. Cook until wine is syrupy, 1 minute. Add the chicken broth. Cover and bring to a boil.
2. Meanwhile, in a bowl, lightly whisk together the chicken, breadcrumbs, egg, Parmesan, parsley, basil, and salt and pepper each. Form 30 meatballs. Add meatballs to the broth. Reduce heat, cover and simmer 7 to 9 minutes or until meatballs are cooked through.
3. Add pasta and tomatoes. Cook, stirring occasionally, until noodles are tender, 3 to 4 minutes. stir in vinegar. Season with salt and pepper. Serve immediately, garnished with basil and parmesan.

CORN SOUP IN SUMMER

Serving:6 -Preparation time: 20 minutes

Ingredients:

- Cut 5 strips of bacon into small pieces
- 3 tablespoons unsalted butter (43 g)
- 1 medium yellow onion, chopped (about 1 1/4 cup)
- 1/2 bell pepper diced
- 1 large poblano chilli, finely chopped
- 1/4 cup all-purpose flour (30 g)
- 3 large cloves of garlic, chopped
- 4 cups low-sodium chicken broth (945 ml)
- 1 cup of water (235 ml)
- 2 cups of coffee creamer (475 ml)
- 1/2 teaspoon smoked paprika
- 1 teaspoon of salt
- 3/4 teaspoon pepper
- 600 g red potatoes, diced
- 7-8 ears of fresh corn, cut off the cob (about 5 cups of corn)

Preparation:

1. Place bacon in a large saucepan or Dutch oven. Turn heat to medium and cook until bacon is crisp and browned. Remove the bacon from the pot and save for later. Do not drain bacon fat.
2. Put the butter in the saucepan and let it melt. Add onion, poblano pepper, and paprika and cook until tender (3-5 minutes).
3. Add the garlic and stir until fragrant (about 30 seconds).
4. Sprinkle the flour over the vegetables and stir until smooth until there are no lumps. Mix or whisk the flour.
5. Stir in the chicken broth, water, and spices (smoked paprika, salt, and pepper).
6. Add the potatoes and corn, bring the mixture to a boil and cook (stirring occasionally) until the potatoes are tender when you pierce them with a fork.
7. Once the potatoes are cooked, carefully place about 3 cups of the soup in a blender and puree until well combined. Alternatively, you can use an immersion blender and puree the soup until it reaches your desired consistency.
8. Pour the pureed mixture back into the soup and stir well. Stir in the reserved bacon.
9. Let the soup simmer (stir occasionally) for 15 minutes before serving.
10. Serve with spring onions, bacon and additional smoked paprika, if you like. Serve with crusty bread.

MEDITERRANEAN ORZO PASTA STEW

Serving: 4 – 6 - Prep time: 30 minutes

Ingredients:

- 2 tablespoons olive oil
- 1 large yellow onion, diced
- 3 cloves of garlic, chopped
- 1 1/2 cups orzo
- 4 cups vegetable broth
- 1 cup feta cheese plus extra for serving
- 1 cup marinated artichokes, drained and roughly chopped
- 1/4 cup Kalamata olives, pitted, finely chopped and set aside for serving
- 1/2 cup sundried tomatoes wrapped in oil, drained and finely chopped
- 1 cup parsley, chopped
- 1/4 cup toasted pine nuts (optional)
- Season with salt and pepper

Preparation:

1. Heat the olive oil in a skillet or Dutch oven over medium-high heat. Stir in the onions and sauté until soft, about 5 minutes.

2. Add the garlic and orzo and cook an additional 3 minutes, stirring frequently. Add the vegetable broth and bring to a boil. Reduce heat and let simmer, stirring frequently (to make sure the orzo doesn't stick to the bottom of the pan). Continue cooking until the orzo is set and slightly chewy and has set into a thick, creamy broth, 10 to 15 minutes.
3. Add feta, artichokes, olives, various tomatoes and parsley and mix well. Season with salt and pepper. Serve each dish with pine nuts and additional olives and sprinkle with feta cheese.

CHICKEN NOODLE SOUP

Serving:8 -Preparation time: 1 hour 15 minutes

Ingredients:

- 2 TBSP. olive oil
- 2 carrots, sliced
- 2 sticks of celery, sliced
- 1 small onion, chopped
- 5 garlic cloves, chopped
- Kosher salt
- Freshly ground black pepper
- 1/4 cup dry white wine
- 8 cups chicken broth
- 1.3 kg boneless skinless chicken breasts
- 2 1/2 cups uncooked egg noodles
- 3 TBSP. Chopped fresh parsley
- 2 TBSP. Chopped fresh dill and 2 tbsp. Fresh Lemon Juice

Preparation:

1. Heat the oil in a large saucepan or Dutch oven over medium-high. Add carrots, celery, onions and garlic. Season with salt and pepper. Cook, stirring occasionally, until tender and golden brown, 8 to 10 minutes.
2. Add wine and simmer until syrupy for 1 minute. Add the chicken broth and chicken pieces. Season with salt and pepper. Bring to a boil over high heat. Reduce heat to low, cover and cook until chicken is tender, 40 to 45 minutes.
3. Remove the chicken and shred the thighs with two forks. Cut the chicken breasts into large, bite-sized pieces and return the meat to the pot. Add the noodles to the soup and cook, stirring frequently, until tender, 6 to 7 minutes. Remove from heat and stir in parsley, dill, and lemon juice. Season with salt and pepper.

FROGMORE GOULASH

Serving: 4-5 - Prep time: 30 minutes

Ingredients:

- 1 large onion, chopped
- 3 celery ribs, chopped
- 2 TBSP. Boil shrimp and crab
- 1 large pepper, chopped

- Salt and pepper

Preparation:

1. Cut hot Polish sausage into pieces.
2. Add halved corn on the cob and cook for 10 minutes:
3. After 2 to 3 minutes, add raw, unpeeled shrimp.
4. Remove from heat and let stand 4 to 5 minutes. Drain the strainer.

SHELL SOUP

Serving:8 -Prep time: 45 minutes

Ingredients:

- Cut 6 slices of lean bacon into strips
- 2 medium carrots, cut into thin rings or half rings
- 1 small onion and 2 celery ribs, finely diced
- 4 tablespoons all-purpose flour
- 1 cup low-sodium chicken stock or broth
- 35 g chopped mussels with their juice from 2 small cans
- 1.5 tsp Worcestershire sauce
- 0.5 tsp Tabasco sauce
- 0.5 tsp dried thyme
- 1.5 tsp salt and black pepper or to taste
- 700 g medium-sized potatoes, peeled
- 500 ml milk of any kind
- 240 ml whipped cream or whipped cream and 1 bay leaf

Preparation:

1. Heat a large saucepan or Dutch oven over medium/high and add the chopped bacon. Fry, stirring occasionally, until fried and crispy. Then place on a plate lined with kitchen paper. Leave 3 tablespoons of bacon fat in the saucepan.
2. Add prepared carrots, onions and celery and continue cooking over medium heat. Dust with 4 tablespoons flour and sauté for another minute, stirring constantly. Add 2 cups chicken broth, 1 cup chopped clams with their juice, 1 bay leaf, 1 1/2 tsp hot sauce, 1/2 tsp Tabasco sauce, 1/2 tsp dried thyme, 1 1/2 tsp salt and 1/4 add tsp black pepper. Bring the soup to a boil.
3. While the soup is heating, cut the potatoes into bite-sized pieces, about 2 cm thick. Place the potatoes in the saucepan and stir in 2 cups milk and 1 cup heavy cream. Prick lightly with a fork (approx. 20 min.). Season to taste with salt and pepper and refine with cooked bacon and fresh coriander.

SEAFOOD STEW

Serving:4 -Prep time: 35 minutes

Ingredients:

- 1/2 cup onion - chopped
- 1/2 cup paprika - chopped
- 1 clove of garlic - chopped
- 425 g tomatoes - chopped
- 225 grams of tomato sauce
- 1/4 cup burgundy
- 1/4 cup oregano - chopped
- 2 tablespoons parsley - chopped
- 1/4 teaspoon crushed red pepper
- 225 g scallops
- 225g medium prawns - peeled and deveined
- 280g baby mussels – drained

Preparation:

1. Coat Dutch Oven with cooking spray. Leave to heat at medium temperature. Add chopped onion, bell pepper and chopped garlic; sauté until tender.
2. Add tomatoes, tomato sauce and burgundy and mix well. Add oregano and next 3 ingredients; mix well.
3. Bring the vegetable mixture to a boil over medium heat. Cover, reduce heat and simmer for 20 minutes.
4. Add scallops, shrimp and clams to the vegetable mixture; bring to a boil. Reduce heat and simmer 7-8 minutes, or until scallops and shrimp are tender. Pour into individual bowls.
5. Stir over medium heat for 3-4 minutes or until sauce thickens. Serve the sauce over the fish.

BOILED BEEF STEW

Serving:4 -Prep time: 1 hour 25 minutes

Ingredients:

- 900 g beef goulash, cut into pieces
- 3 tablespoons all-purpose flour
- 3/4 teaspoon salt
- 2 to 4 teaspoons of canola oil,
- 2 teaspoons beef stock granules
- 2 teaspoons dried parsley flakes
- 1-2 teaspoons of Italian seasoning
- 2 cups of water
- 1 cup Burgundy wine or beef broth
- 3 medium-sized potatoes (approx. 450g to 1.2kg), peeled and quartered
- 1 cup fresh mushrooms, halved
- 1 medium onion, cut into 8 wedges
- 2 medium carrots, cut into chunks
- 2 celery ribs, cut into chunks
- Additional water optional

Preparation:

1. Preheat the oven to 180°C. Mix the beef with flour and salt. Shake off excess. In an ovenproof casserole, heat 2 teaspoons oil over medium-high heat. Brown the beef in batches, adding more oil if necessary. Take out of the pan.
2. In the same pan, add broth, herbs, 2 cups water and wine. Bring to a boil and stir to loosen the browned bits from the pan. Add beef; back to cooking. put it in the oven; bake, covered, 1 hour.
3. Stir in the vegetables, thinning with additional water if desired. Bake, covered, until beef and vegetables are tender, 45-60 minutes.

PEA SOUP WITH HAM

Serve:12 -Prep time: 1 hour 15 minutes

Ingredients:

- 1 package (450 g) dried green peas
- 8 cups of water
- 300 g potatoes (about 2 medium-sized), diced
- 2 large onions, chopped
- 2 medium carrots, chopped
- 2 cups diced ham (280 g)
- 1 celery rib, chopped
- 5 teaspoons low sodium chicken broth granules
- 1 teaspoon dried marjoram
- 1 teaspoon poultry seasoning
- 1 teaspoon of grated sage
- 1/2 to 1 teaspoon pepper
- 1/2 teaspoon dried basil

Preparation:

1. Place all ingredients in a Dutch Oven. Bring to a boil. Reduce heat; simmer, cover and cook until peas and vegetables are tender, stirring occasionally.
1. Tip: Adding just 2 cups of diced ham adds more flavor to the dish.

COCONUT CURRY CHICKEN SOUP

Serving:6 -Prep time: 35 minutes

Ingredients:

- 2 cans of coconut milk
- 1/2 cup red curry paste
- 1 package (225 g) thin rice noodles
- 2 cans of chicken broth
- 1/4 cup brown sugar
- 2 tablespoons of fish sauce or soy sauce
- 3/4 tsp garlic salt
- 3 cups shredded fried chicken
- 2 cups shredded cabbage
- 2 cups sliced carrots
- 3/4 cup bean sprouts
- Fresh basil and coriander leaves

Preparation:

1. Bring the coconut milk to a boil in a Dutch oven. Cook uncovered for 10-12 minutes. Stir in the curry paste until completely dissolved.
2. In the meantime, prepare the noodles according to the package instructions.
3. Add the broth, brown sugar, fish sauce and garlic salt to the curry mixture. reduce the temperature; Simmer uncovered for 10 minutes, stirring occasionally. Stir in the chicken.
4. Drain pasta; Divide among six large soup bowls. Refine with vegetables, basil and coriander.

CREAMY CHICKEN SOUP WITH NOODLES

Serving:8 -Prep time: 50 minutes

Ingredients:

- 6 cups of low sodium chicken broth were used
- 5 cups of water
- Salt to taste
- 3-4 skinless chicken thighs (boneless or boneless)
- 2 tablespoons olive oil
- 1 medium onion, finely chopped
- 3 medium carrots
- 2 grated carrots, 1 carrot cut into thin rings or half circles
- 2 medium celery stalks, finely chopped or thinly sliced
- 2 cups of pasta, e.g. B. Rotini egg noodles or your favorite variety
- 1 cup of corn (400 g)
- 4 tablespoons unsalted butter
- 1/3 cup all-purpose flour
- 1/2 cup cream
- 3 tablespoons fresh or frozen dill
- Favorite condiment without salt

Preparation:

1. In a large stockpot, combine 6 cups broth, 5 cups water, and 1/2 tablespoon salt. Bring to a boil, then add the chicken thighs (no trimming of fat required) and cook uncovered for 20 minutes.
2. Place a large skillet over medium-high and add 2 Tbsp olive oil. Add chopped onions and sauté until tender (5 minutes), then increase heat to medium/high and sauté grated carrots, chopped celery and 5-7 minutes.
3. Remove the chicken thighs from the pot and let them rest. Then use forks or hands to shred the chicken, removing any bones and fat (which should come off easily). Return the shredded chicken to the pot.
4. Add 2 cups of noodles, sliced carrots, and corn to stockpot and simmer on low for 15 minutes, until noodles have reached desired "softness." If you'd like the soup to lighten a bit, you can skim off any excess oil from the top at this point.
5. In a medium saucepan over medium heat, melt 4 tablespoons butter, stir in 1/3 cup flour and mix 1 to 2 minutes or until just golden. Ladle 1 cup of hot stock from the stockpot into the flour mixture, beating

continuously until combined, then add 1/2 cup heavy cream to the stockpot and stir until combined.
6. Season the soup with salt to taste. Add 3 tablespoons of dill, bring to a boil and turn off the heat. Season the soup as you like. Serve with fresh crusty bread.

SAUERKRAUT SOUP

Serving:8 -Prep time: 35 minutes

Ingredients:

- 1 tablespoon olive oil
- 225 g bacon chopped
- 1 stick of celery, finely diced
- 1 medium onion, finely diced
- 2 medium carrots, thinly sliced
- 3 medium 450g potatoes, peeled and cut into chunks
- 1/4 cup quinoa, optional
- 2-3 cups sauerkraut triple drained
- 8 cups low-sodium chicken broth
- 2 cups of water or to taste
- 1 can of white beans

Preparation:

1. Heat 1 tablespoon oil in a large stockpot or Dutch oven. Add chopped bacon until fried.
2. Add chopped celery and onion. Fry until tender and golden brown (5 minutes).
3. Add sliced carrots, potatoes, 1/4 cup quinoa (if using), 8 cups broth, and 2 cups water. Bring to a boil, reduce heat and simmer for 15 minutes.
4. Add 2-3 cups well-washed and drained sauerkraut and half of the cooked bacon, the kidney beans with their juice and 1 bay leaf and continue to cook until the potatoes are tender (about 10 minutes). Season the soup as you like. Serve with fresh crusty bread.

MUSHROOM CREAM SOUP

Serving:4 -Preparation time: 20 minutes

Ingredients:

- 2 tablespoons olive oil
- 2 tablespoons of butter
- 4 cups mushrooms, chopped
- 1 onion, chopped
- 2 cups cream
- 4 cups broth of your choice
- 1 teaspoon Herbes de Provence
- Salt to taste

Preparation:

1. Heat oil and butter over medium-high heat for 30 seconds, then add onions and stir. Add mushrooms and sauté, stirring frequently. Cover and continue cooking over medium-high heat until onions are translucent and mushrooms are brown, 5-6 minutes.

2. Stir every two minutes to avoid burning. Add broth, herbs and salt. Simmer for 10 minutes. Add cream, let simmer for another 5 minutes.
3. Take half of the soup and put it in a blender. Pour the mixed soup back into the unmixed soup and mix well. Serve with hot, crusty bread.

PEA PUREE

Serving: 4 – 6 - Prep time: 50 minutes

Ingredients:

- 2 tablespoons olive oil
- 1 onion, chopped
- 2 cups uncooked peas
- 6 cups of water or vegetable broth
- 1 cup cooked ham, chopped
- 1 carrot, chopped
- Dash cayenne pepper
- Salt to taste

Preparation:

1. Heat oil on medium for 30 seconds, then add onions and stir. Cover and continue cooking over medium-high heat until translucent, 5-6 minutes.
2. Stir every two minutes to avoid burning. Add water or broth, then the split peas. Simmer for 30 minutes. Add the ham and carrot and simmer for another 20 minutes.
3. The soup is ready when the peas are cooked. Add salt and cayenne pepper just before serving.

BIG PUMPKIN SOUP

Serving: 4 – 6 - Prep time: 30 minutes

Ingredients:

- 2 tablespoons of butter
- Cut up 4 cups of fresh pumpkin
- 8 cups of hot water
- 1 cup cream
- Pinch of salt
- Pinch of pepper
- Dash Nutmeg

Preparation:

1. Place the squash in water and simmer, covered, for 20 minutes or until tender. Add salt, pepper and nutmeg and pass through blender. Add the butter and cream and mix again briefly. Serve with a pinch of nutmeg on top.

FRENCH ONION SOUP

Serving:4 -Preparation time: 20 minutes

Ingredients:

- 2 tablespoons of butter

- 4 onions, finely chopped
- 2 tablespoons of flour
- 6 cups beef broth (or hot water)
- Salt and pepper to taste
- 2 cups grated Gruyère cheese
- Baguette slices, cut and toasted

Preparation:

1. Heat butter on medium for 30 seconds, add onions and stir. Cook over medium-high heat until onion becomes translucent, 5-6 minutes.
2. Stir every two minutes to avoid burning. Add flour and stir, sauté until just beginning to brown, about 2 minutes. Add broth (recommended) or hot water and cook for 10 minutes.
3. Season with salt and pepper. Cover the soup with toast and sprinkle with Gruyère. Bake covered at 180 °C for 10 minutes. Serve immediately, making sure to leave some cheese bread on the bottom of each bowl.

SIMPLE PORK UDON

Servings: 4-6 - Prep time: 25 minutes

Ingredients:

- 6 strips of bacon, cut into pieces
- 4 cups vegetable broth
- 2 cups hot water 1 tablespoon soy sauce
- 1/2 cup sake
- 1/2 cup radish, sliced
- 2 cups of small mushrooms
- 1 carrot, chopped
- 1 cup cabbage, chopped
- 2 tablespoons or more red miso paste to taste
- 1/2 cup chopped green onions
- 2 cups of cooked udon noodles

Preparation:

1. Fry the bacon in the pan. Place the vegetable broth, hot water, soy sauce, sake and vegetables in a saucepan and simmer for 20 minutes. Take red miso paste, add 1 cup of the hot broth to a separate bowl and beat until well combined.
2. Remove the soup from the heat, add the miso broth mixture and stir well. Serve over udon noodles with scallions in broth.

LAMB STEW

Serving:8 -Prep time: 1 hour 35 minutes

Ingredients:

- 900 g lamb stew, cut into cubes
- 1 tablespoon of butter
- 1 tablespoon of olive oil
- 450 g carrots, sliced
- 2 medium onions, thinly sliced

- 2 garlic cloves, chopped
- 1-2 cups of low-sodium chicken broth
- 1 bottle of low-sodium chicken broth
- 6 medium-red potatoes, peeled and diced
- 4 bay leaves
- 2 sprigs of fresh thyme
- 2 sprigs of fresh rosemary
- 2 teaspoons of salt
- 1-2 teaspoons of pepper
- 1/4 cup heavy whipping cream

Preparation:

1. Preheat the oven to 180°C. Portion lamb in butter and oil in an ovenproof Dutch Oven. In the same pan, fry carrots and onions until crispy. add garlic; Boil 1 minute.
2. Gradually add broth and beer. Stir in the lamb, potatoes, bay leaves, thyme, rosemary, salt and pepper.
3. Cover and bake 1 1/2 to 2 hours or until meat and vegetables are tender, stirring every 30 minutes. Discard bay leaves, thyme and rosemary. Stir in cream.

BEEF SOUP

Serving:4 -Preparation time: 30 minutes

Ingredients:

- 1.3 kg beef goulash meat
- 3 tsp salt
- 4 tablespoons light olive oil or any cooking oil
- 1 medium chopped onion
- 2 celery ribs finely chopped
- 4 cups beef broth + 4 cups filtered water
- 800 g diced tomatoes
- 2 dry bay leaves
- 1 tsp ground coriander seeds
- 1 tsp smoked paprika
- 2 garlic cloves pressed
- 1/2 cup uncooked white rice
- 2 tablespoons fresh lemon juice from 1 medium lemon
- 1/4 cup fresh parsley, chopped, plus more for serving
- 1/4 cup fresh dill, chopped, plus more for serving

Preparation:

1. Sprinkle the meat with 3 tsp salt and stir. Heat Dutch Oven or Stock Pot to medium/high and add 2 tbsp oil. Once the oil is hot, add the beef in 2 batches and sear until brown on all sides. Remove from the pot and set aside.
2. Add chopped onions and celery with more oil than needed. Fry for 5 minutes until nicely soft.
3. Add canned tomatoes with their juice, 4 cups broth, 4 cups water, 2 bay leaves and browned beef. Bring to a boil, reduce heat, cover and simmer 1 1/2 to 2 hours or until beef is tender.
4. Add 1/2 cup white rice, 2 tablespoons lemon juice, 2 crushed garlic cloves, 1 teaspoon coriander, 1 teaspoon

paprika. Cover and simmer for 20 minutes until the rice is tender.
5. Remove from heat and add 1/4 cup parsley and 1/4 cup dill, then cover and allow to cool an additional 10 minutes before serving. Season with salt and pepper and serve with more fresh herbs if you like.

EASY MUSHROOM MISO SOUP

Serving:4 -Preparation time: 20 minutes

Ingredients:

- 4 cups vegetable broth
- 2 cups of hot water
- 1 tablespoon of soy sauce
- 1/2 cup sake
- 1/2 cup radish, sliced
- 2 cups dried shiitake mushrooms
- 1 cup firm tofu, cut into small cubes
- 2 tablespoons or more red miso paste to taste
- 1/2 cup chopped green onions

Preparation:

1. Soak the shiitake mushrooms in hot water overnight. Place the vegetable broth, soy sauce, sake, radish, and mushrooms in a saucepan with the soaking water and simmer for 10 minutes. Add tofu and simmer for another 5 minutes.
2. Take red miso paste, add 1 cup of the hot broth to a separate bowl and beat until well combined.
3. Remove the soup from the heat, add the miso broth mixture and stir well. Scatter over the broth with the spring onions.

EASY SEAFOOD MISO SOUP

Serving:4 -Preparation time: 20 minutes

Ingredients:

- 4 cups fish soup stock
- 2 cups of hot water
- 1 tablespoon of soy sauce
- 1/2 cup sake
- 1/2 cup radish, sliced
- 1/2 cup small shiitake mushrooms
- 2 cups peeled shrimp, squid, tuna or salmon, cut into chunks
- 2 tablespoons or more red miso paste

Preparation:

1. Put fish broth, hot water, soy sauce, sake, radish and mushrooms in a saucepan and simmer for 10 minutes. Add seafood and cook another 10 minutes.
2. Take red miso paste, add 1 cup of the hot fish stock to a separate bowl and beat until well combined. Remove the soup from the heat, add the miso-broth mixture and stir well. Scatter over the broth with the spring onions.

SPINACH, FETA AND PINE, NO SOUP

Serving: 4 – 6 - Prep time: 30 minutes

Ingredients:

- 2 tablespoons olive oil
- 1 tablespoon butter (optional)
- 6 cups spinach leaves (or 2 heads, washed well)
- 2 tbsp olive oil plus a splash to refine
- 4 cups vegetable broth
- 1 leek, chopped
- Juice of 1 lemon
- 4 teaspoons crumbled feta cheese for garnish
- 4 teaspoons toasted pine nuts for garnish

Preparation:

1. Fry the leeks in olive oil and butter. Add broth, then add spinach leaves.
2. Simmer until tender, about 20 to 30 minutes. Season with salt and pepper, add 1 lemon juice and puree in a blender.
3. Garnish each bowl with a drizzle of olive oil, a spoonful of crumbled feta cheese, and a spoonful of toasted pine nuts. Serve with toasted pita.

EAST BAY BOUILLABAISSE

Serving: 4 – 6 - Prep time: 20-30 minutes

Ingredients:

- 4 to 6 cups of fish stock
- 450 g of mixed fresh fish
- 450 g of mixed fresh shellfish
- 2 cups of hot water as needed
- 1 onion, chopped
- 6 garlic cloves, chopped
- 2 cups tomatoes, chopped
- 4 tablespoons olive oil Splashes of saffron, soaked
- 1/4 cup hot water
- Dash chilli flakes
- Thyme sprig
- Juice of 2 or 3 lemons
- 1 cup white wine salt to taste
- Pepper to taste
- Chopped parsley to refine

Preparation:

1. Heat oil on medium for 30 seconds, then add minced garlic and onion and stir. Cover and continue cooking over medium-high heat until onions become translucent, about 3-4 minutes. Stir every two minutes to avoid burning. Add tomatoes and sauté until soft.
1. Add fish stock, wine, lemon juice, herbs, spices and simmer gently for 10 minutes. Add fish fillets cut into chunks, making sure there is enough liquid to cover the fish and add hot water, boiling for 5 minutes if necessary. Fish is not yet fully cooked. Add mussels and shrimp, stir. Cover and simmer for 5 to 10 minutes

RAINBOW VEGETABLE SOUP

Serving: 6 – 8 -Prep time: 1-2 hours

Ingredients:

- 2 tablespoons olive oil
- 4 cloves of garlic
- 2 onions chopped
- 1 or 2 leeks chopped
- 2 cups assorted mushrooms chopped
- 2 zucchini squash chopped
- 2 yellow pumpkins chopped
- 2 cups chopped tomatoes
- Chop 2 fresh corn kernels and cut off the cobs with a knife
- 4 carrots, chopped
- 1 celery, chopped
- 1 turnip, chopped
- 1 rainbow head or red chard
- 1 cup of cooked chickpeas
- Handful of fresh herbs: tarragon, thyme, rosemary, parsley
- 8 cups of hot water plus as needed
- Salt and pepper
- chopped parsley to refine

Preparation:

1. Heat oil over medium-high heat for 30 seconds, then add chopped garlic, chopped onion, chopped leeks and stir-fry to avoid burning. Cover and continue cooking over medium-high heat until onion and leeks become translucent, about 5-6 minutes. Stir every two minutes to avoid burning.
2. Add your chopped veggies in the following order, browning and stirring for a few minutes between each addition: mushrooms, tomatoes, zucchini squash, yellow squash, carrots, and leafy greens. Cover vegetables with hot water, add fresh herbs, stir well. First make sure that there is about 5 cm of water above the vegetables in the pot.
3. Add your chopped veggies in the following order, browning and stirring for a few minutes between each addition: mushrooms, tomatoes, zucchini squash, yellow squash, carrots, and leafy greens. Cover vegetables with hot water, add fresh herbs, stir well.
4. First make sure that there is about 5 cm of water above the vegetables in the pot. And when water evaporates, there should still be enough water in the pot to keep the veggies covered. Continue to add hot water as needed.
5. Cover and simmer gently for 60 to 90 minutes, stirring every 20 minutes. Add chickpeas and corn during the last 10 minutes of cooking.

VEGETABLE BROTH

Serving: 6 – 8 -Prep time: 1-2 hours

Ingredients:

- 2 tablespoons olive oil
- 4 cloves of garlic, chopped
- 2 onions, chopped
- 1 or 2 leeks, chopped
- 2 cups assorted mushrooms, chopped
- 2 zucchini squash, chopped
- 2 yellow squash, chopped
- 2 cups tomatoes, chopped
- 4 carrots, chopped
- 1 celery, chopped Handful of fresh herbs: tarragon, thyme, rosemary, parsley
- 8 more cups of hot water as needed
- Salt and pepper

Preparation:

1. Heat oil over medium-high heat for 30 seconds, then add chopped garlic, chopped onion, chopped leeks and stir-fry to avoid burning. Cover and continue cooking over medium-high heat until onion and leeks become translucent, about 5-6 minutes. Stir every two minutes to avoid burning.
2. Add your chopped veggies in the following order, browning and stirring for a few minutes between each addition: mushrooms, tomatoes, zucchini squash, yellow squash, carrots, and leafy greens. Cover vegetables with hot water, add fresh herbs, stir well.
3. First make sure that there is about 5 cm of water above the vegetables in the pot. And when water evaporates, there should still be enough water in the pot to keep the veggies covered. Continue to add hot water as needed.
4. Cover and simmer gently for 60 to 90 minutes, stirring every 20 minutes. For vegetable broth, strain the soup through a strainer over a basin to catch the broth. Save cooked vegetables as a garnish with butter or add to the bowl of broth.
5. To reduce, simmer the broth until half the liquid has evaporated. Stock and reduction can be frozen in ice cube trays and stored in pouches for later use in soups, stews and sauces.

MEDITERRANEAN FISH STEW

Serving:6 -Prep time: 35 minutes

Ingredients:

- 1 tablespoon of olive oil
- 1 yellow onion – diced
- 1 green pepper - diced
- 1/2 cup assorted halved tomatoes - chopped
- 2 garlic cloves - chopped
- 1 teaspoon freshly grated lemon zest
- 1 teaspoon crushed red pepper flakes
- 225 g Italian plum tomatoes – seeded, diced (or use canned tomatoes)
- 1 cup of bottled clam juice
- 1 cup of dry white wine
- 450 g firm white fish fillets - cut into pieces
- 450g large prawns - peeled, deveined, tails left intact
- 8 medium or large scallops
- 1/4 cup chopped fresh parsley
- 1/4 cup mayonnaise
- 1 teaspoon additional minced garlic – (optional)
- Crusty bread, couscous or rice

Preparation:

1. Heat the oil in a Dutch Oven on high. Add onions, peppers, and diced tomatoes (reconstitute tomatoes in hot water, wine, or broth before slicing if that's easier). Reduce heat and sauté for 5 minutes, stirring frequently. Add 2 cloves of minced garlic in the last 2 minutes.
2. Add lemon zest, pepper flakes and plum tomatoes; Fry for 2 minutes. Add clam juice and wine. Bring to a boil over high heat, then reduce to low and simmer for 10 minutes. Add fish pieces, shrimp, scallops and parsley; mix well. Cover and simmer for 5 minutes until the seafood is done.
3. In a small bowl, mix together the mayonnaise and additional garlic. Mix well.
4. To serve, pour stew into serving bowls; Cover each with a pinch of mayonnaise. Serve with bread, couscous or rice.
5. Bake until the fish is opaque. Serve sprinkled with black pepper

COUSCOUS STEW WITH SMOKED ALMONDS AND HERBS

Serving: 6 – 8 - Prep time: 15 minutes

Ingredients:

- 2 tablespoons olive oil
- 4 cloves of garlic, chopped
- 2/3 cup slivered almonds
- 1 teaspoon of smoked paprika
- 2 1/4 cups of water
- 2 cups of couscous
- 3/4 teaspoon kosher salt
- 2/3 cup coarsely chopped fresh parsley leaves

Preparation:

1. Heat the oil in a large saucepan or Dutch oven over medium-high heat until shimmering. Add the garlic and almonds and sauté until the garlic is fragrant and the nuts are lightly toasted (about 2 minutes). Add the peppers and sauté for a further 10 seconds.
2. Add the water, stir and bring the mixture to a boil. Reduce heat and stir in couscous and salt. Cover and let stand 5 minutes until liquid is absorbed. Stir in the parsley and serve.

HEARTY BEEF SOUP

Serve:6 – 8

Preparation time: 2-3 hours

Ingredients:

- 3 or 4 large beef bones with marrow
- 450g extra beef goulash, diced
- 2 tablespoons olive oil
- 6 garlic cloves, peeled and quartered
- 1 onion, finely chopped
- 1 carrot, chopped in rounds
- 1 celery, finely chopped
- Handful of fresh herbs: tarragon, thyme, rosemary, parsley
- 1 cup red wine or 1/4 cup sherry
- Madeira salt and pepper to taste
- 1 leek, chopped
- 1 cup mushrooms, chopped and 1 zucchini, chopped
- 1 yellow squash, chopped
- 2 potatoes, chopped
- 2 cups tomatoes, chopped parsley, for garnish.

Preparation:

1. Place beef bones/meat in saucepan and cover with water. Add 1 tablespoon of salt. Bring to a boil and simmer until a foam forms on top (about 10 minutes). Remove the foamy foam with a spoon and repeat this process several times until no white foam rises to the surface (about 30 minutes total).
2. Add chopped onions, carrots, celery and fresh herbs. Simmer gently for 1 1/2 to 2 hours. Add sherry, madeira or wine, stir.
3. Add additional freshly chopped veggies to casual beef bone broth. Simmer gently for another 30 minutes. Vegetables should be tender. Season with salt and pepper. Sprinkle with chopped parsley before serving. Serve hot with crusty bread and butter.

BEEF BONE BROTH

Serving: 6 – 8 -Prep time: 2-3 hours

Ingredients:

- 3 or 4 large beef bones with marrow
- 450 gr. additional beef goulash, diced if desired
- 2 tablespoons olive oil
- 6 garlic cloves, peeled and quartered
- 1 onion, finely chopped
- 1 carrot, chopped in rounds
- 1 celery, finely chopped Handful of fresh herbs: tarragon, thyme, rosemary, parsley
- 1 cup red wine or 1/4 cup sherry
- Madeira salt and pepper to taste

Preparation:

1. Place beef bones/meat in saucepan and cover with water. Add 1 tablespoon of salt. Bring to a boil and simmer until a foam forms on top (about 10 minutes).
2. Remove the foamy foam with a spoon and repeat this process several times until no white foam rises to the surface (about 30 minutes in total). Add chopped onions, carrots, celery and fresh herbs. Simmer gently for 1 1/2 to 2 hours. Add sherry, madeira or wine, stir.
3. Season with salt and pepper. Drain with a colander or serve as is in a bowl with meat or bones. The broth can be strained, then frozen in ice cube trays and stored in bags for later use in soups, stews and sauces. To reduce the strained broth, continue to simmer until half of the liquid has been used up. Freeze in ice cube trays and use for future sauces or soup stock

HEARTY SWEET POTATO CABBAGE SOUP

Serving:6 - Preparation time: 25 minutes

Ingredients:

- 1 large yellow onion
- 4 medium cloves of garlic
- 425g can of black beans
- 2 tablespoons olive oil
- 2 teaspoons dried oregano
- 1 1/2 teaspoons cumin
- 1 teaspoon garlic powder
- black pepper
- 1/8 to 1/4 teaspoon cayenne pepper (optional)
- 1/2 teaspoon kosher or sea salt
- 450 g sweet potatoes (3 cups diced)
- 1 liter (4 cups) of vegetable broth
- 4 cups chopped organic kale (30 g)
- 3 spring onions
- 2 radishes, thinly sliced
- 1 tablespoon lime juice
- 6 tablespoons of yoghurt as a side (optional)
- Hot sauce (optional)

Preparation:

1. Dice the onion. Finely chop the garlic. Dice the sweet potato. Drain and wash beans.
2. In a large saucepan or Dutch oven, heat the olive oil over medium-high heat. Add the onions and sauté for 4 minutes until translucent.
3. Reduce heat to medium, add garlic, oregano, cumin, garlic powder, black pepper and cayenne pepper (optional) and sauté for 30 seconds. Stir in sweet potatoes, add vegetable broth, beans, and Kosher sea salt, and bring to a boil.
4. After boiling, bring to a boil and simmer for 15 minutes until sweet potato is tender. Roughly chop the kale while it cooks. Thinly slice the spring onions and radishes.
5. When sweet potatoes are tender, remove from heat and stir in kale, scallions, and lime juice. Let cool slightly before serving. Add kosher sea salt if desired. Serve with

radishes, a small portion of Greek yogurt (optional) and hot sauce.

MOROCCAN SPICED CAULIFLOWER SOUP

Serving:8 - Prep time: 45 minutes

Ingredients:

- 3 pounds (1.36 kg) whole cauliflower (about 1 1/2 medium heads or 8 cups florets)
- 6 medium cloves of garlic and 6 tablespoons of olive oil
- 1 3/4 teaspoons kosher salt,
- 1 large yellow onion and 1 carrot
- 6 to 7 cups of vegetable broth
- 1 1/2 teaspoons cumin and 1 1/2 teaspoons coriander
- 1 teaspoon ground ginger
- 1 teaspoon turmeric, 1 teaspoon cinnamon and 1/4 teaspoon black pepper
- Sliced spring onions and peppers to refine

Preparation:

1. Preheat the oven to 230°C. Cut the cauliflower into florets. Peel the garlic. Place cauliflower and garlic in a large bowl and toss with 3 tablespoons olive oil and 1 teaspoon kosher salt. Line a baking sheet with parchment paper or a silicone mat and spread the cauliflower on it in an even layer. Roast for 30 to 35 minutes, until slightly very tender, stirring once.
2. Meanwhile, dice the onion. Peel and dice the carrot. In a large saucepan or Dutch oven, heat 2 tablespoons olive oil over medium-high heat. Sauté onion and carrot until onion is translucent, about 5 minutes. Add 6 cups of veggies and cumin, coriander, ginger, turmeric, cinnamon, and black pepper and bring to a boil. Simmer for 10 to 15 minutes while the cauliflower roasts. Add the remaining roasted cauliflower and garlic to the broth. Add 1 cup broth, 1 tablespoon olive oil, and 3/4 teaspoon kosher salt. Blend until smooth with a hand blender.
3. Serve immediately, garnishing with the reserved cauliflower, chopped spring onions, additional olive oil (if desired) and a sprinkling of paprika

VZiti stew with sausage

Serving:6 - Preparation time: 30 minutes

Ingredients:

- 450 gr. sweet Italian sausage
- 1/2 medium yellow onion, chopped
- 2 garlic cloves, chopped
- 1 (450 gr.) may have diced tomatoes
- 1 (450 gr.) can of tomato sauce
- 2 tablespoons of tomato paste
- 1 teaspoon of Italian spices
- 1 teaspoon of sugar and 3/4 teaspoon of salt
- 1/4 teaspoon red pepper flakes
- 1 1/2 cups of water
- 3 cups uncooked ziti

- 1/3 cup grated parmesan
- 225 gr. Whole milk mozzarella cheese, cut into small cubes
- 1 cup of ricotta cheese

Preparation:

1. Place the sausage in a Dutch Oven and cook over medium-high heat. Break up the sausage with a wooden spoon while it cooks. Once the sausage is about half cooked, add the onion. Cook for 2 to 3 more minutes and add garlic. Boil 1 minute. Add diced tomatoes, tomato sauce, tomato paste, Italian seasoning, sugar, salt, and red pepper flakes. Simmer for 10 minutes.
2. Add water and ziti. Stir well so the ziti are submerged. Cook 8 to 10 minutes, or until noodles are almost set and slightly chewy. (You still want to be fairly firm as it will continue to cook for a while.) Remove the Dutch Oven from the heat. Stir in the parmesan and mozzarella. Topped with a spoonful of ricotta. Place the Dutch Oven in the oven under the grill until the cheese is hot and melted on top.

GOLDEN CHICKEN BROTH

Serving:6 - Prep time: 2-3 hours

Ingredients:

- 1 whole chicken, cut into pieces
- 2 tablespoons olive oil
- 1 onion, finely chopped
- 2 carrots, chopped
- 1 turnip, chopped
- 1 handful of fresh herbs: a mixture of tarragon, thyme, rosemary, basil, parsley

Preparation:

1. Put the chicken in the pot and cover it with water so that the water level is about 5 cm above the level of the chicken. Add 1 tablespoon of salt and bring to a boil. Bring to a boil and cook for 20 minutes, removing any foam that may collect on top of the soup. This may take a few minutes, but it's worth it to keep the broth clear. Add the chopped onion, carrot and fresh or dried herbs.
2. Stir well and simmer over low heat for another 1 1/2 hours. Place a large basin or saucepan in your sink (large enough to hold all of the chicken broth) and cover with a colander. Strain the chicken soup through the strainer to catch the broth in the bowl below.
3. Your chicken and herbs stay in the colander and all of your broth is separated into the bowl. Serve the broth as is and add any desired meat that you set aside in the colander. You can also add pre-cooked pasta or a handful of thin vermicelli to the broth. Refrigerate the chicken and broth separately. The broth can be strained, then frozen in ice cube trays and stored for later use in soups, stews and sauces.

Golden Chicken Broth

Serving:6 - Prep time: 2-3 hours

Ingredients:

- 1 whole chicken, cut into pieces
- 2 tablespoons olive oil
- 1 onion, finely chopped
- 2 carrots, chopped
- 1 turnip, chopped
- 1 handful of fresh herbs: a mixture of tarragon, thyme, rosemary, basil, parsley

Preparation:

1. Put the chicken in the pot and cover it with water so that the water level is about 5 cm above the level of the chicken. Add 1 tablespoon of salt and bring to a boil. Bring to a boil and cook for 20 minutes, removing any foam that may collect on top of the soup. This may take a few minutes, but it's worth it to keep the broth clear. Add the chopped onion, carrot and fresh or dried herbs.
2. Stir well and simmer over low heat for another 1 1/2 hours. Place a large basin or saucepan in your sink (large enough to hold all of the chicken broth) and cover with a colander. Strain the chicken soup through the strainer to catch the broth in the bowl below.
3. Your chicken and herbs stay in the colander and all of your broth is separated into the bowl. Serve the broth as is and add any desired meat that you set aside in the colander. You can also add pre-cooked pasta or a handful of thin vermicelli to the broth. Refrigerate the chicken and broth separately. The broth can be strained, then frozen in ice cube trays and stored for later use in soups, stews and sauces.

Carrot-Ginger Soup

Serving:4 - Preparation time: 30 minutes

Ingredients:

- 2 tablespoons olive oil
- 1 large yellow onion, finely chopped
- 4 cups carrots, chopped
- 1 thumb-sized piece of freshly peeled ginger, chopped
- 2 cups vegetable broth
- 2 cups of hot water, plus if needed
- 1 teaspoon of turmeric powder
- 1 teaspoon of cumin powder
- Juice of 1 lemon
- Salt and pepper to taste
- Chopped parsley to refine
- Dollop of sour cream (optional)

Preparation:

1. Heat oil on medium for 30 seconds, then add chopped onions and stir. Cover and continue cooking over medium-high heat until translucent, about 5-6 minutes. Stir every two minutes to avoid burning.

2. Add the chopped carrots, chopped ginger, spices and liquids. Cover and simmer over medium heat for 30 minutes, stirring every 10 minutes.
3. When the carrots are soft, remove from the heat. Cover and leave to cool for 10 minutes. Put in a blender. Add salt to taste. Serve with a pinch of sour cream or yogurt and chopped parsley.

Spicy Tomato Soup

Serving:4 - Prep time: 40 minutes

Ingredients:

- 4 tablespoons olive oil
- 2 garlic cloves, finely chopped
- 1 onion, finely chopped
- 4 cups tomatoes, peeled and chopped (fresh or canned).
- 1 cup fresh basil leaves.
- 4 cups vegetable broth or hot water.
- Salt and pepper to taste
- Chopped parsley for garnish
- Sour cream, to refine (optional)

Preparation:

1. If using fresh tomatoes: The first step is to remove the tomato skin. Fill a saucepan with water and bring to a boil. Submerge fresh whole tomatoes in the boiling water for about a minute.
2. Drain and let cool. Chop the tomatoes once they are peeled. Heat oil on medium for 30 seconds, then add chopped garlic and chopped onion and stir. Cover and continue cooking over medium-high heat until onions become translucent, about 5-6 minutes.
3. Stir every two minutes to avoid burning. Add your tomato chunks and sauté until tender, about 5 minutes. Add about half your fresh basil and enough broth/water to cover the mixture. Simmer for 30 minutes. Leave on for 10 minutes and run through a blender. Serve with some black pepper and a sprig of fresh basil.

Creamy Mixed Vegetable Soup

Serving: 6 – 8 - Preparation time: 60 minutes

Ingredients:

- 3 tablespoons olive oil
- 1 tablespoon butter (optional)
- 3 garlic cloves, finely chopped
- 1 onion, finely chopped
- 1 leek, cut into thin rings
- 2 carrots, cut into thin rings
- 1 head of anise, halved or quartered
- 2 yellow pumpkins, cut into thin rings
- 1 or 2 potatoes, cut into small cubes
- 2 cups tomatoes, chopped
- 1 tablespoon of dried oregano
- Hot water

- Salt and pepper to taste
- 1/2 cup yogurt, full fat and chopped parsley for garnish

Preparation:

1. Heat oil and butter over medium-high heat for 30 seconds, then add chopped garlic, chopped onion, chopped leeks and sauté, stirring frequently. Cover and continue cooking over medium-high heat until translucent, about 5-6 minutes. Stir every minute to avoid burns. If possible, add your chopped veggies in the following order, lightly browning and stirring between each addition: mushrooms, zucchini or yellow squash, tomatoes, root greens, leafy greens.
2. When all the veggies are in the pot, add dried herbs and add enough hot water to cover 1 to 2 inches (about 5 cm) above the veggies. Cover the pot, reduce the heat and simmer for an hour, stirring every 10 minutes. When the veggies are done, after about an hour, bring them to a boil (note: there's no harm in slow-cooking the veggies for two hours), add the yogurt, salt, and pepper. Mix everything together for an amazingly creamy and delicious vegetable soup. Refine with parsley and sour cream as desired

CALIFORNIA CAULIFLOWER SOUP

Serving:4 - Preparation time: 30 minutes

Ingredients:

- 3 tablespoons olive oil
- 1 tablespoon butter (optional)
- 1 large yellow onion, finely chopped
- 1 head cauliflower, chopped (any color)
- 2 cups vegetable broth
- 2 cups hot water, plus additional salt and pepper as needed
- Parsley for refinement
- Sour cream to refine

Preparation:

1. Heat oil and butter over medium-high heat for 30 seconds, then add chopped onions and stir. Cover and continue cooking over medium-high heat until translucent, about 3-4 minutes.
2. Stir every minute to avoid burns. Add your cauliflower pieces. Fry for a few minutes, stirring occasionally.
3. Cover with broth and hot water. The liquid should only cover the vegetables. Cover the pot and simmer every 5 to 10 minutes until the cauliflower is tender (about 20 minutes total).
4. Add cayenne pepper, salt and pepper to taste. Mix the soup with a blender. Refine with chopped parsley, sour cream and another dash of cayenne pepper.

FRENCH LEEK POTATO SOUP

Serving: 4 - 6 - Prep time: 40 minutes

Ingredients:

- 3 tablespoons olive oil
- 1 tablespoon butter (optional but recommended)
- 2 to 3 leeks, chopped
- 2 potatoes, diced
- 4 cups vegetable broth or hot water (or a combination)
- Additional hot water, salt and pepper as needed
- Parsley and cream for refinement (optional)

Preparation:

1. Sauté leeks in olive oil (and butter if using) over medium-high heat until translucent (about 10 minutes, stirring frequently). Cover to speed up cooking. Add potato cubes and stir. Add broth and water until vegetables are covered with liquid, cover and simmer for about 30 minutes.
2. Stir occasionally. When the potatoes are soft, the soup is cooked. Allow the soup to cool slightly, then set aside a cup of the cooked vegetables. Run the remaining soup mixture through a blender.
3. Add some salt while mixing. Pour the mixed soup back into the stockpot and toss with the reserved chunks of vegetables. This gives the soup a very nice, hearty texture.
4. If you prefer a creamier soup, just mix everything together at once. Sprinkle with chopped parsley and some cream if you like. Serve immediately with crusty French bread and salted butter.

CHICKEN SOUP

Serving:4 - Preparation time: about 1 hour

Ingredients:

- 2 chicken breasts
- 1 onion
- 2 cloves of garlic
- 2 cans of chili peppers
- 1 can of tomatoes
- 1 can of beans (black)
- 1 can of chicken broth
- ½ teaspoon chili powder

Preparation:

1. Place 12 briquettes under the Dutch Oven and light.
2. Rinse the chicken breast under cold water, dry thoroughly and cut into small pieces.
3. Peel and dice the onion. Also chop the garlic cloves. 4. Place the chicken breasts and onions in the Dutch Oven. Add the remaining ingredients and mix well.
4. Place 11 briquettes under and 17 briquettes on top of the Dutch Oven and let the soup simmer for about 60 minutes.
5. Arrange on plates and serve with some yoghurt or cheese.

POTATO SOUP

Serving:8 - Preparation time: about 1 hour

Ingredients:

- 2 carrots
- 3 cloves of garlic
- 4 onions
- 2 bay leaves
- 2 pairs of Cabanossi
- 2 winning couples
- 1 leek
- 2 kg of potatoes
- 200 g bacon (smoked)
- 2 tablespoons sunflower oil
- 1 bunch of parsley
- 1 lovage
- 2 liters of water
- Some nutmeg
- Some chives
- 1 pinch of salt and pepper

Preparation:

1. Peel and dice the potatoes. Chop carrots, celery, leeks, garlic and onions. Put the oil in the Dutch Oven and heat. Add the onions, garlic, celery, carrots, celery and carrots and sauté briefly. Refine everything with salt, pepper and nutmeg. Place the bay leaves, parsley and lovage in the Dutch Oven. Deg, lazing with water.
2. Add bacon and simmer for about 40 minutes. Remove the bay leaves and bacon from the Dutch oven and puree the rest. Cut the bacon and sausage into small pieces and add to the soup. Let everything simmer for another 15 minutes. Divide the potato soup among plates and serve with chives.

HEARTY SOUP WITH RED CABBAGE AND APPLES

Serving:4 - Preparation time: 30 minutes

Ingredients:

- 3 onions
- 4 potatoes
- 500 g red cabbage
- 1 liter of vegetable broth
- 250 ml of red wine
- 3 apples and oranges
- 1 teaspoon of coriander
- 2 tablespoons acacia honey
- 4 tablespoons olive oil
- 1 tablespoon fruit vinegar
- 1 pinch of salt and pepper

Preparation:

1. Cut open the red cabbage, clean and cut into strips. Also dice potatoes and onions.

2. Put olive oil in the Dutch Oven and heat. Add the onions and sauté them. Add red cabbage and potatoes and sauté briefly. Pour red wine and vegetable broth over everything. Refine with salt, pepper, fruit vinegar and acacia honey. Cover the Dutch Oven and let the soup simmer for about 30 minutes.
3. Halve the orange. Squeeze half and cut off the other half.
4. Serve red cabbage soup with oranges.

CHEESESOUP

Serving:4 - Preparation time: 15 minutes

Ingredients:

- 4 spring onions
- 200g Gouda
- 100 grams of butter
- 100 grams of flour
- 100 grams of pumpkin
- 1 cup of milk
- 1 liter of vegetable broth

Preparation:

1. Peel the spring onions and cut into small pieces.
2. Put butter in the Dutch Oven and heat. Add the spring onions and sauté briefly.
3. Add the flour to the milk and dissolve in it. Put in the Dutch Oven together with the vegetable broth.
4. Grate the pumpkin and add it as well. Let everything simmer for about 15 minutes.
5. Scatter cheese on top and stir in gently.
6. Divide the cheese soup among plates and serve with bread

KOHLRABI SOUP

Serving:4 -Preparation time: 25 minutes

Ingredients:

- 1 onion
- 600 grams of kohlrabi
- 20 grams of butter
- 200 grams of cream
- 800 ml vegetable broth
- ½ bunch parsley
- 1 teaspoon lemon zest
- Some chili powder
- Some oil Some nutmeg
- 1 pinch of salt and pepper

Preparation:

1. Put the oil in the Dutch Oven.
2. Chop the onions and kohlrabi and sauté briefly in the Dutch oven. Pour the vegetable broth over everything and cook for about 20 minutes.
3. Remove the kohlrabi and set aside.

4. Add cream and heat. Add butter and stir well. Season with salt, pepper and chilli powder.
5. Divide the kohlrabi soup among plates and serve with parsley and lemon

COCONUT SOUP

Serving:4 -Prep time: 35 minutes

Ingredients:

- 2 stalks of lemongrass
- 4 cloves of garlic
- 2 limes
- 1 onion and 1 pepper
- 1 chili pepper
- ½ bunch coriander
- 1 can of bamboo shoots
- 10 corn on the cob (mini)
- 4 spring onions
- 100 g bean sprouts
- 100 g glass noodles
- 1 liter of vegetable broth
- 1 liter coconut cream
- Some ginger (3 cm)

Preparation:

1. Place charcoal on the grill and light it. Place the Dutch Oven on the grill. Chop the lemongrass, onion and garlic, as well as the lime, chili peppers and ginger.
2. Put the oil in the Dutch Oven and heat. Put all the cut ingredients with the coriander sprigs in the Dutch Oven and toast briefly. Turn occasionally. Pour vegetable broth and coconut cream over everything and simmer for about 15 minutes.
3. Core and dice the peppers. Also cut the spring onions and corn into small pieces. Place the contents of the Dutch Oven in a bowl and season with salt and pepper.
4. Add the peppers, spring onions, corn, bamboo shoots and soybean sprouts to the Dutch Oven and simmer for a few minutes. Divide the soup among plates and serve with coriander.

GYROS SOUP

Serving:4 - Prep time: 1 hour

Ingredients:

- 2 peppers (red)
- 2 peppers (yellow)
- 2 onions
- 1 cup processed cheese
- 1 bottle of gypsy sauce
- 1 liter of water
- 3 cups whipping cream
- 1 bouillon cube
- 1 kg pork neck
- Some oil
- 1 pinch of salt and pepper

Preparation:

1. Cut the pork neck into small pieces and refine with gyros spice. Place the briquettes in the kindling stove and let them shine through. Place fully heated coals under the Dutch Oven.
2. Put the oil in the Dutch Oven and heat. Add the pork neck and sauté. Remove the meat from the Dutch Oven and set aside.
3. Chop the onions and peppers and add to the Dutch Oven. Chop and add garlic. Pour water, cream and melted cheese over everything. Add the bouillon cubes and gypsy sauce and mix well. Close the lid and let everything simmer for about 30 minutes.
4. Add meat and simmer for 30 minutes. Arrange on plates, season with salt and pepper and serve with some bread.

ONIONSOUP

Serving:5 - Prep time: 45 minutes

Ingredients:

- 300 grams of onions
- 100 grams of carrots
- 80 g diced bacon
- 60 g Emmental cheese
- 20 grams of garlic
- 20 grams of butter
- 20 grams of sugar
- 20 grams of garlic
- 2 tablespoons canola oil
- 800 ml chicken broth
- 300 ml root beer
- 100 ml of white wine
- 4 slices of toast
- 2 sprigs of thyme
- 2 bay leaves
- A few chili flakes
- 1 pinch of salt and pepper

Preparation:

1. Place the Dutch Oven on the grill. Preheat to 200°C.
2. Fry the bacon cubes in a little oil in the Dutch oven.
3. Peel and dice the onions and carrots and place in the Dutch Oven. Add sugar and caramelize everything. Deglaze the contents with malt beer.
4. Add garlic and chili and deglaze with white wine. Refine with bay leaves and thyme and simmer for about 20 minutes.
5. Salt Pepper Onion Soup, divide onto plates and serve with toast.

OX TAIL SOUP

Serving:10 - Preparation time: about 3 hours

Ingredients:

- 3 carrots
- 1 celery
- 1 leek
- 6 allspice corns
- 2 onions
- 1 bouillon cube (fat)
- 1 kg of oxtail
- 2 liters of water
- 100 ml of red wine
- 3 tbsp oil
- 1 pinch of sea salt and pepper

Preparation:

1. Put the oil in the Dutch Oven and heat it up. Briefly serve the oxtails in it.
2. Cut the vegetables and leeks into small pieces and place in the Dutch oven. Add water and bouillon cube. Let simmer for about 3 hours.
3. Separate the meat from the bone and place back in the oven. Refine everything with red wine, salt and pepper, spread on plates and serve with some bread.

LENTIL SOUP

Serving:10 -Prep time: 1 hour 30 minutes

Ingredients:

- 7 potatoes
- 5 cloves of garlic
- 3 onions
- 5 bay leaves
- 1 kg of soup vegetables
- 700 grams of lentils
- 600 g cabanossi
- 450 g pork belly
- 250 ml vinegar
- 1 tbsp oil
- 1 pinch of salt and pepper

Preparation:

1. Put the lentils, bay leaves and garlic cloves in a saucepan of boiling water. Let everything simmer for about 30 minutes.
2. Wash and dice vegetables and pork belly.
3. Put the oil in the Dutch Oven, heat and leave out the bacon bits. Add onions and sauté. Add the onions and potatoes to the lentils.
4. Chop and add the Cabanossi. Put everything in the Dutch Oven, close the lid, light the briquettes and simmer for about 50 minutes.
5. Salt, pepper and serve.

FISH SOUP

Serving:6 - Prep time: 45 minutes.

Ingredients:

- 1 kg of fish fillet
- 250 grams of shrimp
- 4 cans of tomatoes
- 2 cloves of garlic
- 2 zucchini
- 2 onions
- 1 glass of fish broth
- 3 tablespoons tomato paste
- 2 tablespoons oyster sauce
- 1 jar of olives (black)
- 2 tablespoons oregano
- 2 tbsp curry
- 1 tbsp rosemary
- 1 tbsp thyme
- 1 bottle of white wine
- 1 pinch sugar (brown)
- 1 pinch of salt and pepper

Preparation:

1. Put olive oil in a Dutch Oven and heat.
2. Peel and chop the onions and garlic and place in the Dutch oven with the tomato paste. Add all remaining ingredients (except fish fillet and shrimp) and simmer for about 30 minutes.
3. Cut the fish fillet into small pieces and simmer in the oven with the shrimp for about 10 minutes.
4. Divide the fish soup among plates and enjoy with 1 glass of white wine.

CHEESE LEEK SOUP

Serving:2 - Preparation time: 25 minutes

Ingredients:

- 450 grams of minced meat
- 400 g processed cheese
- 5 potatoes
- 2 leeks
- 1 onion
- Some nutmeg
- Some olive oil
- 1 pinch of salt and pepper

Preparation:

1. Allow 14 briquettes to burn in the chimney starter.
2. Cut the leeks, onions and potatoes into small pieces.
3. Place the Dutch Oven on the chimney starter.
4. Put the olive oil in the Dutch Oven, heat it up and fry the minced meat briefly. Add onions and sauté briefly. Add the leeks and potatoes and deglaze everything with the vegetable broth. Let the contents cook for about 15 minutes.

5. Add the melted cheese and briefly boil again. Refine with salt, pepper and nutmeg and serve with a few tomato flakes.

MUSHROOM SOUP

Serving:2 - Preparation time: 30 minutes

Ingredients:

- 300 g mushrooms (brown)
- 1 onion
- 1 clove of garlic
- 500 ml mushroom broth
- ½ teaspoon of beef
- Some oil Some parsley
- 1 pinch of salt

Preparation:

1. 1st X-ray, 7 briquettes in the chimney starter.
2. Wash the mushrooms and dry them carefully. Dice half the mushrooms and slice the other half. Peel and dice onions and garlic.
3. Place the Dutch Oven on the briquettes and heat for a few minutes. Add oil and heat. Put the onions and garlic in the Dutch Oven and sauté for a few minutes. Add the mushroom cubes and sauté.
4. Add the mushroom slices and season with Beef Symphony and a pinch of salt. Deglaze everything with the mushroom broth and bring to a boil.
5. Close the lid and place 3 of the 7 briquettes on the Dutch Oven. Let the soup simmer for about 20 minutes, spread on plates and refine with parsley.

PUMPKIN SOUP

Serving: 10 - Preparation time: 20 minutes

Ingredients:

- 2 pumpkins (Hokkaido)
- 3 cloves of garlic
- 2 onions
- 1 carrot
- 1 celery
- 1 orange, 1 ginger root
- 1 liter of water
- 200ml cream
- 3 potatoes
- 200 grams of chestnuts
- 3 tablespoons sunflower oil
- Some parsley
- Some pumpkin seed oil
- 1 pinch of salt and sugar

Preparation:

1. 1. Cut the pumpkin into small pieces. Peel and dice onions, garlic and leeks. Dice carrots, celery and potatoes.

2. 2. Put the sunflower oil in the Dutch Oven and heat it up. Add onions and garlic and sauté. Add the leek and celery. Caramelize with sugar and deglaze with water and orange juice.
3. 3. Add the pumpkin, carrots and celery and simmer at 180°C for about 50 minutes.
4. 4. Place the chestnuts on the grill for about 25 minutes, heat them up and then peel them. Salt and pepper the pumpkin soup and refine with cream, puree and serve with chestnuts.

PIZZA SOUP

Serving:6 - Preparation time: 20 minutes

Ingredients:

- 1 kg minced meat (beef)
- 100 g diced ham
- 2 cloves of garlic
- 2 onions and peppers
- 2 cans of mushrooms
- 1 cup cream & crème fraîche
- 400 g processed cheese
- 700ml of water
- 1 pack of Italian herbs
- ½ bottle of gypsy sauce
- 1 bottle of BBQ sauce
- 1 packet of tomatoes (sifted)
- 1 pinch of salt and pepper

Preparation:

1. Wash the vegetables and cut them into small pieces.
2. Place the briquettes in the chimney starter and light them. Place the Dutch Oven on the chimney starter.
3. Place the diced ham in the Dutch Oven. Add the ground beef and fry. Place the onions and garlic in the Dutch Oven. Season everything with salt and pepper. Deglaze with the tomato puree.
4. Add peppers, mushrooms and some water. Add the remaining ingredients and remove the fire pot from the chimney starter.
5. Close the lid and place 12 briquettes under and 16 briquettes on top of the Dutch Oven. Let the soup simmer a little longer, divide onto plates and serve with some bread.

SPAGHETTI STEW

Serving:4 -Preparation time: 25 minutes

Ingredients:

- 450 g lean ground beef (90% lean)
- 3-4 cups sliced fresh mushrooms
- 3 cups of tomato juice
- 1 tin of diced tomatoes (225 g) without adding salt, drain
- 1 can (225 g) unsalted tomato sauce
- 1 tablespoon dried chopped onion

- Salt
- Garlic powder
- 1/2 teaspoon ground mustard
- Pepper
- 1/8 tsp ground allspice
- 170g uncooked multigrain spaghetti, broken into pieces
- Optional fresh mozzarella or shaved parmesan cheese

Preparation:

1. In a Dutch oven, cook the beef and mushrooms over medium-high heat until the meat is no longer pink. Add tomato juice, tomatoes, tomato sauce, onions and spices.
2. Bring to a boil. Stir in spaghetti. Cover and simmer for 12-15 minutes or until spaghetti is tender. Serve with cheese if desired.

ZUCCHINI SOUP WITH SAUSAGE

Serving:4 - Preparation time: 30 min

Ingredients:

- 6 medium zucchini
- 4 sausages
- 1 liter chicken broth
- 150 ml cream
- 4 slices of white bread dill
- Paprika powder
- Salt and pepper
- Butter for frying

Preparation:

1. Wash zucchini, remove stalk and cut into small pieces. Dice the white bread slices and cut the bockwurst into pieces.
2. Simmer the zucchini pieces in the broth over low heat for about 20 minutes. Add cream and season with paprika powder, dill, pepper and salt. Puree the whole thing.
3. Finally, add the pieces of sausage to the soup.
4. Slices of white bread roasted in butter go very well with the soup. To do this, heat the butter in the Dutch oven and fry the pieces of white bread on all sides.
5. Serve the soup with the pieces of white bread and enjoy.

CHEESE SOUP

Serving:6 - Preparation time: 50 min

Ingredients:

- 500 g minced pork
- 125 g beef jerky
- 2 onions
- 3 leeks
- 1 can of corn
- 1 can of tomato passata
- 1 cup cream

- 250 grams of mushrooms
- 2 points (1.14 liters). herbal melted cheese
- 1 bouillon cube
- 1 liter of water
- Paprika powder
- Salt and pepper
- Oil for frying

Preparation:

1. Peel and dice the onion. Dice the beef jerky. Wash and slice the leek. Wash and quarter the mushrooms. Drain corn.
2. Heat the oil in the Dutch oven. Fry the onions, minced meat, leek and beef jerky.
3. Then add the tomato passata, water and bouillon cube and simmer for 30 minutes with the lid closed and low heat from below.
4. Finally add the cream, cheese and mushrooms and bring to the boil. Season with salt, pepper and paprika.
5. Serve and enjoy.

PUMPKIN POTATO SOUP

Serving:4 - Prep time: 40 minutes

Ingredients:

- 1 Hokkaido pumpkin
- 6 potatoes
- 3 onions
- 1 clove of garlic
- 750 ml vegetable stock
- 2 cm piece of ginger
- 1 tsp salt
- Pepper
- 1 tablespoon curry powder
- Some cream

Preparation:

1. Wash and roughly chop the pumpkin. Wash, peel and coarsely dice the potatoes. Peel and roughly chop the onions and garlic. Peel and chop ginger.
2. Bring the vegetable stock to a boil in the Dutch Oven over medium-high heat. Add the potatoes, squash, onions, ginger, and garlic and simmer, uncovered, until potatoes are tender, about 30 minutes.
3. Then puree all the ingredients and season with salt, pepper and curry powder. Refine with a little cream if you like.
4. Serve and enjoy.

CHICKEN COCONUT SOUP

Serving:4 - Prep time: 55 min

Ingredients:

- 400 g chicken breast
- 220 ml coconut milk
- 500ml of water
- 2 tablespoons clarified butter
- 2 onions
- 2 cloves of garlic
- 2 chili peppers
- 8 grams of ginger
- 2 tsp lemon juice
- 2 tsp curry powder
- Salt and pepper.

Preparation:

1. Peel and chop the garlic, onion, ginger and chili into small pieces.
2. Heat the Dutch Oven with ghee and fry the chicken breast. Add the garlic, onion, ginger and chili pepper and sauté as well.
3. Add water and simmer, with the lid closed, over low heat for about 25 minutes.
4. Remove the chicken breasts from the Dutch Oven, cut into small pieces and return to the pot. Season with salt, pepper, curry powder and lemon juice and mix well.
5. Serve and enjoy the finished soup.

SPICY CARROT SOUP

Serving:4 - Preparation time: 30 min

Ingredients:

- 800 grams of carrots
- 40 g of pumpkin seeds
- 3 chili peppers
- 2 tablespoons nut oil
- 400 ml cream
- 100 ml milk
- 4 tablespoons vegetable broth
- 3 cm ginger
- 1 teaspoon dates - balsamic vinegar

Preparation:

1. Peel carrots and cut into small pieces.
2. Heat the Dutch oven. Roast the pumpkin seeds and place in a small bowl.
3. Put the nut oil in the Dutch Oven and heat. Add the carrots and chillies and cook.
4. Remove the mixture and puree with an immersion blender.
5. Boil the vegetable stock, milk and cream in the Dutch oven. Add the mashed carrot mixture and mix. Boil again. Finished!
6. Enjoy and serve the finished soup.

SPANISH BEAN SOUP

Serving:4 - Prep time: 40 minutes

Ingredients:

- 4 chicken breast fillets
- 2 bulbs of fennel
- 2 onions
- 2 carrots
- 2 lemons
- 4 tablespoons olive oil
- 2 tablespoons of fennel seeds
- 200 ml vegetable broth
- 1 sprig of dill
- Salt and pepper

Preparation:

1. Peel the onion, carrot and fennel and cut into small pieces. Cut the lemon into small slices. Season chicken breast with salt and pepper.
2. Heat the olive oil in the Dutch Oven. Fry the onion, fennel, fennel seeds, carrots and lemon. Add the chicken breast and sauté for 2 minutes.
3. Then bake with the lid closed over low heat from above and below (approx. 6 briquettes each) for approx. 15 to 20 minutes.
4. Serve the finished dish decorated with dill and enjoy.

GARLIC SOUP

Serving:4 - Preparation time: 50 min

Ingredients:

- 200 g of smoked ham
- 5 cloves of garlic
- 4 tablespoons olive oil
- 5 hard-boiled eggs
- 1.5 l vegetable broth
- Salt and pepper
- Paprika powder

Preparation:

1. Peel the garlic cloves and cut into small pieces.
2. Heat the olive oil in the Dutch Oven. Add the garlic and ham and sauté.
3. Add vegetable broth and mix well. Season with salt, pepper and paprika.
4. Let the soup simmer from below with the lid closed and low heat for about 20 minutes.
5. Peel the hard-boiled eggs and add to the soup.
6. Serve and enjoy the finished soup.

POTATO SOUP WITH SAUSAGES

Serving:4 - Prep time: 90 minutes

Ingredients:

- 10 potatoes
- 1 bunch of soup vegetables
- 2 bay leaves
- Salt and pepper
- 4 sausages
- 1 liter of vegetable broth
- 2 carrots
- Nutmeg

Preparation:

1. Peel and dice potatoes and carrots. Wash and chop the soup vegetables. quarter sausages.
2. Put all the ingredients together in the Dutch Oven and cook for about 1 hour. Season with salt, pepper and nutmeg.
3. Before serving, remove the bay leaves. Finished!

CHICKPEA SOUP

Serving:4 - Preparation time: 30 min

Ingredients:

- 300 g chickpeas, cooked
- 2 sweet potatoes
- 2 cm piece of ginger
- 2 onions
- 500 ml coconut milk
- 600 ml vegetable broth
- 3 tablespoons coconut oil
- 1 tsp nutmeg
- Salt and pepper

Preparation:

1. Peel and finely chop the onion and ginger. Peel the sweet potato, wash and cut into small cubes.
2. Heat the oil in the Dutch oven. Fry onions and ginger. Add sweet potato and deglaze with vegetable broth. Simmer for about 15 minutes over medium heat.
3. Add chickpeas and simmer for another 5 minutes.
4. Remove from the embers. Add coconut milk and puree in blender until creamy. Season to taste with nutmeg, salt and pepper.
5. Serve in deep plates and enjoy.

LENTIL SOUP

Serving:4 - Preparation time: 70 min

Ingredients:

- 400 grams of lentils
- 4 medium potatoes
- 4 carrots

- 1.5 l vegetable broth

Preparation:

1. Peel potatoes and carrots, wash and cut into small cubes.
2. Pour the vegetable stock into the Dutch Oven and bring to the boil.
3. Add potatoes, carrots and lentils and simmer for 60 minutes with closed lid and medium heat.
4. Arrange on deep plates and enjoy.

SUGAR PEA SOUP WITH MINT

Serving:4 - Preparation time: 20 min

Ingredients:

- 4 shallots
- 20 g organic butter
- 400 g frozen organic peas
- 750 ml vegetable stock
- 200 ml organic cream
- 2 tablespoons of linseed oil
- Salt and pepper
- Mint to decorate.

Preparation:

1. Dice shallots. Heat the butter in the Dutch oven and sauté the shallots until translucent.
2. Add the peas and sauté.
3. Boil the vegetable broth, add to the peas and simmer for 5 minutes.
4. Puree the pea stock and pass through a fine sieve. Season with salt and pepper.
5. Finally, cut the mint leaves into fine strips and add to the soup.
6. Whip the cream until stiff and pull it through the hot soup.
7. Serve and enjoy.

TOMATO COCONUT SOUP

Serving:4 - Preparation time: 20 min

Ingredients:

- 4 spring onions
- 400ml tomatoes, strained
- 250 ml coconut milk
- 150 ml vegetable broth
- 2 tablespoons freshly squeezed orange juice
- 1 clove of garlic
- 2 pinches of Sambal Oelek
- 3 pinches of cumin
- Salt and cayenne pepper
- Coconut oil for frying

Preparation:

1. Wash the spring onions and cut into fine rings. Peel and press the garlic.
2. Heat the oil in the Dutch oven and sauté the spring onions and garlic for about 3 minutes until translucent.
3. Add tomatoes, coconut milk, vegetable stock and orange juice and mix well.
4. Let everything simmer on low heat for 5 to 6 minutes. Season with salt, cumin, cayenne pepper and sambal oelek and taste.
5. Serve and enjoy.

FRESH PEAR SOUP

Serving:4 - Preparation time: 50 min

Ingredients:

- 4 pears
- ½ celery
- 4 potatoes
- 2 onions
- 2 tablespoons canola oil
- 1.5 l vegetable broth
- 100 g of crème fraîche
- 1 tsp oregano
- Some lemon juice
- Pepper and salt
- Nutmeg

Preparation:

1. Peel and roughly dice the potatoes. Peel and chop the onions. Roughly dice the celery. Wash and dice the pear.
2. Heat the oil in the Dutch oven. Sweat onions. Then add the potatoes and celery and sauté.
3. Then add the pear pieces, sauté briefly and then deglaze with vegetable stock. Simmer everything together for about 30 minutes.
4. Stir in the crème fraîche and season with oregano, nutmeg, salt, pepper and lemon juice.
5. Serve and enjoy.

CHEESE LEEK SOUP

Serving:4 - Preparation time: 50 min

Ingredients:

- 300 g Emmental cheese
- 4 spring onions
- 1 liter of vegetable broth
- ¼ Hokkaido pumpkin
- 250 ml milk
- 70 grams of butter
- 70 grams of flour

Preparation:

1. Cut the spring onions into rings. Finely grate the pumpkin.

2. Heat the butter in the Dutch Oven. Add spring onions. Then slowly add the flour and mix well. Gradually add the milk and continue to stir well so that a creamy mass is formed.
3. Add broth and bring to a boil. Add the pumpkin shavings and simmer uncovered for about 15 minutes. Stir in cheese and cook and stir until melted.
4. Serve and enjoy.

RED CABBAGE SOUP WITH APPLES

Serving:4 - Preparation time: 50 min

Ingredients:

- 500 g red cabbage (fresh)
- 2 onions
- 6 potatoes
- 3 tablespoons olive oil
- 1 liter of vegetable broth
- 100 ml white wine (dry)
- 2 oranges
- 1 cm ginger
- 1 tablespoon of raspberry vinegar
- 3 apples
- 1 tablespoon maple syrup
- Salt and pepper

Preparation:

1. Halve the red cabbage, remove the stalk and cut into thin strips. Peel and finely chop the onions and ginger. Peel and dice the potatoes. Peel 1 orange and cut into pieces. Squeeze 1 orange. Wash and roughly chop the apples.
2. Heat the oil in the Dutch oven. Fry onions and ginger. Add the potatoes and red cabbage and sauté for about 5 minutes.
3. Deglaze with white wine and let it boil down. Then add the vegetable stock, raspberry vinegar, maple syrup, salt and pepper and simmer with the lid closed for about 30 minutes.
4. Add orange juice and apples and simmer for another 10 minutes.
5. Serve with orange slices and enjoy.

SPICY MEAT SOUP

Serving:6 - Preparation time: 150 min

Ingredients:

- 500 g turkey
- 3 onions
- 1 teaspoon of vegetable stock powder
- 500 grams of mushrooms
- 2 peppers
- 1 can of tomato passata
- ½ can of pineapple
- 300 g peas (frozen)
- 250ml salsa

- 200 ml curry ketchup
- 500 ml milk
- 500 ml cream
- Some water
- 2 tablespoons olive oil

Preparation:

1. Rinse and dice the meat. Clean the peppers and mushrooms and cut into large cubes.
2. Heat the oil in the Dutch oven and fry the meat with the peppers. Season with salt, pepper and bouillon powder.
3. Add the remaining ingredients to the Dutch Oven except for the water and mix well.
4. Pour enough water into the pot to cover the mixture.
5. Simmer over medium heat from below and high heat from above for about 1 ½ to 2 hours.
6. Serve and enjoy.

TOMATO SOUP

Serving:4 - Preparation time: 20 min

Ingredients:

- 1 can of tomato passata
- 1 may have chopped tomatoes
- 1 can of kidney beans
- 1 clove of garlic
- 1 can of corn
- 1 onion
- 500 ml vegetable broth
- 100 g of crème fraîche
- 2 tablespoons olive oil
- Paprika powder
- Salt and pepper

Preparation:

1. Peel and finely chop the onion and garlic.
2. Heat the oil in the Dutch Oven and sauté the onions and garlic. Deglaze with the two cans of tomatoes and the vegetable broth.
3. Add corn and kidney beans. Then stir in the crème fraîche. Season to taste and simmer with the lid on for about 10 minutes.
4. Serve and enjoy.

GARDEN SOUP

Serving:4 - Prep time: 80 minutes

Ingredients:

- 6 turnips
- 4 carrots
- 2 onions
- 4 tomatoes
- 4 celery
- 300 grams of yoghurt

- 500 ml vegetable broth
- 2 tablespoons canola oil
- 2 tablespoons of white wine vinegar
- Salt and pepper

Preparation:

1. Peel and chop onions. Peel and dice the carrots. Wash tomatoes and celery and cut into pieces. Wash beetroot and cut into small pieces.
2. Heat the oil in the Dutch oven. Add onions and sauté. Place the remaining vegetables in the Dutch Oven and fry.
3. Deglaze with vegetable broth and white wine vinegar and let everything simmer for about 40 minutes. Season with salt and pepper.
4. Fold in the yoghurt. The soup is ready.
5. Serve and enjoy.

BEETROOT SOUP

Serving:4 -Preparation time: 35 min

Ingredients:

- 500 g beetroot
- 2 cm ginger
- 2 potatoes
- 2 tsp lemon juice
- 2 tsp olive oil
- 1 tsp turmeric
- 1 tsp coriander powder
- 600ml of water
- Salt and pepper

Preparation:

1. Wash potatoes and beetroot and cut into small pieces.
2. Heat a Dutch Oven with oil and add ginger, turmeric and coriander and sauté.
3. After about 1 minute add the potatoes and beets and let simmer. Simmer for 20 minutes over medium heat with the lid closed. Season to taste with lemon juice and salt.
4. Puree the entire mixture with an immersion blender.
5. Serve and enjoy the finished soup.

CHICKEN MUSHROOM SOUP

Serving:4 - Prep time: 40 minutes

Ingredients:

- 2 chicken breast fillets
- 1000 grams of mushrooms
- 200 grams of peas
- 500ml of water
- 500 ml milk
- 200 g processed cheese
- 2 carrots
- 2 onions
- 1 clove of garlic

- 2 tablespoons of fresh herbs
- 3 tablespoons canola oil
- Paprika powder
- Chili flakes
- Salt and pepper

Preparation:

1. Dice the chicken breast. Slice the mushrooms. Peel onion and garlic and chop finely. dice carrots
2. Put oil in the Dutch Oven. Add the onions, garlic and chicken to the Dutch Oven and sauté. Add mushrooms and carrots and sauté.
3. Taste, laze with water and milk. Then add peas. Finally stir in the melted cheese.
4. Let everything boil again. Season with salt, pepper, chilli flakes, paprika powder and herbs.
5. Serve and enjoy.

POTATO AND CHEESE SOUP WITH CORN

Serving:6 - Preparation time: 50 min

Ingredients:

- 2 tablespoons canola oil
- 500 grams of potatoes
- 750 ml milk
- 2 cans of corn
- 180 g grated mozzarella
- 1 tablespoon flour
- 2 onions
- 500 g of crème fraîche
- Salt, pepper, nutmeg
- Mixed herbs

Preparation:

1. Peel and chop onions. Peel and dice the potatoes.
2. Heat the oil in the Dutch oven. Sweat onions. Dust the potatoes with flour and place in the Dutch Oven.
3. Carefully stir in the milk and season with salt, pepper and nutmeg. Cook.
4. Then add the corn, cheese, herbs and crème fraîche and simmer for about 20 minutes.
5. The soup is ready when the cheese has melted and the potatoes are cooked.
6. Serve and enjoy.

MANGO SOUP

Serving:4 - Preparation time: 30 min

Ingredients:

- 1 mango
- 500 g mini carrots
- 1 tablespoon of olive oil
- 2 onions
- 200ml of water
- Herbal salt and pepper

- 2 tablespoons of balsamic vinegar

Preparation:

1. Peel the mango and cut into small pieces. Wash the mini carrots and cut into small pieces.
2. Peel the onion and cut into small pieces. Place in the Dutch Oven with a little olive oil and fry.
3. After 2 minutes add water, carrots and mango pieces.
4. After another 2 minutes add the remaining ingredients, season and simmer for 10 minutes.
5. Serve and enjoy the finished soup.

FISH SOUP

Serving:4 - Preparation time: 20 min

Ingredients:

- 400 g mare fruit
- 3 onions
- 2 carrots
- 500 ml fish stock
- 200 g of tomato passata 2 cloves of garlic
- 1 tsp thyme
- 1 orange
- Salt and pepper
- 2 fennel

Preparation:

1. Peel, wash and cut vegetables into small pieces.
2. Heat the fish stock in the pot and add the vegetables.
3. Finely chop the garlic and onion and add to the pot.
4. Add the defrosted fish to the saucepan, mix well and leave for 5 minutes.
5. Squeeze the orange, add it and mix well. Season with salt and pepper.
6. Serve and enjoy the finished soup.

MUSHROOM SOUP

Serving:4 - Preparation time: 50 min

Ingredients:

- 2 onions
- 400 grams of mushrooms
- 200 grams of mushrooms
- 1 liter of vegetable broth
- 2 tablespoons olive oil
- Salt and pepper

Preparation:

1. Peel the onions and cut them into small pieces.
2. Heat some olive oil in the Dutch Oven. Fry the onions. Wash, cut and add mushrooms and mushrooms.
3. Add vegetable broth and mix well. Simmer with the lid on for about 50 minutes.
4. Puree the soup with a hand blender and season with salt and pepper.

5. Serve and enjoy the finished soup.

POTATO SOUP WITH SPINACH

Serving:4 - Preparation time: 25 min

Ingredients:

- 600 g spinach leaves
- 200 grams of potatoes
- 1 liter of vegetable broth
- 1 tablespoon coconut oil
- 200 ml coconut milk
- 1 tsp curry powder
- 2 teaspoons lemon juice
- Salt and pepper

Preparation:

1. Wash spinach. Peel the potatoes, cut into small pieces and cook in boiling water in the Dutch oven. Put aside.
2. Heat coconut oil in the Dutch Oven. Add the spinach and potatoes and sauté.
3. Add vegetable broth and bring to the boil.
4. Mix everything well with a mixer until a creamy mass is formed.
5. Add coconut milk and season with curry powder, salt, pepper and lemon juice and mix well.
6. Serve and enjoy the finished soup.

VEGETABLE SOUP WITH INSERT

Serving:4 - Preparation time: 50 min

Ingredients:

- 2 tsp marjoram
- 600 ml vegetable broth
- 1 turnip greens
- 50 g Parmesan cheese
- 2 green onions 4 carrots
- 4 potatoes
- 200 g cherry tomatoes
- 1 tablespoon of olive oil
- Salt and pepper

Preparation:

1. Wash vegetables and potatoes and cut into small pieces.
2. Pour some olive oil into the Dutch Oven. Add vegetables and sauté.
3. Pour in vegetable stock and season with marjoram, salt and pepper.
4. Allow the soup to simmer for a few minutes, decorate with Parmesan and serve and enjoy.

COCONUT PUMPKIN SOUP

Serving:4 - Preparation time: 35 min

Ingredients:

- 2 shallots
- 1 clove of garlic
- 1 Hokkaido pumpkin
- 2 carrots
- 60 ml orange juice
- 2 cm ginger
- 300 ml vegetable broth
- 250 ml coconut milk
- 1 tsp curry powder
- Some coconut oil
- Salt and pepper
- Nutmeg

Preparation:

1. Peel and finely chop the shallots, ginger and garlic. Wash and chop the Hokkaido pumpkin. Peel and finely chop the carrots and ginger.
2. Put the ginger, garlic and shallots in the Dutch Oven and sauté in a little oil. Add the pumpkin and carrot and sauté.
1. Taste, laze with vegetable broth and coconut milk and simmer over low heat for about 25 minutes.
2. Add orange juice.
3. Then puree everything with a blender. Season with salt, pepper, curry powder and nutmeg.
4. Serve and enjoy.

PEA SOUP

Serving:4 - Preparation time: 20 min

Ingredients:

- 300 g green peas
- 300 grams of potatoes
- 1 onion
- 2 carrots
- 750 ml vegetable stock
- 1 tsp olive oil
- Salt and pepper

Preparation:

1. Wash, peel and cut the carrots, onions and potatoes into small pieces.
2. Bring the peas to a boil in the Dutch oven together with the vegetable stock.
3. Add the potatoes and other vegetables. Bring everything to a boil over medium heat and season.
4. Add olive oil and puree everything with a hand blender. Boil again.
5. Serve and enjoy

DANDELION SOUP

Serving:4 - Preparation time: 60 min

Ingredients:

- 150 grams of dandelion
- 300 g arugula
- 2 onions
- 2 cloves of garlic 4 potatoes
- 1 tsp olive oil
- 600 ml vegetable broth
- Salt and pepper

Preparation:

1. Wash and finely chop the dandelion and rocket. Wash potatoes and cut into small pieces. Peel onion and garlic clove and cut into small pieces.
2. Sweat the onions, garlic and potatoes in a pan with a little oil.
3. Add all other ingredients and simmer for 15 minutes with the lid closed over low heat.
4. Remove and puree with a hand blender. Season with salt and pepper. Finished!
5. Alternatively, when there's no outlet outside, it can be enjoyed as a single-ingredient broth.

CORN SOUP

Serving:4 - Preparation time: 30 min

Ingredients:

- 2 cans of corn
- 2 onions
- 3 cloves of garlic
- 2 tablespoons of olive oil 500 ml of vegetable broth
- 100 ml coconut milk
- 4 tsp lemon juice
- Salt and pepper

Preparation:

1. Remove the corn from the can and drain off the liquid. Peel onions and garlic and cut into small pieces.
2. Put the corn, onions and garlic in the pot and sauté with a little olive oil. Season with salt and pepper.
3. Add the vegetable broth and simmer over medium heat, uncovered, for about 10 minutes.
4. Then add coconut milk and lemon juice. Let simmer for another 5 minutes.
5. Serve and enjoy the finished soup.

I love COOKING

110

BREAD, DESSERTS, AND CAKES

APPLE STRUDEL

Serving:4 - Prep time: 80 minutes

Ingredients:

- 1 kg of apples
- 80 grams of butter
- 50 g breadcrumbs
- 50 grams of raisins
- 50 g chopped hazelnuts
- 100 grams of sugar
- Brand of a vanilla bean
- 2 tablespoons lemon juice
- Cinammon
- 5 tablespoons of lukewarm water
- 1 pinch of salt
- 200 grams of flour
- 60 grams of butter
- Egg yolk

Preparation:

1. For the dough: Put the flour, water, salt and melted butter in a bowl and knead into a smooth, slightly elastic dough. Form the dough into a ball and let it rest in a warm bowl for 30 minutes.
1. 1st 2.   For the strudel: wash the apples, peel, core, cut into small pieces and mix well with the lemon juice and vanilla pulp. Lay out the strudel dough on a kitchen towel to form a thin square and brush with a little butter. Spread the breadcrumbs, raisins, pieces of apple, sugar, hazelnuts and cinnamon evenly over the dough. The edges should remain about 3-4 cm free. Roll up the strudel with the kitchen towel from the long side and press well together at the end. Line the Dutch Oven with kitchen paper and heat from the bottom over low heat and from the top over medium heat. Brush the outside of the strudel with egg yolk and place it in a ring in the Dutch oven. Bake with the lid on for about 40 minutes until the strudel is golden brown. Serve and enjoy. Vanilla ice cream goes very well with it.

APPLE COMPOTE

Serving:4 - Preparation time: 15 min

Ingredients:

- 750 grams of apples
- 5 tablespoons of water
- 1-2 tablespoons of cane sugar
- Cinammon

Preparation:

1. Wash the apples, remove the core, core and cut into small pieces.

2. Simmer in the Dutch Oven with water and sugar for about 10 to 15 minutes until the apples are soft.
3. Then puree with a magic stick and serve with cinnamon and enjoy.

BAKED APPLE WITH MARZIPAN

Serving:4 - Preparation time: 30 min

Ingredients:

- 4 apples
- 60 grams of walnuts
- 60 grams of raisins
- 1 tablespoon of honey
- Cinammon
- 60 g raw marzipan mass
- 20 grams of butter
- 2 tablespoons chopped almonds
- 200 ml apple juice

Preparation:

1. Wash and core the apples.
2. Mix the walnuts, raisins, honey, butter, marzipan, cinnamon and almonds well and fill into the apples.
3. Heat the Dutch Oven, put the apples and the apple juice in the Dutch Oven.
4. Simmer the baked apples for about half an hour over low heat from below and medium heat from above and with the lid closed.
5. Serve and enjoy.

CREME BRULEE

Serving:4 - Prep Time: 2 hrs 40 mins

Ingredients:

- 30 grams of sugar
- 30 grams of cane sugar
- 250 ml cream
- 3 egg yolks
- 1 vanilla bean

Preparation:

1. Scrape the pulp out of the vanilla bean and heat it up in the Dutch oven together with the cream. At the same time, mix the egg yolk and sugar into a creamy mass.
2. Then slowly add the vanilla cream to the egg yolk mixture. Not too fast so the egg doesn't curdle.
3. Pour the mixture into 4 ovenproof ramekins. Then lightly cover the bottom of the Dutch Oven with water and put in the molds. Allow to set in the Dutch Oven over medium heat for approx. 35 minutes.
4. Let cool outside for at least 2 hours.

5. Then spread some cane sugar on the surface of the molds and caramelize the cane sugar with a Bunsen burner.
6. Serve and enjoy!

RICE PUDDING WITH WARM CHERRIES

Serving:4 - Prep time: 45 minutes

Ingredients:

- 400 g rice pudding
- 1 liter of milk
- ½ vanilla bean
- 3 tablespoons of sugar
- Zest of half a lemon
- 300 g cherries (from the jar)
- ½ pack vanilla pudding powder

Preparation:

1. Scrape the seeds out of the vanilla pod and place in the Dutch Oven along with 2 tablespoons of sugar, milk, rice pudding and lemon zest. Cook over low heat from below and medium heat from above for about 35 to 40 minutes. Stir occasionally. Remove, pour into bowls and let cool.
2. Now put the remaining sugar, the cherries with their juice and the vanilla pudding powder in the Dutch Oven and simmer gently for about 10 minutes. Finished!
3. Serve both together and enjoy.

VANILLA PUDDING

Serving:4 - Preparation time: 30 min

Ingredients:

- 6 tablespoons of sugar
- 80 grams of butter
- 50 g cornstarch
- 300 ml milk
- 2 egg yolks
- 1 packet of baking powder
- 1 vanilla bean
- 100 grams of flour

Preparation:

1. Mix butter and sugar well. Then add the egg yolks and stir until creamy. Then mix the flour, cornstarch and baking powder and add to the remaining ingredients along with the vanilla seeds and milk.
2. Pour the pudding mixture into the Dutch Oven and simmer until the pudding has thickened, about 20 minutes. Finished!
3. Serve chilled and enjoy.

STRAWBERRY SEMOLINA

Serving:4 - Preparation time: 10 min

Ingredients:

- 140 g soft wheat semolina
- 4 eggs
- 3 pinches of stevia
- 1 tsp cinnamon
- Some lemon juice
- 1 liter of milk
- 400 grams of strawberries
- 1 pinch of salt

Preparation:

1. Separate eggs. Beat the egg whites and put the yolks in a bowl. Cut strawberries into pieces.
2. Bring the milk to a boil in the Dutch Oven. Mix the soft wheat semolina, salt and stevia and add to the milk. Simmer for 1 minute while stirring constantly.
3. Add the semolina pudding to the egg yolk and mix well. Gently fold in the egg whites and finally fold in the strawberries.
4. Serve sprinkled with cinnamon and enjoy.

CHOCOLATE PUDDING WITH COCONUT FLAKES

Ingredients:

- 1l almond milk
- 4 tablespoons of cornstarch
- 5 tablespoons of sugar
- 2 tablespoons of baking cocoa
- 6 tablespoons coconut flakes.

Preparation:

1. Mix 12 tablespoons of almond milk with cocoa powder, coconut flakes, cornstarch and sugar with a whisk.
2. Bring the remaining almond milk to a boil in the Dutch oven.
3. Once the almond milk has boiled, add the cocoa-starch mixture to the milk and simmer with a whisk for 30 seconds, stirring constantly.
4. Remove from the embers and place in bowls.
5. Serve and enjoy.

PUMPKIN BREAD

Serving:6 - Prep time: 180 minutes

Ingredients:

- 700 g Hokkaido pumpkin
- 30 grams of butter
- 20 grams of fresh yeast
- 100 ml milk
- 400 grams of rye flour
- 350 grams of wheat flour
- 2 tablespoons of salt
- 3 sprigs of rosemary
- A pinch of sugar
- 4 tablespoons olive oil

Preparation:

1. Cut the pumpkin into pieces and wrap in aluminum foil and bake in the Dutch oven for about 60 minutes until the flesh is soft. Removed. Put in the blender with a little olive oil, rosemary and sugar and puree well.
2. Put the butter, milk and yeast in the Dutch Oven and heat slightly. Add the pumpkin flesh, flour and salt and knead everything into a nice dough. Leave face down for 40 minutes.
3. Remove and place in a casserole dish. Then leave uncovered for another 60 minutes.
4. Then place in the Dutch Oven and bake over low heat from above and below (approx. 6 briquettes below and 7 briquettes above) for 60 minutes.
5. Leave to cool. Finished!

FLAX BREAD

Serving:4 - Prep time: 90 minutes

Ingredients:

- 250 grams of flax flour
- 120 grams of almond flour
- 40 g coconut flour
- 4 eggs
- 7 grams of yeast
- 1 tsp sugar
- 300 ml almond milk
- 2 tsp salt

Preparation:

1. Put all the ingredients in a bowl and knead into a dough.
2. Cover the dough and let it rise in a warm place for about 60 minutes.
3. Knead the dough again and place in the Dutch Oven. Dust the Dutch Oven with some flour beforehand. Bake the bread for about 45 minutes over low heat from below and medium heat from above.
4. Allow the finished bread to cool, serve and enjoy.

BEER BREAD

Serving:4 - Preparation time: 18h

Ingredients:

- 150 grams of wheat flour
- 350 grams of rye flour
- 10 grams of yeast
- 2 tablespoons of salt
- 80 ml root beer
- 200ml water (lukewarm)
- 50 g of pumpkin seeds

Preparation:

1. Knead the yeast, salt, flour, malt beer, pumpkin seeds and water into a dough. Leave covered in the fridge overnight.
2. Fill the dough into a loaf tin and bake in the Dutch oven for about 45 minutes at high heat from above and medium heat from below.
3. Halfway through cooking, look under the lid and turn the heat down a little if needed.
4. Leave to cool. Finished!
5. Serve and enjoy.

QUARK BREAD

Serving:4 - Prep time: 90 minutes

Ingredients:

- 300 g low-fat quark
- 8 eggs
- 100 grams of almonds
- 100 grams of flaxseed
- 2 tablespoons flour
- 1 packet of baking powder
- 1 tsp salt
- 2 tablespoons sunflower seeds
- Butter

Preparation:

1. Place cottage cheese, eggs, and baking powder in a bowl and mix well.
2. Add the other ingredients and mix well.
3. Grease a baking pan with butter and pour the batter into the baking pan. Sprinkle with sunflower seeds.
4. Place the baking tin in the Dutch Oven and bake at medium heat from above and below for approx. 90 minutes.
5. Let the finished bread cool and serve

PUMPKIN SEED BREAD

Serving:4 - Preparation time: 75 min

Ingredients:

- 500 g spelled flour
- 500ml of water
- 75 g of flaxseed
- 100 g of pumpkin seeds
- 25 grams of sesame
- 1½ tsp salt
- 1 packet of baking powder
- 1 tsp olive oil

Preparation:

1. Mix flour and baking powder.
2. Mix in the flaxseeds, pumpkin seeds, sesame and salt.
3. Add lukewarm water and knead well by hand.
4. Place the bread mixture in an oiled loaf pan and lightly brush the surface of the mixture with water.
5. Place in the Dutch Oven and bake for 60 minutes over medium heat from below and high heat from above.
6. Allow warm bread to cool, serve and enjoy

SPICY CHEDDAR BREAD

Serving:4 - Prep time: 1 day 50 minutes

Ingredients:

- 3 cups whole wheat flour
- 1 tsp yeast
- 1 tsp salt
- 1 cup cheddar cheese
- 2 chili peppers
- 1 medium jalapeño
- 1 ½ cups of warm water

Preparation:

1. 1. Dice the grated cheese. Cut the jalapeño into rings. Cut chili peppers into small pieces.
2. 2. Set aside 4 tablespoons of cheese and the jalapeño.
3. 3. In a large bowl, mix together the flour, salt, and yeast. Then add the remaining cheese and the chillies and mix well.
4. 4. Add water and stir until a slightly sticky dough forms. Leave covered overnight.
5. 5. Then shape into a large loaf and place in the already preheated Dutch Oven. Bake on medium heat for 30 minutes on top and bottom.
6. 6. Then pour the remaining cheese and jalapeño over the dough and bake for another 10 to 15 minutes on low heat from below and high heat from above. Finished!

SUNFLOWER BREAD WITH POPPY SEEDS

Serving:1 - Preparation time: 80 minutes; Rest time: 1 hour

Ingredients:

- 500 g flour type 405
- 80 g spelled flour
- 300 ml water, lukewarm
- 20 grams of dry yeast
- 1 tsp sugar
- 1 tablespoon apple cider vinegar
- 2 tablespoons olive oil
- 50 grams of poppy seeds
- 150 g sunflower seeds
- 1 tsp salt
- Baking paper

Preparation:

1. First knead half of the poppy seeds together with the other ingredients into a dough.
2. Cover and let rise for an hour in a warm place.
3. Then knead the dough well and form it into a loaf.
4. Sprinkle this bread with the remaining poppy seeds.
5. Now line the Dutch Oven with the baking paper.
6. Add the bread and bake with the lid closed for 70 minutes at 190° Celsius.

GRAIN BREAD

Serving:1 - Prep time: 75 minutes; Rest time: 1 hour

Ingredients:

- 600 g flour type 550
- 350 grams of cornmeal
- 500 ml water, lukewarm
- 250 ml buttermilk, lukewarm
- 1 yeast cube
- 1 tsp sugar
- 2 tsp salt
- Baking paper

Preparation:

1. First, all the ingredients are put in a bowl and kneaded together well.
2. Then cover the dough and let it rise for 30 minutes.
3. Knead the dough again and let it rise for another 30 minutes.
4. Now the Dutch Oven is lined with baking paper.
5. A loaf of bread is formed from the dough and placed in the Black Pot.
6. Bake with the lid closed for 65 minutes at 190° Celsius.

HERB BREAD

Serving:1 - Preparation time: 60 minutes; Rest time: 1 hour

Ingredients:

- 700 g flour type 405
- 400 ml water, lukewarm
- 2 packets of dry yeast
- 100 g herbs, chopped
- Baking paper

Preparation:

1. First, all the ingredients are put in a bowl and kneaded together well.
2. Then cover the dough and let it rest in a warm place for 1 hour.
3. Then carefully knead the dough again and shape it into a loaf.
4. Now line the Dutch Oven with the baking paper and place the loaf inside.
5. Bake with the lid closed for 50 minutes at 190° Celsius.

CHILI BREAD

Serving:1 - Preparation time: 80 minutes; Rest time: 30 minutes

Ingredients:

- 700 g flour type 405
- 400ml of water
- 2 packets of dry yeast
- 1 tablespoon of salt
- 2 tablespoons chili, dried
- 2 peppers, red and yellow
- 1 tablespoon of sugar
- 1 tsp marjoram, dried
- Baking paper

Preparation:

1. First, the peppers are washed, deseeded and cut into cubes.
2. Place the remaining ingredients in a bowl and add the diced peppers.
3. Need everything in a batter.
4. Cover and let rise in a warm place for 30 minutes.
5. Then form into a loaf.
6. Line the Dutch Oven with baking paper and place the bread inside.
7. Bake with the lid closed for 70 minutes at 175° Celsius

MUESLI BREAD

Serving:1 - Preparation time: 70 minutes; Rest time: 1 hour

Ingredients:

- 250 g fruit muesli
- 650ml buttermilk
- 380 g almond flour
- 50 grams of sugar
- 1 tablespoon oat bran
- 2 eggs
- 1 packet of baking powder
- ½ tsp salt
- 1 packet of vanilla sugar
- 60 grams of raisins
- Baking paper

Preparation:

1. First, put the granola, buttermilk, oat bran, and eggs in a bowl and mix together.
2. Cover and leave this mixture to rise for an hour.
3. Then add baking powder, salt, vanilla sugar, raisins, almond flour and sugar to the muesli mixture and knead.
4. Form a loaf of bread from the dough.
5. Line the Dutch Oven with baking paper and place the bread inside.
6. Bake with the lid closed for 60 minutes at 175° Celsius.

MULTIGRAIN BREAD

Serving:1 - Prep Time:

Ingredients:

- 300 g flour type 405
- 350 g flour type 550
- 1 yeast cube, fresh
- 500 ml vegetable stock, lukewarm
- 1 tablespoon of salt
- 80 g sunflower seeds
- 80 g of pumpkin seeds
- 50 grams of flaxseed
- 2 tbsp sesame seeds
- Baking paper

Preparation:

1. First, the yeast cube is crumbled and added to the vegetable broth. Stir briefly and let the yeast dissolve.
2. Put all the other ingredients, except for the sesame seeds, in a bowl, add the yeast mixture and knead well.
3. Then cover the dough and let it rise in a warm place for 1 hour.
4. Form the dough into a loaf and sprinkle with sesame seeds.
5. The Dutch Oven is lined with baking paper and the loaf of bread is placed inside.
6. Bake with the lid closed for 50 minutes at 190° Celsius

GARLIC CIABATTA

Serving:1 - Prep Time:

Ingredients:

- 500 g flour type 405
- 18 g yeast, fresh
- 350ml of water
- 2 tablespoons apple cider vinegar
- 1 tsp salt
- 5 cloves of garlic
- 1 teaspoon fresh thyme
- 1 tablespoon olive oil
- Baking paper

Preparation:

1. First chop the garlic finely.
2. Turn the lid upside down and pour in the oil. Add the garlic along with the thyme and sauté.
3. Then put the flour, yeast, water, apple cider vinegar and salt in a bowl and knead well. Cover the dough and let it rise for 30 minutes.
4. After this time add the garlic and knead again.
5. Now seal the dough airtight and let it rest for 12 hours.
6. The next day, gently shape the dough into a loaf.
1. 7th 7.   Line the Dutch pot with parchment paper and place the loaf on top.
7. Bake for 45 minutes with the lid closed and 190° Celsius.

PULLED BREAD WITH HERBS AND CHEESE (1300G)

Serving:4 - Prep time: 45 minutes

Ingredients:

- 750 g wheat flour type 550
- 1 yeast cube
- 500 ml warm water
- 4 tablespoons of sugar
- 4 tsp smoked salt
- 2 tablespoons of oil
- Oil for brushing
- 1 pot of basil
- 1 sprig of sage
- Thyme
- Rosemary
- 100 g Parmesan cheese

Preparation:

1. Knead all the ingredients for the dough, herbs and cheese in a food processor on medium speed for about 5 minutes. If the dough is a bit sticky, add flour. Let the dough rise for 1 hour.
2. Shape the dough into small balls and brush with the remaining oil. Line the Dutch Oven with baking paper and place balls next to each other in the pan.

3. Close the lid, distribute the charcoal. After half an hour the bread is ready.

YEAST BRAID (1800 G)

Serving time: 18 - Prep time: 90 minutes

Ingredients:

- 1 kg wheat flour (type 405)
- 1 yeast cube
- ½ liter of milk
- 150 grams of butter
- 100 grams of sugar
- 2 tsp salt
- 3 eggs
- 1 tablespoon grated lemon zest
- 2 tablespoons of sugar

Preparation:

1. Dissolve the yeast with the sugar in a mug of lukewarm milk. Add lemon zest and 2 eggs, mix with hand mixer.
2. Sift flour into a mixing bowl. Add the yeast-egg-milk mixture, the softened butter and some salt. Knead for about 10 minutes. Let the dough rise for 2 hours. You should roughly double.
3. Knead on a floured surface and divide into 3 equal portions. Shape each portion into a strand. The 3 strands can now be braided into a braid.
4. Rub the inside of the Dutch Oven with plenty of flour. Lay out with baking paper. Place the braid in a spiral. Whisk an egg with a pinch of sugar and salt and brush the yeast braid with it. Sprinkle with sugar if you like. Close the Dutch Oven and let it rise for 30 minutes.
5. Put on the embers. Bake for about 45 minutes. Let the bread cool on a wire rack.

WHITE BREAD (850 G)

Serving:8 - Preparation time: 30 minutes

Ingredients:

- 500 g flour type 405 (does
- also half and half with wholemeal flour)
- 350ml of water
- 1 packet of dry yeast
- 1 tablespoon of sugar
- 1 tsp salt
- 2 tablespoons of oil

Preparation:

1. Mix the sugar with the dry yeast and 3 - 4 tablespoons of lukewarm water.
2. Place all other ingredients in a mixing bowl or food processor, then add the yeast mixture while stirring or kneading. Work the dough into a nice smooth mass. Let the dough rise for 30 minutes.

3. The dough is then placed in the mold and the top of the dough scored lightly with a sharp knife. This gives a nice crust when baking.
4. The Dutch oven is now on the embers and the white bread then needs about 50 minutes. After baking, remove the bread from the tin and let cool on a wire rack.

TOMATO BREAD (1,000 G)

Serving:10 - Preparation time: 30 minutes

Ingredients:

- 500 g flour type 405
- 350ml of water
- 20 grams of fresh yeast
- 160 g sun-dried tomatoes in oil
- 1 tablespoon of sugar
- 1 tsp salt
- 2 tablespoons olive oil
- 2 tablespoons Italian bruschetta –

Preparation:

1. First, completely dissolve the yeast with sugar in a cup of lukewarm water.
2. Combine flour, spices, olive oil and salt in a mixing bowl or food processor. Cut the sun-dried tomatoes into fine pieces and drain the oil in a sieve. Add the tomato pieces to the flour mixture and stir. Add the water-yeast-sugar mixture while stirring and knead everything with the food processor to a smooth dough.
3. Put the dough in the pot and let it rise in a warm place for 1 hour.
4. When the dough has risen nicely, it goes straight onto the embers. Line the Dutch Oven with baking paper. After about 1 hour you can use a wooden skewer to check whether the bread is done and the crust is nice and crispy. If some dough still sticks to the wooden skewer, extend the baking time by another 10-12 minutes.

MIXED RYE BREAD (400 G) BAKED IN THE OVEN

Serving:4 - Prep time: 105 minutes

Ingredients:

- 50 grams of rye flour
- 300 grams of wheat flour
- 10 grams of salt
- 1 packet of dry yeast
- 1 cup of warm water
- 1 packet of sourdough

Preparation:

1. Mix flour, salt and dry yeast in a bowl. Add the sourdough and the water and knead everything into a

dough. Cover the bowl and let the dough rise for an hour.
2. Knead the dough again on a floured work surface and shape into a loaf. Leave on for 30 minutes.
3. At the same time, preheat the oven with the Dutch Oven in it to 260 °C.
4. Place the bread in the Dutch Oven and bake for 30 minutes with the lid closed. Then bake for another 10 minutes without a lid so that the bread gets a nice colour.
5. During the baking time without the lid in the oven, check again and again whether the bread has the desired color.

CRUSTY BREAD (1,300 G) BAKED IN THE OVEN

Serve:13 - Prep time: 2 hours

Ingredients:

- 750 g flour type 550
- 500 grams of lukewarm water
- 60 grams of sunflower oil
- 2 packets of dry yeast
- 2 tsp salt

Preparation:

1. Dissolve yeast in a cup of lukewarm water. Mix all ingredients by hand until a sticky dough forms. Cover the mixing bowl and let the dough rise in a warm place for 30 minutes.
2. With floured hands and a spatula, remove the dough from the bowl. Flourless pieces over and over again until the clump of dough is completely loosened. Place the dough on the floured work surface.
3. Stretch the dough a little. Then fold the ends towards the middle to make a three-layer loaf. Dust lightly with flour to prevent the dough from sticking to the work surface. Then fold the dough again from top to bottom. Place the bread, smooth side up, in the warm Dutch oven lined with parchment paper.
4. Now put on the cold lid. The pot goes into the lukewarm oven. In about half an hour, the yeast will lift the dough and form beautiful loaves. Just check from time to time how big the dough piece has become and remember that the bread will rise a little while baking.
5. Bake the bread in the oven at 220°C for 45 minutes with the lid closed. Remove the bread from the oven and remove the lid. The bread has risen nicely and looks great, but still has a lot of steam.
6. So the whole pot, without the lid, goes back into the oven for 15-20 minutes at 160 °C. This will make the crust crispy and firm.
7. Let the bread cool on a wire rack

YOGHURT – BREAD (APPROX. 800G)

Serving:8 - Prep time: 150 minutes

Ingredients:

* 220 grams of lukewarm water
* 20 grams of fresh yeast
* 350 g wheat flour type 550
* 150 g spelled flour
* 140 g whole milk yoghurt
* (3.5 – 4.0% fat)
* 2 tsp salt
* 2 tablespoons balsamic vinegar
* 1.5 tsp baking malt
* 1 tsp honey

Preparation:

1. 1. Dissolve the yeast in lukewarm water. Place the remaining ingredients in a bowl and mix. Slowly add the yeast water and knead all the ingredients together.
2. 2. Cover the dough and let it rest in a floured bowl for about 1.5 hours. The risen dough is then folded, i.e. right to middle, left to middle, top to bottom and bottom to top. Then the bread is formed into a round shape and spread with the smooth side up with the whole milk yoghurt. Line the Dutch Oven with baking paper.
3. 3. Flour the top of the bread and carve a diamond pattern. The fire pot is closed and filled with the glowing briquettes
4. 4. The yoghurt crust should cool down for 1-2 hours before slicing.

PEACH CRUMBLE DESSERT

Serve:12 - Prep time: 35 minutes

Ingredients:

* 6 cups sliced peeled ripe peaches
* 1/4 cup packed brown sugar
* 3 tablespoons all-purpose flour
* 1 teaspoon of lemon juice
* 1/2 teaspoon grated lemon zest
* 1/2 teaspoon ground cinnamon
* 1 cup of sugar
* 1 teaspoon of baking powder
* Salt
* 1/4 teaspoon ground nutmeg
* 1 large egg, room temperature, lightly beaten
* 1/2 cup butter, melted and cooled
* Vanilla ice cream, optional
* Refine:
* 1 cup all-purpose flour.

Preparation:

1. Preheat the oven to 190 °C. Place the peaches in a greased shallow Dutch oven, cast-iron skillet, or casserole dish. In a small bowl, combine brown sugar, flour, lemon juice, lemon zest, and cinnamon; sprinkle over the peaches.
2. Mix flour, sugar, baking powder, salt and nutmeg. Beat in the egg until the mixture resembles coarse crumbs. Scatter over the peaches. Pour butter over the topping.
3. Bake for 35-40 minutes. Serve with ice if desired.

COOKIES WITH SAUCE

Serving:6 - Preparation time: 15 minutes

Ingredients:

* 1 packet of biscuits
* 1 tbsp oil
* 450 g crumbled sausage
* ¼ cup flour
* 2½ cups milk
* ½ teaspoon onion powder
* ⅓ tsp thyme
* 1 tsp pepper
* ⅓ tsp salt

Preparation:

1. Rub the bottom and sides of the oven with oil so that the
2. Cookies don't stick.
3. Arrange the biscuits in the Dutch oven so that they are barely touching. They will stretch, so leave some space between them.
4. Bake the cookies for 10 minutes, then check. Add time as needed.
5. In a separate pan, fry the sausage at medium temperature for 5-6 minutes.
6. Stir in the flour, mix with the sausage and coat in breadcrumbs. Begin adding the milk little by little, making sure to stir constantly.
7. Boil the mixture and wait until the mixture starts to thicken. stir constantly. Reduce temperature and simmer for 2 minutes. Season with salt, pepper, onion powder and thyme.

TASTY FEAST

Serving:3 – 4 - Prep time: 1 hour

Ingredients:

* 400g frozen buttermilk pancakes
* 4 eggs
* 1½ cups of coffee creamer
* 8 oz package of cocktail size smoked sausages, chopped
* 1½ cups shredded cheddar cheese
* Maple syrup

Preparation:

1. 1. Lightly oil the Dutch Oven. You can also line with aluminum foil and spray. Remove the pancakes from

the box, unwrap and carefully separate. Set aside to partially thaw.

2. 2. In a large bowl, beat eggs and creamer with a whisk. Roughly chop the pancakes. Add pancake pieces and chopped sausage to egg mixture; shake to coat.
3. 3. Leave on for 5 minutes. Pour the mixture into the prepared Dutch Oven.
4. 4. Bake at 180°C for 40 minutes. Sprinkle with cheese, cover and cook for a further 10-15 minutes until edges are set and light golden brown. Leave to rest for 10 minutes.
5. 5. Cut into squares; Serve with maple syrup.

LEMON BLUEBERRY COOKIES

Serving:9 - Preparation time: 20 minutes

Ingredients:

- 2 cups all-purpose flour
- ½ cup granulated sugar
- 2 teaspoons of baking soda
- ½ tsp baking powder
- ¼ tsp salt
- 225 g lemon yoghurt
- 1 egg
- ¼ cup butter, melted
- 1 tsp grated lemon zest
- 1 cup fresh or frozen and thawed blueberries
- Glaze:
- ½ cup powdered sugar
- 1 tablespoon lemon juice
- ½ tsp grated lemon zest

Preparation:

1. Lightly oil the Dutch Oven or place baking foil in it and spray.
2. Whisk together the flour, sugar, baking powder, and salt in a large bowl.
3. In another bowl, whisk together yogurt, egg, melted butter, and 1 teaspoon lemon zest until well combined.
4. Add liquid ingredients to the flour mixture; Stir until just moistened, then fold in the blueberries. Place ⅓ cups into prepared Dutch oven.
5. Bake at 200°C for at least 18 minutes or until golden brown. In a small bowl, mix the glaze ingredients together. Stir gently with the whisk. Drizzle the glaze over the warm cookies.

SAUSAGE AND FRIED POTATO WEDGES

Serve:12 - Prep time: 45 minutes

Ingredients:

- 450 g breakfast sausage
- ½ onion, diced
- 24 eggs
- 1 can of cream of mushroom soup
- 1 cup of milk
- 2 cups of cheese
- 1 pepper, diced
- 1 bag of hash browns
- 1 tablespoon seasonal salt

Preparation:

1. Place the sausage and ¼ of the onion in the Dutch Oven at 190 °C
2. Cook for 20 minutes or until sausage is brown.
3. In a separate bowl, mix together all the eggs, cream of mushroom soup, and milk. Add salt, the rest of the onion and paprika.
4. Remove the sausage and onion mixture from the Dutch Oven. Take half of the sausage and layer it on the bottom of the Dutch Oven. Next, place a quarter bag of rösti on top. Pour the egg mixture over the hash browns and meat layer, and sprinkle 2 handfuls of cheese over the egg mixture.
5. Add the remaining amount of sausage, onions and bacon for this layer. Place the remaining hash browns on top, place the lid on the Dutch oven and bake at 180°C for 45 minutes or until the eggs are cooked through.
6. Take the Dutch Oven out of the oven and remove the lid. Spread again with cheese. Cover for a few minutes until the cheese melts. Take out, let cool and cut into slices.

SOURDOUGH FRENCH TOAST

Serving: 4 - 6 - Prep time: 1 hour.

Ingredients:

- ½ loaf of sourdough bread
- 4 eggs
- 1 cup of milk
- ¼ cup cream
- ⅔ cup white sugar
- 1 tablespoon of vanilla
- ¼ cup flour
- ¼ cup brown sugar
- ½ teaspoon of cinnamon
- ⅛ teaspoon salt
- Add ½ butter, cut into pieces
- Glaze:
- ¾ cup powdered sugar
- 1.5 tablespoons milk (more if needed)

Preparation:

1. Use cooking spray to coat the oven. Tear the bread into bite-sized pieces and place evenly in the Dutch Oven. In a separate bowl, whisk together the eggs, milk, cream, sugar and vanilla. Pour the bread evenly over it.
2. Cover with the lid and let cool overnight. Combine flour, brown sugar, cinnamon, and salt in a bag. Add the chopped butter pieces to the flour mixture. Use your hands to crumble the butter and mixture inside the bag.

3. If you want the frosting, you can make it by mixing the 3 tbsp milk into the powdered sugar. To bake, remove the Dutch Oven and bag from the fridge. Sprinkle the crumb mixture evenly on top. Bake for 1 hour at 180°C.

TRAPPER BREAD

Serving:1 - Preparation time: 2 hours

Ingredients:

- 1 kg of wheat flour
- 600ml of water
- 1 packet of yeast
- 1 pinch of salt and sugar

Preparation:

1. Place the Dutch Oven on the embers and preheat.
2. Place the ingredients in a bowl and knead. Form the dough into a loaf, sprinkle with flour and place in the Dutch Oven. Bake bread for about 45 minutes.
3. Dust again with a little flour and bake for another 45 minutes at 220 °C.
4. Trapper bread goes perfectly with soups, chili or stews.

NAAN BREAD

Serving:6 - Prep time: 1 hour 30 minutes

Ingredients:

- 500 grams of wheat flour
- 125 g natural yoghurt
- 150 grams of butter
- 10 grams of yeast
- 5 cloves of garlic
- 200 ml milk
- some flour
- 1 pinch of salt and sugar

Preparation:

1. Pour the milk into a bowl, add the yeast and sugar and dissolve, stirring constantly. Cover everything and set aside for about 15 minutes.
2. Place the flour, yoghurt, 50 g butter and a pinch of salt in a bowl and make a well in the centre. Add the yeast mixture and knead into a dough. Cover and leave to rise for about 60 minutes.
3. Divide the dough into 6 equal parts and form into flatbreads. 4. Live and heat the charcoal under the Dutch Oven.
4. Heat the garlic and butter in the Dutch Oven and place in a separate bowl.
5. Fry the flatbreads individually with the garlic butter for about 5 minutes on both sides.
6. Serve with chili or stew and enjoy.

MIXED RYE BREAD

Serving:1 - Preparation time: about 12 hours

Ingredients:

- 355 grams of rye flour
- 390 grams of water
- 235 grams of wheat flour
- 12 grams of salt
- 5 g rye sourdough

Preparation:

1. Put the ingredients in a bowl and mix the dough. Then cover and let rise for 12 hours.
2. Occasionally e.g. Sprinkle flour on a work surface and shape the dough into a ball. Dust a bowl with flour and pour in the batter. Cover again and let rest for 12 hours.
3. Place the Dutch Oven in the oven and preheat to 250°C and put the dough in the Dutch Oven, lower the temperature to 230°C and bake the mixed rye bread for about 30 minutes.
4. Remove the lid from the Dutch oven and bake the bread for another 15 minutes.
5. Finally allow to cool, cut the bread and cover the slices.

CRUSTY BREAD

Serving:1 - Preparation time: about 23 hours

Ingredients:

- 760 grams of flour
- 1 bread
- 500 g water (lukewarm)
- 60 grams of sunflower oil
- 1.5 packets of dry yeast
- 2 teaspoons of salt

Preparation:

1. Put the ingredients in a bowl and mix well. Cover and let the dough rise for about 30 minutes.
2. Preheat the Dutch Oven in the oven to 50 °C.
3. Sprinkle flour on a work surface, shape the dough and fold the ends towards the middle. Put the dough and some flour in the Dutch Oven. Seal the bread and bake for about 30 minutes.
4. Raise temperature to 450°F and bake crusty bread for another 45 minutes.
5. After 60 minutes, the crusty bread can be sliced and topped.

TYROLEAN FARMER'S BREAD

Serving:1 - Preparation time: 1 hour 20 minutes

Ingredients:

- 750 grams of wheat flour
- 75 g diced ham
- 1.5 packets of dry yeast
- 3 tablespoons fried onions
- 1 tablespoon soy sauce
- 2 teaspoons of salt
- 1 teaspoon of cumin
- 1 teaspoon of fennel seeds
- 1 tsp sugar
- ½ teaspoon pepper (black)

Preparation:

1. Chop the spices and mix with the flour and fried onions. In another bowl add warm water, dry yeast and sugar and stir. Add soy sauce and let stand 5 minutes.
2. Fry the diced ham briefly, add to the flour with a little water and mix well. Cover the dough and let it rest for 1 hour. Sprinkle flour on the countertop, spread out the dough and fold both sides in 1/3. Form a round loaf.
3. Cut off the sides of the parchment paper and place in the Dutch Oven. Preheat the oven to 220 °C, place the bread in the Dutch Oven and place in the oven. Close the Dutch Oven and bake for about 45 minutes. Bake uncovered for another 15 minutes.
4. Allow the bread to cool, then slice and top

BAKED APPLE

Serving:2 - Preparation time: 30 min

Ingredients:

- 4 apples
- 60 grams of walnuts
- 60 grams of raisins
- 1 tablespoon of honey
- Cinammon
- 60 g raw marzipan mass
- 20 grams of butter
- 2 tablespoons chopped almonds
- 200 ml apple juice

Preparation:

1. Wash and core the apples.
2. Mix the walnuts, raisins, honey, butter, marzipan, cinnamon and almonds well and fill into the apples.
3. Heat the Dutch Oven, put the apples and the apple juice in the Dutch Oven.
4. Simmer the baked apples for about half an hour over low heat from below and medium heat from above and with the lid closed.
5. Serve and enjoy.

PLUM CRUMBLE

Serving:2 - Prep time: 40 minutes

Ingredients:

- 1 kg of plums
- 6 tablespoons of honey
- 1 tablespoon of starch
- 80 grams of rolled oats
- 50 g ground almonds
- 40 g flaked almonds
- 30 grams of butter
- 1 pinch of salt
- Cinammon

Preparation:

1. Preheat the Dutch Oven from the top and bottom to medium-high.
2. Wash the plums, stone them, cut into small pieces and mix with 3 tablespoons of honey.
3. For the crumble: Mix together the rolled oats, honey, ground almonds, slivered almonds, starch, butter, salt and cinnamon.
4. Place the plums in the Dutch Oven, pour the crumble over the plums and bake with the lid on for about 30 minutes until the crumble is lightly browned.
5. Serve and enjoy.

BLACK BREAD

Serving:4 - Preparation time: 75 min

Ingredients:

- 500 g spelled flour
- 500ml of water
- 75 g of flaxseed
- 100 g of pumpkin seeds
- 25 grams of sesame
- 1½ tsp salt
- 1 packet of baking powder
- 1 tsp olive oil

Preparation:

1. Mix flour and baking powder.
2. Mix in the flaxseeds, pumpkin seeds, sesame and salt.
3. Add lukewarm water and knead well by hand.
4. Place the bread mixture in an oiled loaf pan and lightly brush the surface of the mixture with water.
5. Place in the Dutch Oven and bake for 60 minutes over medium heat from below and high heat from above.
6. Allow warm bread to cool, serve and enjoy.

DUTCH OVEN BREAD

Serving:4 - Prep time: 90 minutes

Ingredients:

- 250 grams of flax flour
- 120 grams of almond flour
- 40 g coconut flour
- 4 eggs
- 7 grams of yeast
- 1 tsp sugar
- 300 ml almond milk
- 2 tsp salt

Preparation:

1. Put all the ingredients in a bowl and knead into a dough.
2. Cover the dough and let it rise in a warm place for about 60 minutes.
3. Knead the dough again and place in the Dutch Oven. Dust the Dutch Oven with some flour beforehand. Bake the bread for about 45 minutes over low heat from below and medium heat from above.
4. Allow the finished bread to cool, serve and enjoy.

RYE BREAD WITH MALT BEER

Serving:4 - Preparation time: 18h

Ingredients:

- 150 grams of wheat flour
- 350 grams of rye flour
- 10 grams of yeast
- 2 tablespoons of salt
- 80 ml root beer
- 200ml water (lukewarm)
- 50 g of pumpkin seeds

Preparation:

1. Knead the yeast, salt, flour, malt beer, pumpkin seeds and water into a dough. Leave covered in the fridge overnight.
2. Place the dough in a loaf tin and bake in the Dutch Oven for about 45 minutes over high heat from above and medium heat from below.
3. Halfway through cooking, look under the lid and turn the heat down a little if needed.
4. Leave to cool. Finished!
5. Serve and enjoy.

Printed by BoD™in Norderstedt, Germany